From the Great Wall to Wall Street

Wei Yen

From the Great Wall to Wall Street

A Cross-Cultural Look at Leadership and Management in China and the US

Wei Yen
California, USA

ISBN 978-3-319-81420-9   ISBN 978-3-319-33008-2   (eBook)
DOI 10.1007/978-3-319-33008-2

© The Editor(s) (if applicable) and The Author(s) 2017
Softcover reprint of the hardcover 1st edition 2016
This book was advertised with a copyright holder in the name of the publisher in error, whereas the author holds the copyright.
This work is subject to copyright. All rights are solely and exclusively licensed by the Publisher, whether the whole or part of the material is concerned, specifically the rights of translation, reprinting, reuse of illustrations, recitation, broadcasting, reproduction on microfilms or in any other physical way, and transmission or information storage and retrieval, electronic adaptation, computer software, or by similar or dissimilar methodology now known or hereafter developed.
The use of general descriptive names, registered names, trademarks, service marks, etc. in this publication does not imply, even in the absence of a specific statement, that such names are exempt from the relevant protective laws and regulations and therefore free for general use.
The publisher, the authors and the editors are safe to assume that the advice and information in this book are believed to be true and accurate at the date of publication. Neither the publisher nor the authors or the editors give a warranty, express or implied, with respect to the material contained herein or for any errors or omissions that may have been made.

Printed on acid-free paper

This Palgrave Macmillan imprint is published by Springer Nature
The registered company is Springer International Publishing AG
The registered company address is: Gewerbestrasse 11, 6330 Cham, Switzerland

Acknowledgements

Writing a book that traverses different cultures requires an open mind, and I have many people to thank for that. First, I like to thank my late father, Jimin Yen, and my mother, Joyce Yen, for instilling in me the proper values when I was growing up. My mother in particular encapsulated both Chinese and American values as a graduate of the first Chinese women's college, Ginling College in Nanjing. As a Chinese son, I wish to honor them with this book. I also like to thank my wife, Leesa, for her unwavering support, understanding and patience during the past three years, when I was absorbed with the pleasure of thinking and writing, and my sons James and Alex for always believing in their dad. I also want to thank my brother, Craig, for inspiring me all through my life, and my teachers at Hong Kong's Pui Ying Middle School for teaching me the invaluable Chinese lessons.

In the US I also have many people to thank: Gary Brooks for his patience in accepting me into his family and teaching this newcomer the American ways; Ron and Ginny Littlefield, Fred Rock and many others in the great state of Maine for having faith in me and being true friends; Ray Farinato in Connecticut for surviving with me in a changing corporate world; Jess Belser at Rothschild Ventures for allowing me to have an exciting beginning in the financial industry; Jim Parish and Rob McCreary at Moody's for taking me under their wings and teaching me the fine art of credit analysis; and John Neibuhr at Lehman for hiring me the first time in New York, and then having the faith to hire me again in Hong Kong. Their fairness and trust in me has strengthened my faith in the US system. In Hong Kong, I like to thank Ju Weimin and Chairman Chang Zhenming of CITIC for entrusting me with the task of rebuilding the finance function of CITIC Pacific at a critical juncture in its development history.

Turning a collection of random thoughts and notes over a 15-year period into a book required serious professional help. In this regard I wish to thank Craig Pepples for reviewing the first draft and giving me valuable feedback; Skip Press for editing the earlier drafts and suggesting the use of a pendulum approach to compare the two cultures; John Stuart for suggesting the main title; Stephen Partridge at Palgrave Macmillan for taking a risk on me as a first-time author, and who together with Josephine Taylor helped to shape the manuscript into its current form; and finally Sarah Schott for her excellent index editing.

Contents

1 Introduction   1

2 Chinese Characteristics   7

3 Games people play   23

4 Geography of Management   43

5 The Power of the Whole   97

6 The Irrationality of Being Rational   105

7 Union of Men and Heaven   119

8 Contemporary Expressions of Tradition   133

9 Etiquette with Chinese Characteristics   165

10 The Chinese Model   179

11 Moral Hazard or Moral Imperative?   195

12 Exporting China Inc   221

13 Cross-Cultural Lessons   239

14 Two Systems: One World   255

Index   261

About the Author

Born in China, raised in Hong Kong and educated in the US, Wei Yen has spent half his life and his career living and working in both the US and Asia.

Wei has 23 years of financial industry experience, including as Managing Director for Moody's Asia Pacific, where he ran its Asian financial institution rating practices, and as Managing Director for Lehman Brothers Asia and Nomura International, where he advised Asian clients on rating and corporate finance. He was also a member of Lehman's Asia Commitment Committee. Wei also held corporate positions as Chief Financial Officer for iSwitch Corp., a Mainland Chinese technology company, and as Group Treasurer for CITIC Pacific Limited, a Hong Kong-listed subsidiary of the conglomerate CITIC Group.

Before relocating to Asia in 1997 with Lehman Brothers, Wei was a biotech venture capitalist in New York for Rothschild Ventures, and Corporate High-Yield Analyst for Moody's, covering the technology and chemicals sectors. Earlier in his career he was a research physicist and business manager for the American Cyanamid Company.

Wei received his BS in physics from SUNY at Stony Brook, PhD in physics from the University of Maine and MBA in finance from Pace University. He lives in Southern California.

List of Figures

Fig. 3.1 The yin and yang symbol   26
Fig. 4.1 Business success factors   57

List of Tables

Table 14.1 Differences in management emphasis   258
Table 14.2 Cross-cultural comparison of management styles   259

1

Introduction

In the not too distant future, China will overtake the US to become the largest economy in the world. While Asians have rarely questioned China's growth potential, its rapid ascent has caught many Westerners by surprise. Numerous observers have attributed its rise to an industrious people making up for lost time working under an authoritarian regime. From time to time, they also sound the alarm about its demise. However, the culture behind China's resiliency has rarely been discussed.

I grew up in Hong Kong, where I received a local K-12 education. As I am familiar with its culture, China's accomplishments were not a surprise to me. Having attended college in the US and later worked both there and in Asia for US and Chinese companies, I had the opportunity to compare the Chinese and Western management styles up close. I came to the realization that, even though the two styles are quite different, they are not necessarily mutually exclusive. Each has something to offer the other. This book explains my path to this understanding. Decision-makers may consider using this book to supplement their own methods of analysis to obtain a richer perspective.

In the 1950s, as now, Hong Kong's schools were divided into English and Chinese streams. English schools were more preferable for career-minded families. However, my parents enrolled me in a Chinese school all the way through high school because they wanted me to fully understand my own cultural heritage. As my family came from Northern China, I spoke Mandarin at home and Cantonese with my friends elsewhere. I also took additional English lessons with ladies affiliated with churches and volunteer organizations.

Traditional Chinese disciplinarians ran my school. Students had to have clean-cut appearances at all times. They had to stand to the side and bow to the teachers when they walked by. Long hair, short skirts and Beatles music were not allowed; these were considered decadent influences from the West. Violators were punished, and very often humiliated in front of their classmates.

In school, we were taught to be considerate and have proper manners at all times. We had to show respect to our parents, teachers and the elderly, per Chinese traditions. The curriculum emphasized Chinese literature and history, plus math and science. My Chinese teachers were like a walking encyclopedia on China. They seemed to know the details of every event that occurred in its long history, including the juicy bits. They also always had impeccable manners and a wonderful sense of humor. They were like Koi fish swimming contentedly in a pond, serenely at peace with themselves and their surroundings. Nothing seemed to bother them, nor did they bother anyone else. They operated smoothly in their environment and exuded qualities that traditional scholars might describe as a harmony between men and their ideal world—that is, the union of men and heaven. As an easily excitable teenager, I wondered if I could feel that way one day.

In my Chinese classes, we studied the *Analects* of Confucius and works by Mencius, the Taoist (Daoist) Lao Tzu (Laozi), plus Zhuangzi and other Chinese classics. Much of it was taught by traditional rote learning. Repetitive as it was, it did give me a solid grounding in the language and culture.

In 1967 I went to the US to attend college. At the time, the country was deeply divided by the Vietnam War. In fact, it seemed the whole world was in tumult during the 1960s. In Hong Kong, the leftists took a page from China's Cultural Revolution and agitated against colonial rule. They planted homemade bombs in the streets, and held demonstrations that inevitably led to riots. There were curfews all the time and the atmosphere was strained beneath the calm that the authorities were desperately trying to maintain. Given this uneasy backdrop, going away to college didn't seem like a bad idea.

What little I knew about the US didn't prepare me for what I was about to experience. When I arrived in San Francisco, my older brother picked me up at the airport. After we had settled down and had a bite to eat, we went straight to the Haight-Ashbury district, named after the intersection of two streets in San Francisco. In 1967 the Haight was a hippie paradise. Young men and women came from all over the US and elsewhere to live the life of the free. They would smile at an awkward teenager fresh off the plane and say hi. I had no idea that we had walked straight into the country's famous Summer of Love. It was a real eye-opener for me.

In Hong Kong I was not supposed to smile at strangers because that would imply I wanted to get something from them. In San Francisco I was surprised by how people could get along with others by being themselves. The song "San Francisco (Be Sure to Wear Flowers in Your Hair)" by Scott McKenzie was constantly in the air and we were indeed greeted, smiled at and given flowers by strangers. Everyone was relaxed and doing their own thing, and no one was bothered by or bothering others.

Having been brought up in a traditional Chinese setting, I was expected to behave properly and be conscious of how others viewed me at all times. In San Francisco, I found I could feel free and content, just by being myself. It was an interesting introduction to the US.

It was not until I had lived among Americans for several years that I began to appreciate the essence of their culture. I learned that beneath the in-your-face brashness and individualistic demeanors that might be misconstrued as offensive by a newcomer, Americans believed deeply in a set of core values. The phrase "I will fight for your right to have free speech" says it all. In the US, individuality is respected and conformity is not required—very different than what I was taught.

I began to examine the values I was brought up with and compare them with the new ones I encountered. After straddling both cultures for a while, at times feeling like someone with a split personality, I managed to strike a balance. I came to realize that adopting a new culture was not an either/or proposition. Different cultures can co-exist. With some work, one can harmonize them and enjoy the best of both worlds.

After graduate studies, I began my career with a traditional Fortune 500 industrial corporation in the US. Later I moved on to a series of jobs in banking and finance, in New York and later in Hong Kong. For 15 years I travelled extensively in Asia, working with different clients in China, Taiwan, Hong Kong, Japan, Korea, Thailand, Indonesia, Vietnam and Malaysia. They included many private and state-owned companies in a variety of industries.

I interacted frequently with senior managers of major Asian corporations and ministry officials charged with regulating their businesses. I observed how they strategized, dealt with business issues and made decisions. After a while, I realized that, even though these companies were located in different countries, almost all of their senior management teams shared one thing in common—their Confucian heritage. This common cultural platform served to complement their Western business training, and it provided them with a richer perspective from which to manage their businesses.

I also experienced Chinese corporate culture first hand when working in a private company in Shenzhen, China, and later with a Hong Kong-listed subsidiary of a major Chinese state-owned enterprise (SOE). In Asia I witnessed the rise of its economies from the ruins of the Asian financial crisis. I saw how China, one of the oldest civilizations, transformed into a modern market economy in leaps and bounds, in a manner the Chinese would describe as crossing the river by feeling the stones underneath one's feet.

China retains what works and jettisons what doesn't, while improvising along the way. It manages to adopt modern Western practices but also maintains an essential Chinese identity.

As I am comfortable with both cultures, I found myself explaining to my non-Chinese colleagues what our Chinese clients said and meant. Likewise, my Chinese friends and clients often asked me the same questions about Westerners. Both sides have a fair number of misconceptions about the other. This gave me the idea of writing about cross-cultural management comparisons.

This book is not about which culture is better but rather what we can learn from each other. I hope we can build on the common goodness that is in all of us and develop an appreciation of our differences. Because there is little written about the Chinese management style, I have made it a major focus of this volume. Some of the ideas can be applied to other East Asians, such as Korean and Japanese, because both have been influenced by Chinese culture in the past. For simplicity, I call them East Asians or just Asians.

I have also gone into the Chinese culture a little more than most business books. I believe it is crucial that we, as decision-makers, appreciate the cultural basis of not just how but also why people make their decisions. I have also taken the liberty to translate some of the ancient Chinese passages to give them a more contemporary twist.

I should point out that some of the Chinese traditions, such as the Middle Way, or the dialectics of Taoism, have appeared in other cultures. However, in China, these traditions are deeply ingrained in people's everyday lives.

Last, it is my sincere hope that this book will engender debates and additional research on the subject of cross-cultural management. The old Chinese saying "Throw a piece of brick at someone in the hope of attracting a piece of jade in return" fairly describes my motivation.

For simplicity, I generally use the word he, and not she or he and she, when I describe an individual, and Westerners to describe people of European descent, such as North Americans, British, continental Europeans, folks from Oceania and others. I have not included Indian and Middle Eastern cultures, which are significant in their own rights, because I simply don't know much about them, and excluding them does not seem to affect the major thesis of this book.

I hope that you will enjoy the ideas here as much as I have enjoyed developing them.

2

Chinese Characteristics

The Rise of China

In *Global Trends 2030*, the US National Intelligence Council predicts China will surpass the US before 2030 to become the world's largest economy, if gross domestic product (GDP) is measured by the market exchange rate method, and even earlier (in 2022) if GDP is measured by the purchasing power parity method. Even though China's ongoing economic rebalancing has made forecasting its GDP a hazardous exercise, it seems reasonable to speculate that one day China will regain the status as the largest economy in the world, just on account of its massive population, and continuing efforts to reform.

In 2012 the World Bank published a joint study with the Development Research Center of China's State Council, describing what China would look like in 2030. It stated unequivocally that the country had to adjust its development focus away from investments and towards consumers. If it is able to make such a transition, it will have a much more balanced economy. As a global economic power, China will have a massive influence on all of us. Martin Jacques, in *When China Rules the World*, describes the country as capable of having both a gravitational pull and a centrifugal impact on the rest of the world.

At a minimum, China will pull the West towards its growing market of 1.36 billion consumers, the biggest, most contiguous and the most culturally homogeneous market in the world. Outside of its borders, China will increasingly push and engage others with its growing clout in economic, military and political arenas.

As China moves closer to becoming the world's largest economy, its businesses will increasingly compete with those of the West in all layers of the value-added chain, from low to high end, and from low to hi-tech. Its consumers will drive demand for all kinds of commodities, properties, electronics, luxury goods and financial assets. Its students will compete with Western children in college admissions and jobs. Its technology industry will vie with those in the West to come up with the fastest computers and the latest electronic gadgets. Its power plants and production facilities, and the growing fleets of automobiles, will put massive amounts of greenhouse gases into the atmosphere. Last, its government will increasingly compete with other governments to exert its influence regarding issues of politics, the military, finance and soft power.

In short, China will influence Western lives in more ways than we can imagine. It will no longer be the country that only exports manufactured products overseas, generates huge trade surpluses and buys foreign government debt. Depending on which perspective we choose, China can be a foe, a partner or both. Everyone's interests will be more and more co-mingled and our existence synergetic. It is absolutely imperative for us to understand how the Chinese think, and the cultural mindset that drives their decision processes.

The last two-and-a-half centuries saw the West thoroughly dominate the globe. Its presence permeates science and medicine, business and finance, law and education, and just about every realm of human activity. Its military power is massive. Its political power is second to none. Its financial prowess is gargantuan, and its culture pervasive. In short, the West has influenced just about every aspect of how we all look and think, as well as our work and personal conduct.

Whether they realize it or not, most Asians are already heavily immersed in Western culture. They wear Western-style clothing, eat Western fast foods, watch Western television programs and movies, listen to Western music, go to Western churches and argue in Western-inspired courts, often in English. In comparison, few Westerners have experienced Chinese culture up close, unless they have lived in China or Asia. The occasional trips to Chinese restaurants or chats with Chinese colleagues at the office is not a representative experience. As such, few Westerners are ready to face a growing China.

Many Westerners also have an uninformed view of what China is, and why its government and people behave the way they do. Because of this lack of understanding, they often struggle to understand where China has come from, and where it may be headed in the future. There are also fears of an ideology-driven global competitor that doesn't quite play by the established rules. Moreover, because Westerners tend to employ a predominantly Western mindset to analyze China, the conclusions they draw don't always match up with the facts.

China has a continuous history of almost 5,000 years, one of the longest in the world. The nation has survived numerous regime changes, countless wars, natural disasters, famines and foreign invasions, yet it has managed to stay together as a union. The glue that binds its people so miraculously together through all these travails is China's unique culture. This same culture will continue to influence how Chinese people live, and how they conduct business and formulate policies in the future.

It has been only 100 years between the demise of the last Chinese dynasty and the present day, a tiny timespan in the context of China's long history. The gap between China's Open Door policy and today is even more miniscule. To the point, China will remain culturally Chinese, despite massive efforts to turn it into a different nation in a very short period of time. It may adopt some Western practices, but over time these imports will take on Chinese characteristics and be melded into the Chinese mainstream. And even though Chinese people may wear Western-style clothes, eat Western food and speak Western languages, their souls will remain quintessentially Chinese.

Bertrand Russell, the great British mathematician and philosopher, was very insightful regarding China. In 1922, after spending a year living and lecturing there, he published *The Problem of China*. In it, Russell argues that if China could assimilate what is the best of the Western civilization with its own fine traditions, it could result in a very splendid union.

The question is which cultural elements are responsible for China's longevity and current success. Will what has worked before continue to work for the Chinese in the future?

The Chinese government attributes its economic success to "socialism with Chinese characteristics". This politically correct phrase connotes a sense of legitimacy, but it is also intentionally vague. Although the 38-year-old slogan is constantly on the lips of officials, they have never provided it with a precise definition.

A Different Mindset

To Westerners, the Chinese decision-making process is often shrouded in mystery. They often find it like a black box, with input going in and output coming out, but no telling what's going on inside. Likewise, the Chinese find it difficult to decipher Westerners' true intentions. To them, Westerners are too narrowly focused on a small number of issues and oblivious to the broader context. Therefore they must have some hidden agendas. A better understanding of the two cultures can help dispel some common misconceptions and improve the way we communicate. It can also open up creative ways for problem-solving.

If a person has only two options to choose from, and they are the polar opposites of each other, the result may be distinct but not necessarily optimal. This type of binary decision-making, where options are limited by design, is very Western. Traditional Chinese don't like to make decisions this way. They are wholistic thinkers who prefer the more balanced middle way.

When opportunities and risks co-exist, should someone go after perceived opportunities, maximize the return of his efforts and let others deal with the consequences? Or should he look wholistically and choose a path balancing both risks and opportunities, and the self and the greater good? Most Westerners would probably choose the first, while most Chinese would prefer the latter. This, I believe, reflects the major differences between the Western and traditional Chinese ways of thinking.

All managers are responsible to their stakeholders. In a Western company, this may be interpreted as delivering sustainable risk-adjusted returns to the company's shareholders. To increase profits, management must grow revenue or cut costs. When the economy is bad and growth is difficult to achieve, management should close plants and fire workers to save costs and protect the bottom line. Such right-sizing activities are routinely carried out in US companies.

However, for Chinese managers, shareholders are not the only important stakeholders. Social stability, which reflects a commonly accepted sense of fairness, is a traditional Chinese value that enters prominently into management considerations. As a result, management may be less willing to close plants and drastically cut the workforce during bad times. This results in weaker performance but a more harmonious workplace. Alibaba's Jack Ma, who describes his three stakeholders as customers, employees and shareholders—in that order—echoes this traditional Chinese value hierarchy.

Chinese Characteristics

China may be modernizing rapidly but its soul remains quintessentially Chinese. One of the early Western observers of China was Arthur Henderson Smith, an American missionary who had preached for decades in that country. In his 1894 book *Chinese Characteristics*, he describes the Chinese as a people who were overly polite, too conscious about saving face, suspicious of each other, fixated on filial piety, and lacking in public spirit, among other qualities that were objectionable to a Western clergyman. Even with the passage of time, his observations remain quite astute. However, his prediction that in order for China to survive as a nation it must be Christianized and fully adopt Western ways has yet to be proven.

As a people, the Han Chinese, who represent over 92 percent of the population, are very good at taking in foreign ideas and melding them into their own culture. The Mongols, who invaded China in the thirteenth century, and the Manchus, who did the same in the seventeenth century, are typical examples. Their once alien cultures, with their own languages and religions, have long been assimilated into the Chinese mainstream.

The hotpot, a hearty Chinese dish where diners cook their own food in hot boiling soups (think fondue with soup), came with the Mongolians. It is a welcome reprieve from the harsh wintry conditions of Northern China. However, the dish is now served everywhere in China with different regional characteristics. In Southern China, the hotpot is light and delicate, with lots of vegetables and seafood. In Western China's Sichuan, it is a cauldron of a fiery lip-numbing concoction laden with chilli and peppercorns. Away from food, the qipao, a traditional Manchurian outfit for women, has slimmed down into a formal dress worn by Chinese women today for special occasions.

Even Christmas, the quintessential Western holiday for the remembrance of Christ, has taken on Chinese characteristics. The Chinese word for Christmas Eve is Pingan Ye (平安夜), or the evening of peace. It has since evolved into a winter version of Valentine's Day for young couples. It also serves as an opportunity for people to exchange apples and wish each other a peaceful season, because the Chinese word for Christmas Eve rhymes with the word pingguo (苹果), which translates as apples.

China did not merely import foreign lifestyles. During the early part of the twentieth century, it also took on many Western ideas, including communism. Through trial and error, it has managed to keep what has worked and jettison what didn't, including the ideology of binary class struggle. Today, many Western imports have taken on unique Chinese characteristics and become part of the mainstream.

In 1978, China's paramount leader, Deng Xiaoping, coined the phrase "socialism with Chinese characteristics". He wanted to get the Chinese people excited about economic development, and to move away from ideological struggles that did nothing to improve their livelihoods. To do that, he modified socialism, a Western import, to make it more Chinese.

The Chinese responded enthusiastically to Deng's call and the economy took off. Deng was brilliant in that he realized that in order for China to move forwards, it must not give up its past. Also, whatever China imports from the West must be compatible with its own traditional values. However, Deng left the high-context slogan open to interpretation.

A group of fat-cat businessmen smoking big cigars while deciding how much people should pay for everything is the image of capitalism to a lot of Chinese brought up in an earlier era. However, socialism with Chinese characteristics has replaced the egregious businessmen, many of them foreign-trained, with China's native sons. Deng's insightful slogan managed to remove the age-old hang-up about business, from Confucianism to socialism, and transformed it into an activity worthy of a national purpose. Chinese businessmen today are obviously there to make a profit, but in so doing they are also helping their fellow countrymen to advance. Since Deng made his famous statement over 35 years ago, China has managed to narrow its performance gap with developed countries. In the process it has also lifted several hundred million people out of abject poverty. Just what are the so-called Chinese characteristics that were responsible for this economic miracle?

Will the Chinese people continue to embrace traditional values while wearing suits, drinking soda and talking on smartphones—all foreign imports? Will Chinese consumers forsake frugality, go into debt and spend like their Western counterparts? Will they demand a broader set of rights that consumers generally expect in a market economy? Will a model re-emphasizing traditional values drive sustainable growth even though it has caused stagnation in the past? Also, just how competitive is the Chinese model compared with the Western model? These subjects are provocative and worth exploring.

To appreciate how the Chinese have managed to accomplish so much in such a short time, we need to understand how they work and make decisions. We can achieve this by looking at their management mindset and, in turn, the Chinese culture.

The Chinese and many Asians prefer a wholistic management model, which relies on sharing both gains and pains. It is fundamentally different from the Western model, which is analytical and relies on individuals competing in a system that fairly rewards hard work and risk-taking. Most of the developed world runs on the Western model. The US, in particular, with its strong business culture and academic institutions, continues to be at the forefront in the development of the science of management. The Chinese model, however, remains little studied.

The Chinese model does have merits. The steady performance of the Chinese economy since the global financial crisis of 2008 contrasts vividly with the rapid decline of Western economies. This has given the Chinese more confidence in their own model against those of their international peers. It has also revived an interest in the study of *Guoxue* (国学), or traditional Chinese culture.

As a management model must reflect the culture it comes from, Chinese and Western models are necessarily different. Yet each has something to offer the other. The Chinese can benefit from the West's rigorous problem-solving and execution skills, its free markets, and its comprehensive legal framework. However, the West's contentious culture can become too adversarial at times. Its combative style, where there must be a clear winner and loser in each contest, can result in management paralysis and missed opportunities, especially in the political arena. The West can also benefit from an appreciation of tolerance, a more balanced view of life, and the Chinese concept of harmony that comes from a people who have lived on the same piece of land for thousands of years.

A cross-cultural review of management styles will illuminate just how traditional Chinese culture can add value. It can also show how Chinese managers compare with their Western counterparts in developed markets overseas that Chinese companies are venturing into, or in a more open China, where rules and regulations are harmonizing towards global standards.

Chinese Soft Power

According to Joseph Nye, a nation's soft power is what it uses to spread its influence beyond its borders, without resorting to coercion or payments. Within this definition, culture is the most important component of a nation's soft power, followed by political values and foreign policies.

According to a 2013 Pew Research study, people from across the globe continue to appreciate US pop culture and to admire its scientific and technical achievements. However, only developing countries in Latin America and Africa view China favorably. Opinions about China from some developed countries in Europe and the Americas have actually deteriorated over a recent six-year period.

Soft power reflects that special ability to get other people to do the things you want them to do willingly and voluntarily. Although we can all feel the pull of soft power, we can't quantify it easily. By way of a financial analogy, soft power can be viewed as an intangible asset on a country's balance sheet. It contributes significantly to the country's net worth and influence but is difficult to quantify precisely.

One of the most important intangible assets any company can have is its brand.

A well-known brand creates value by effortlessly drawing consumers to its products. When people think of Coca-Cola or Mercedes, they immediately conjure up the lifestyles these famous brands represent. When they purchase these products, they are in a position to partake in their associated lifestyles. When people think of the US, they think of freedom and individualism, and what these qualities represent. When people think of China, they see an ancient culture with a fast-growing economy run by communists. How much more confusing can the Chinese brand be?

At the moment, Chinese soft power is noticeably less visible than its very tangible economic accomplishments. When foreigners come to China, they see cities full of new subways and gleaming tall buildings, and a society full of contradictions between the old and new, East and West, and rich and poor. But the Chinese brand is amorphous and unclear. This doesn't help them understand China easily. The Chinese have also been unable to explain themselves clearly and convincingly. Most adults are preoccupied with their own pursuits of wealth and success, and have little time to harmonize this modern lifestyle with their own traditional culture.

Because of the Cultural Revolution, those in power missed out on a formal education in the Chinese classics during their formative years. Since they were not taught the substantive parts of their culture, they often appear superficial and unconvincing. The government is keenly aware of this soft power gap and is actively promoting Chinese culture at home and abroad. By doing so, it hopes to project a softer image than one of a fast-growing but soulless economic power.

Teaching Chinese culture and language overseas is an effective way of spreading the culture. The Chinese government, through its Hanban unit under the Ministry of Education, established the first Confucius Institute in 2004. At the end of 2013, the number has reached 440 in 120 countries. There is a plan to further increase the number of these institutes to over 1,000. Although many governments have also established their cultural units overseas, such as Alliance Francaise, Goethe-Institute, and the British Council, the growth of the Confucius Institute is much more ambitious.

But Chinese culture is not just about speaking Mandarin, reading Chinese books, or learning about its festivals or foods; it's more about the Chinese soul, or the resilient philosophical ideas that have allowed Chinese people to follow their own way of life over the centuries. These same Chinese characteristics, such as benevolence, perseverance, family values and tolerance, should also allow future generations of Chinese people to behave in much the same way as their ancestors.

However, Chinese culture is not an easy sell to foreigners. Aside from the difficult language and its many subtleties, a major handicap is the lack of suitable Chinese role models for foreigners to identify and resonate with.

Mickey Mouse and Monkey King

US soft power dominates the globe. Its pop culture is the most dynamic and pervasive form of Western culture today. Chinese culture is little known in the West, despite being one of the oldest.

It is arguably much easier for a foreigner to appreciate US pop culture than traditional Chinese culture. I will attempt to illustrate why by using a popular icon from each.

By doing this I am not suggesting that cartoon characters are the best cultural representatives: there are more elegant high-culture examples that appeal to the educated. However, pop culture icons do demonstrate the effectiveness of soft power, how they can resonate with young audiences and why China is lacking in this space.

Mickey Mouse is one of the most recognizable characters in US pop culture. Everyone loves the charming little critter, with its big ears, little white vest and gloves, and child-like antics. The way Mickey manages to outsmart his much larger nemesis, Pete the black cat, delights fans all over the world. Walt Disney's creation managed to turn a pest into a mischievous, humanized figure that appeals to people of all ages and cultures. Mickey represents the little guy who manages to succeed despite being outsized. Those of us who have been in similar situations can easily identify with him.

True to their founding spirit, Americans have a love for the underdogs, who triumph over their much stronger adversaries. It is an enduring theme in books, movies and songs. To succeed in spite of the circumstances is also the spirit of the American Dream.

The Chinese also have their traditional heroes, but they are more frequently featured in tales focused on rags-to-fame than on rags-to-riches themes. A typical theme is a poor student who studies hard, does well in exams and becomes an important government official.

One of the most popular characters in Chinese literature is Sun Wukong, or the Monkey King, from the classic novel *Journey to the West*. Sun is a cunning monkey who has been given supernatural powers by Taoist immortals. He can perform many incredible feats, including turning himself into one of his 72 disguises to deceive his much stronger opponents.

True to his monkey nature, Sun is a naughty little fellow with no respect for the authorities. His antics infuriate the Buddha so much that he is imprisoned under a big mountain. To redeem himself he has to accompany a Tang Dynasty monk (Zuanzang) on his trip west in the seventh century to acquire sacred Buddhist texts. Sun's wit and power manage to protect the Tang monk on his treacherous journey from Changan (today's Xi'an) to Afghanistan and India, and it allows him to bring back the valuable Buddhist sutras to China.

Chinese children and adults all marvel at how the Monkey King can perform his feats and outsmart his more powerful opponents. Secretly, they wish they could have some of his magical power too: it would make their lives much easier.

In this respect, the stories of Mickey Mouse and the Monkey King are similar. Both characters are small in stature but are able to compensate for that by being smart and cunning. The difference is that Mickey Mouse uses the quickness and smartness of a typical house mouse to overcome his adversaries, while the Monkey King relies on supernatural powers given to him by the gods.

The Monkey King has human emotions—he is, after all, a deity. As such, he can be admired but not emulated. No one can imagine he can perform any of Monkey King's incredible feats because humans don't have supernatural powers. However, you can easily replicate some of Mickey Mouse's antics. In fact, some of us might have played similar tricks on our poor siblings or friends when we were young. In this respect, Mickey is like most of us.

The beauty of US pop culture, and one of the reasons why it is so popular, is that it appeals to the basic feelings all of us have, regardless of whether we are talking about the individual spirit, pop music or Mickey Mouse's survival antics. Because the messages are so down to earth, they are appreciated by a large number of people regardless of where they come from.

In contrast, anything deemed worthy in China must not be ordinary. In traditional Chinese culture, only top dogs can get respect, while underdogs only get pity. Traditionally, there are very few commoner role models. Young people have only scholars, war heroes or sages to look up to. In fact, most commoners mentioned in Chinese history had tragic lives.

Chinese culture is also quite complex, and is relatively difficult to appreciate through indirect means. For example, a young person who has never been to the US can have a pretty good idea what the country is about by watching its films, listening to its music, wearing its fashion and eating its fast food. But the same person will have difficulties grasping what China is by going through the same routines because what's behind the culture is not obvious. This is one of the reasons why promoting Chinese culture overseas is such a difficult proposition.

Appreciate the Culture Slowly

China's long history and foreign influences make for a complex culture. To appreciate Chinese culture, you should take your time.

Chinese people love their history, and they refer to it all the time. To them, history is what justifies the present, and what gives them a sense of purpose for the future. To the Chinese, history is a continuum of events, and Chinese culture is built on such continuity. It has a purpose and the people are part of it.

2 Chinese Characteristics

Westerners don't refer to their history all that much. Very few Western countries have such a long, unbroken history as China. Westerners, especially Americans, also tend to be more individualistic: they believe that what they do is more important than what their forefathers did before them, so why dwell on history?

Traditional Chinese culture offers wonderful insights and wisdom that differ from what most Westerners are used to. Those in the west like things that are precise and logical. They prefer quick answers and instant gratification. Chinese culture offers none of that. Chinese people live in a high-context world full of ambiguities. Pushing precision doesn't work well with the them: it boxes them in. When people are boxed in, friction inevitably increases and harmony becomes elusive.

This typical Chinese attitude was born out of necessity. For so many Chinese to live in such close proximity and get along, each person must erect a mental comfort zone to buffer himself from others.

The Chinese comfort zone is different from the Western concept of personal space that describes the physical distance people need between them to feel comfortable in social settings. It also doesn't have much to do with the concept of privacy that Westerners have taken as a given. This is why Westerners often find it difficult to understand how Chinese people can tolerate congested places, loud noises or being stared at. The Chinese comfort zone is a mental buffer built on a high level of tolerance that allows people to be alone even in crowds.

Chinese culture is also more than just a collection of wisdom and rules. Let's examine Chinese medicine and food as examples of this subtlety.

Chinese medicine is a wholistic way of managing health. While the practice is not that precise, and scientific evidence behind it is not that conclusive, proponents of Chinese medicine, including herbal medicine and acupuncture, swear by its efficacy. Unlike Western medicine, which treats specific illnesses, the goal of Chinese medicine is to strengthen a patient's body by restoring its balance of yin and yang. The theory is that over time a balanced body in harmony with nature should be able to cure itself. However, because of its non-specific nature, Chinese medicine also takes a lot longer to work, if it works at all.

Acupuncture is the practice of sticking thin needles into a person's body to cure an illness. The Chinese believe that the body's vital energy, qi, travels via meridians located throughout the body. Illness can result from blockages of someone's qi and blood flow that can be brought on by weather or fatigue, for example. By sticking needles into a subset of 361 acupuncture points around the body, a practitioner can stimulate the body's natural responses by restoring its proper flow of qi.

Chinese food is also holistic by design. Chinese people consider food not only as a means to satisfy hunger and provide nutrition but also as a way to be in tune with nature. Food ingredients are often selected from fresh, seasonal produce and cooked with medicinal herbs to supplement what the body requires at different times of the year. Because of that, each food also has many medicinal purposes and the Chinese often use food and medicine interchangeably.

The early Greeks also believed in food as medicine. Hippocrates, the Greek physician considered to be the father of Western medicine, said, "Let food be thy medicine and medicine be thy food", which reflects a similar idea. In contrast, modern dietary practice has broken down food into components of protein, fat, carbohydrate, fiber, vitamins and minerals. The wholeness of food is often lost in this type of analysis.

Besides flavors, Chinese food should consist of contrasting textures, and be a harmonious synthesis of the goodness of all the fresh ingredients. In addition to taste, food must also be appealing to look at. A good chef should be able to deliver a presentation that is both visually inviting and contextually meaningful to wow the guests.

Although China is famous for its cuisine, it doesn't have that many fast foods. The Chinese prefer to sit down and enjoy their food while it is hot, and to achieve harmony between the body and food. Eating and running would result in poor digestion, so that's not encouraged. Cold food, such as sandwiches, is less desirable because it can perturb the warm digestive system. It also doesn't quite agree with the older generations. They would never eat cold food, drink ice water or cold soda, or eat ice cream during the winter. These foods just don't align with the natural order. Most prefer hot tea or warm water instead of cold drinks.

By contrast, Americans eat their favorite foods at any time of the year. Many Chinese people don't understand why Americans drink icy sodas or eat big ice creams in winter. To them, this is quite unnatural.

To the Chinese, eating is not just a means of satisfying hunger; it is also a ritual that allows them to be better in tune with nature. Unlike typical Western fast food where you can have a hunger-satisfying but average eating experience chomping down an endless assortments of baked buns, ground beef, cheese, eggs, bacon, lettuce, salami and tomatoes, you must take time to enjoy a typical Chinese dish, such as mapo doufu.

This simple yet tasty dish consists of cubes of soft tofu, a bit of ground pork, fermented bean paste and chilli powder tossed together in a hot wok for a few minutes, prepared faster than it takes to cook a hamburger. The tender but bland-tasting tofu acts as a flavor absorber for the fresh pork, salty bean paste and hot chilli. It is the contrasting textures and tastes that make the dish interesting. To enjoy, you should hold the tofu in your mouth to experience its silky texture while savoring the different flavors it carries, before swallowing it down with a mouthful of hot rice.

Finally, you should slowly sip a cup of hot tea, and contemplate the balance of the dish's flavors and textures, or its yin and yang. If you gulp down Chinese food like fast food, you acquire calories but miss the finer aspects of the eating experience.

Other examples of traditional Chinese culture will be discussed in the next chapter.

Bibliography

GLOBAL TRENDS 2030: ALTERNATIVE WORLDS, *A Publication of the National Intelligence Council,* p. 15, December 2013, NIC 2012-001.

The World Bank, Development Research Center of the State Council, the People's Republic of China, *China 2030, Building a Modern, Harmonious, and Creative High-Income Society,* 2012.

Martin Jacques, *When China Rules the World,* P. 511, Penguin Books, 2012.

Bertrand Russell, *The Problem of China, Questions, P. 6, Chapter 1,* George Allen & Unwin Ltd, 1922.

Arthur Henderson Smith, *Chinese Characteristics,* copyright 1894 by Fleming H. Revell Company, Digitized by Google.

Plant Cultures, *Chili Pepper—History,* www.kew.org./plant-cultures

Joseph S. Nye, *Soft Power, The Means to Success in World Politics*, Public Affairs, a member of the Perseus Books Group, New York, preface, p. 6, 11, 2004.
Pew Research Global Attitudes Project, Ch. 2 and 3, 2013.
Vice Premier calls for further development of Confucius Institute, Xinhuanet, 7 Dec 2013.
Dustin Roasa, *China's Soft Power*, Foreign Policy 18 Nov 2012.
Journey to the West, Wikipedia, reviewed Jan 2016.
Acupuncture, baike.baidu.com, reviewed Oct 2014.
Quotes by Hippocrates, www.goodreads.com, reviewed Feb 2015.

3

Games People Play

In the *Tao Te Ching*, Lao Tzu says that the weak can triumph over the strong and the gentle can overcome the uncompromising. This saying illustrates succinctly the traditional Chinese attitude towards conflict. Below I use three representative examples—the martial art of tai chi, board game of Weiqi and the book *The Art of War*—and their Western equivalents to show how Chinese and Westerners differ in their approaches to managing contest.

Tai Chi: The Ultimate Soft Power

The Chinese are famous for their many different martial arts, made popular in part by the proliferation of Kung Fu movies. Most of these movies are well made, entertaining and true to the art they represent. However, such screen fantasies often give the impression that the Chinese love to fight all the time, and brute force is the preferred way to settle differences. In reality that is hardly the case.

In fact, all Chinese martial arts stress the importance of self-restraint and the avoidance of conflict whenever possible. This is true even for the most famous martial arts spokesman, Bruce Lee. In his movies, Lee often portrays a humble character who resorts to fighting only when he is cornered and pushed too hard; and then and only then does he move swiftly to teach his enemies a lesson they won't forget.

Tai Chi (Taiqi, 太极), also called shadow boxing, is a traditional Chinese exercise-cum-martial art. Legend has it that a Taoist monk invented it to mimic animals in nature, and to help ward off the mountain chill. Tai Chi is as much a Taoist philosophy of life as an exercise for health and physical fitness. Its elegant moves exemplify the harmony of opposites, and the metamorphosis of one into the other, according to the Tao. Many patterns in the way Chinese people conduct themselves in business and everyday life also resemble Tai Chi, so it is worth looking into.

The direct translation of Tai Chi is "grand ultimate", and indeed Chinese martial artists generally hold it in high esteem. Tai Chi moves are slow and deliberate, and not very menacing in appearance. This is quite different from most of the fast and furious forms of martial art, such as boxing, where the objective is to knock out the opponent as quickly as possible with brute force.

The objective of Tai Chi is less about winning an outright fight and more about maintaining a proper balance at all times. He who disrupts the balance will lose the contest. If an opponent becomes too aggressive, or has a lapse in concentration, he will lose.

In Tai Chi, what matters is not brute force but soft power. A Tai Chi practitioner derives power from his ability to maintain proper balance, even when under attack. When a person is able to maintain his balance under stress, he is in control of the situation instead of merely reacting to it. This is the essence of Tai Chi. Tai Chi may look weak but in reality it is quite powerful. It looks passive but in fact it is in control.

Yin and Yang in Motion

In Tai Chi, a strong offensive move may invite a deadly counter-attack, while a skillfully executed counter-move can turn things around for the defender. When someone attacks his opponent by kicking or throwing a punch at him, he is executing a yang move. However, his attack inevitably exposes his ribcage or groin to the opponent's counter-attack. So the harder he strikes, the less balanced and more vulnerable he becomes. His aggression has simultaneously given rise to a vulnerability, which is a yin characteristic.

Within any motion, both yin and yang co-exist. The more a person retreats from confrontations, the more powerful he becomes. This may seem odd to Westerners, who would only retreat when they lose. So how can retreating from aggression be a sign of strength? Shouldn't it be a sign of weakness instead?

According to Newton's Law, "For every action there is an equal and opposite reaction." In Newtonian mechanics, and in many ways Western thinking, you can be either the action or the reaction, but not both at the same time. However, the Chinese think of them together.

Consider the familiar yin and yang diagram: there is yin within yang and yang within yin. These two opposing forces are constantly jostling with each other to reach a dynamic balance, where no one side can take over the opposite side completely by force. If it tries to do that, it will inevitably expose its own weaknesses and, at the same time, encourage the opposite within it to grow. So the two opposites have to evolve slowly together in order for changes to be made.

In comparison, the Western contest can be described as a circle split somewhere in the middle, with white on one side and black on the other. If either one side has a numerical advantage, it will win the contest and the minority will have to concede. There is always a winner and a loser in this contest. Even though this method of determining the outcome of a contest is precise, it can ignore the middle simply because of how the opposites are defined.

On 23 June 2015, British voters chose to leave the European Union (EU), an economic entity it joined since 1975. The esult of the so-called Brexit votes was 51.9 percent for leaving and 48.1 percent for staying, against predictions of several popular polls before the ballot was taken. This non-binding result has caused the British pound and world stock indices to fall sharply. While the markets have recovered since then, they have yet to stabilize, and will likely remain fragile for a long period of time. It is incredible that such a momentous decision could be determined by such a polarizing ballot and with such a slim margin of victory.

The question remains whether the side with the most area (or votes), of say 51 percent, and the winner by this definition, is really representative of the whole? If so, then who looks after the other 49 percent? Or is this black and white method the best way to handle any contest, where the absolute winner is to represent the interest of the majority? In contrast, the traditional Chinese yin and yang approach focuses on the overall balance, not the absolute. Everyone is both a winner and loser at the same time (Fig. 3.1).

In the traditional Chinese yin and yang symbol, notice the undulating movement of the opposites in a harmonious balance. There is yang within yin, and vice versa.

In Tao, the relationship between action and reaction is not as mathematically precise as in physics. However, both action and reaction are essential for any motion to occur. Without the opposites constantly engaging each other, and occasionally morphing into one another, there can be no motion.

According to *I Ching* (the ancient Book of Changes), "Yin and Yang constitute Tao (阴阳之为道)." This suggests the Tao, or nature's way, has always within it two opposing yet complementary elements. In the *Tao Te Ching*, Lao Tzu also says that opposites drive the Tao, and yielding is how the Tao can be applied. And as the popular sayings go, a single hand cannot clap, and it takes two to tango.

This ancient wisdom makes it abundantly clear that opposites are parts of the whole, and a necessary part of life.

Tai Chi is what the Chinese call an internal style of martial art, where a person's mental state is just as important as his physical abilities. Unlike most sports that rely on power and instincts acquired through repetitive

Fig. 3.1 The yin and yang symbol

drills, in Tai Chi, a practitioner directs the movement of his limbs deliberately with his thoughts. In this respect, Tai Chi is also mind over body.

Tai Chi has many important health benefits, even though it looks decidedly non-cardiovascular. Its circular movements strengthen the practitioner's back and posture, and the constant bending of the knees builds up one's legs and stamina. What's more, the Chinese believe that Tai Chi can help regulate the body's flow of qi, or its vital energy. Rebalancing the body's qi with Tai Chi, herbal medicine or other forms of manipulation such as acupuncture or therapeutic massage can restore health.

The Three Ps of Tai Chi

Tai Chi moves are mostly circular in appearance and defensive in nature. They can be categorized into three broad categories: parry, push and pull. Together they can be called the three Ps of Tai Chi.

Parrying is a very efficient means of self-defense. It uses a small tangential force to deflect a direct attack away from the body, without confronting it head on. Parrying eliminates a challenge by changing its course, thus removing it as a threat. Parrying is also part of the repertoire of seasoned politicians. Another way to describe them is slippery.

In boxing, which dates back to ancient Greece, the goal is to deliver a knockout punch that leaves the opponent reeling onto the mat, down for the eight count. Obliterating an opponent in the shortest amount of time is the best strategy for winning a boxing match. At the end, there can be only one winner. The other, by definition, is the loser.

As Vince Lombardi, the famous American football coach, once said, "Winning isn't everything, it is the only thing." To win at all costs is the attitude of a lot of Westerners in business and politics. You either win or you lose. There is no middle way.

If someone does not wish to be seen as a loser, then he must try his hardest to win, preferably by knocking out his opponent. The win–win approach in business is a more recent phenomenon. The Chinese have been practicing it for a long time.

The strategy of Tai Chi is very different than that of boxing. Instead of beating the opponent into submission with brute force, Tai Chi lets the practitioner turn an opponent's aggressive energy against him. As a result, the harder the opponent strikes, the harder he falls.

The three Ps are carried out over and over again, until one of the two players loses his balance and gets thrown off. This approach is also quite consistent with other Chinese traditions.

The Chinese military strategist, Sun Tzu, in his seminal work *The Art of War*, says that when the enemy is greedy, lure him; when he is in disarray, attack him. This is also the game plan of Tai Chi, where you play along with your opponent and only take advantage of him when he is weakened or over-extended. To be a good Tai Chi practitioner, you have to be patient and firmly grounded. Those who are not good at these will not last long. Not surprisingly, there are many similarities between Tai Chi and how Chinese people manage.

The Three Ps of Chinese Business

Tai Chi resembles the way many Chinese people conduct themselves in both business and everyday life. In meetings, open confrontation is frowned upon and cordiality must be maintained at all times. You should never lose your temper in meetings because it disrupts the very harmony that everyone tries so hard to maintain. Worse, it creates an opening for your opponents to take advantage of you.

Negotiation with Chinese people is always a drawn-out affair. It is never straightforward. The list of discussion items keeps getting longer all the time as a diversionary tactic. The deadline Westerners consider inviolable becomes a moving target—that is, a delaying tactic. By applying diversionary (parry) and delaying (pull) tactics, Chinese businessmen can fake out their opponents and put themselves in a better position to push their own agenda. In business Tai Chi, one side pushes and the other side defends, and the roles alternate over and over.

An attacking move might be complaining about the quality of a product or service, and asking for concessions, such as lower prices or better terms. A defensive might be changing the topic to something else while brushing the request aside.

Sensing the advance, the defender parries the opponent's push away to avert any immediate harm, then follows by a pull to expose the opponent's weakness and lures him into a compromising position. This can be seen in the following exchanges.

The customer complains angrily, "Your product is terrible; it left a foul residue in my machines." This sets the stage for a push to fell the opponent, such as, "For us to ever consider using your product again, you must remedy the situation and do better."

Of course, the manager is well aware of how the game is played. Feeling vulnerable and the push coming, he parries the attack and says, "That's strange! We have never had any complaints from our other long-term customers. Perhaps it's how your mechanics applied it in your shop that caused the residue to appear. If you don't mind, we can send some technicians over to check it out. By the way, we won't be responsible if the product is applied incorrectly." After the push is parried away, the manager adds, "Just so you know, our order book for this product is getting full. Unless we receive your order by this Friday, I cannot guarantee you that we can ship your order before next month." So the exercise goes on and on, until both sides are exhausted and see no advantage in continuing. Only then can an agreement be struck.

In negotiations, a skillful Tai Chi player will always outmaneuver the anxious party. A real-life example comes from 1968, when the US was mired in the Vietnam War with over 0.5 million troops stationed in that Southeast Asian country. In May that year, President Lyndon Johnson, who decided not to run for re-election, wanted his successor to have a clean slate to begin his new term with. So he initiated a peace talk with North Vietnam, the patron of the Vietcong, who were waging guerrilla warfare against the South Vietnamese government.

There were four parties in the talks: the US, North Vietnam, South Vietnam and the Vietcong.

To show their commitment to the negotiating process, the North Vietnamese rented a villa in Paris. The American negotiators, who were anxious to wrap up talks quickly, stayed in hotels. Knowing that Johnson was about to leave office and anxious to strike a deal, the Vietnamese parried away US initiatives. They took their time to pull the Americans deeper and deeper into the negotiating process with seemingly trivial matters.

The Vietnamese were also Confucians who demanded that the names and protocols be proper before they would proceed with the real talks. So the parties spent several months haggling over the shape of the negotiating table and seating arrangements. Meanwhile, the Vietcong and North Vietnamese continued their ground offensives in the south. The off-and-on peace talks continued until January 1973, when all parties finally signed an accord that signaled the end of American involvement in Vietnam, more than 3.5 years after the talks had begun.

This type of practice is not limited to Asia.

In 1941, at the height of the Second World War, Hitler invaded the Soviet Union, Germany's one-time ally. With his crack army divisions, Hitler wanted to defeat the Soviets in quick blitzkrieg fashion as he had earlier in Western Europe. Stalin initially resisted but he soon realized he was no match for Nazi firepower, so he pulled his troops eastward to retreat from the advancing Germans. Stalin also made sure that nothing was left behind, so there was no food or fuel—absolutely nothing for the invading Germans to capture.

Hitler kept pushing and pushing, hoping to score a quick win. Stalin kept pulling and pulling, until the Germans were terribly extended, cold and depleted by the harsh Russian winter. Only then did the Russians counter-attack and push the Germans out of their country.

The three Ps are routinely practiced in China, in family rooms and across conference tables. The best businessmen in China are skillful practitioners of the art. They are patient and calm, and will only strike when their opponents are vulnerable.

However, if only one of the parties knows Tai Chi and the other does not, then all bets are off. The innocent party is now fair game to be exploited and must submit to the superior player.

This is also one of the reasons why there are so many fake products in China, from hi-tech replicas to medicines and foodstuffs. In these markets, ordinary folks have no real power to speak of. They cannot push the manufacturers to be more ethical, nor can they rely on the regulators to pull for them. For a variety of reasons, including corruption, Chinese regulators have not been as effective as they should have been. As consumers have little economic or political pull, they are fair game to be exploited by unscrupulous manufacturers.

Yin and Yang Politics

In many situations involving the contest of two parties with similar abilities, the Tai Chi principle applies. A practitioner may evade, pull or push his opponent, but he doesn't really wish to obliterate him.

Destroying an enemy may deliver a moment's peace, but it can end up creating more enemies and no lasting peace. Like a magnet, cutting away one pole does not separate it into two separate poles: it merely creates more magnets. Similarly, eliminating an opponent may take away his physical presence but it will cause his ideas to multiply.

There is a better way. You can eliminate an opponent by making him more like you, or you can take the things that are positive about him and learn to behave more like him. This can be achieved through a mutually beneficial transformation via a deliberate process of dialog and adaptation. In so doing, you not only eliminate an immediate threat but also create an ally in the process.

At the end of the exercise, both you and your enemy will have changed for the better. This multi-tasking diplomacy exercise can best be done through a deliberate process, in good old Tai Chi fashion. Abraham Lincoln said this succinctly, "Am I not destroying my enemies when I make friends of them?"

So instead of cutting a big magnet into small magnets, and weakening them all, why not join the smaller pieces together to create a really big magnet? The resultant aggregate will be much stronger than the individual pieces, and also much easier to handle.

If we focus only on our own narrow interests and lose sight of the big picture, we risk losing our balance and weakening ourselves in the process.

An example is the US presidential campaign, the biggest peacetime contest on earth.

Every four years, Democrats and Republicans square off to put their respective nominee into the Oval Office, arguably the most powerful office in the world. At the beginning of past election campaigns, the two camps were usually poles apart in their politics. Republicans wanted to have a smaller government, reduce the budget deficit and reduce taxes to spur job growth in the important private sector. Democrats wanted to push for infrastructure investment, immigration and healthcare reform, not to mention narrowing the widening wealth gap.

After the campaigns were kicked into high gear, the rhetoric of the two camps became increasingly heated. But when it got closer to election day, both parties would have gradually softened their initial stances and shifted more towards the political center, where the majority of Americans reside.

For argument's sake, let's assume the Republicans can be characterized as yang, and the Democrats as yin. Although these two parties had been contesting each other fiercely and vociferously, closer to election day they began to look more like each other. Both sides wanted to appeal to the swing voters, represented by a substantial middle class with middle-of-the-road values. Finally, on election day, after all the votes had been tallied, a new President was elected to the highest office in the land for the next four years.

In order for Tai Chi to work, all participants must agree to a common principle, which is to maintain their balance while jostling with each other. The 2011 budget battle between President Barack Obama and the Republican-controlled Congress failed to meet the Tai Chi criteria. The partisan politics and take-no-prisoners attitude got the best of both sides.

The politics of the parties became dangerously polarized and extreme. They drifted further apart instead of coming together at the middle. The result was a stalemate when, for the first time, rating agency Standard and Poor's stripped the US government of its coveted AAA sovereign credit rating. Afraid of a repeat of the Lehman Brothers collapse, the markets sold off. American politicians, imbued with their must-win attitude, have grown to relish this kind of open warfare. However, as the markets have shown, the results were more destabilizing than constructive.

The situation did not get any better the second time round. In October 2013, President Obama and the Republicans went at it again. This time the Republicans wanted to repeal the president's signature legislation, the Affordable Care Act, by tying it to the approval to extend the US debt ceiling.

Again, both sides claimed the moral high ground and, as always, the rhetoric became increasingly heated. Republicans argued that a rising debt burden would choke off the nation's nascent economic recovery and unfairly shift the liabilities to future generations of Americans. Democrats claimed economic recovery was under way, and now it was time to address some long-standing issues, such as affordable healthcare. The fight was high drama, with both sides appealing to their bases for support.

Finally, on 16 October 2013, exactly one day before the US debt ceiling was to be breached, Congress reached an agreement for a temporary suspension until February 2014. In the interim, the US government had a partial shutdown for 16 days during which some non-essential services were curtailed. This episode resulted in the temporary furlough of 800,000 federal employees and a significant loss of economic activity.

In the end, the president and the Democrats prevailed, but US prestige suffered greatly, especially overseas. Foreigners began to view the US government, long the shining beacon of a functioning democracy, as being represented by teams of squabbling politicians who refuse to work together. The budget debacle took the US to the brink of a credit default and raised questions about the government's willingness to honor its financial obligations.

To most investors, the credit risk of US Treasury obligations does not reside in the US government's ability to pay. The government can issue more debt whenever necessary to fund its obligations since it has the largest economy in the world, and the US dollar is the world's main reserve currency. Domestic and foreign investors have never shied away from buying new US Treasury issues. And if the Congressional Budget Office's forecast is correct, the US federal deficit is expected to shrink in the current decade, which will reduce the need to borrow over time. This is good for the outlook of US credit.

Asians are raised as consensus-builders. Their culture requires them to seek commonalities before looking for differences. They may jostle with each other and play endless rounds of Tai Chi, but they are unlikely to throw any hard punches. Therefore, they find it difficult to understand why US politicians behaved the way they did. The very public manner in which the budget debate took place was also quite disruptive.

One of the reasons why sensitive matters should be discussed in private is that it allows experts to do their jobs without others interfering with them. Privacy also allows participants to back down gracefully from their entrenched positions without appearing weak in front of their constituents. Most importantly, it allows people to keep their backs straight and and not to lose face in compromising situations. If reputation is damaged, goodwill is lost. If goodwill is lost, it is difficult for people to work together openly.

In *The Art of War*, Sun Tzu says not to chase after an enemy who is cornered. Just like an animal, an enemy who has nowhere to go will fight his hardest to survive. Therefore, it is essential to offer an adversary a graceful way to back down. There is no need to humiliate him, least of all in public. Otherwise, he will fight his hardest to get away.

The US debt-ceiling debacle raised serious concerns about the government's ability to function at the highest level. Having learnt a lesson, lawmakers decided to discreetly deal with their next budget challenge, which was to temporarily extend the US debt ceiling, to January 2014.

This was accomplished without much fanfare by a team of congressional leaders comprising both Republicans and Democrats. In February 2014, another agreement was reached and passed by both houses to extend the debt ceiling to 2015. While the ultimate prize of a permanent resolution of the US debt-ceiling problem is still elusive, and the problem will likely resurface, this deal gave the government a year's worth of extra breathing room to prepare for it. (In 2015, Congress agreed to raise the debt ceiling for another two years.) The success of the congressional teams testifies to the importance of working on a set of common agendas while using diplomacy to resolve sensitive issues.

Weiqi: Winning by Suffocation

One can look at a traditional Chinese board game, Weiqi (围棋), to see how the Chinese like to deal with conquest. Many scholars have compared chess and Weiqi. Henry Kissinger, in *On China*, uses them to describe the differences between Chinese and Western mindsets. In chess, either the international version or the Chinese version, the goal is to capture the king or emperor to win the game. In Weiqi, however, the goal is to capture more territory than the opponent.

3 Games People Play

Weiqi, also called Go in Japan, is a deceptively simple board game that can become complicated very quickly. Two opposing players take turns placing white and black round stones on the intercepts of a 19 by 19 grid drawn on a square board. Unlike chess, where the coveted location is in the middle of the board, Weiqi players like to control the corners and edges. That's because the center is too prominent because it is exposed on all four sides and therefore more susceptible to attack.

Unlike chess, there are no queens, knights or pawns, and no checkmate for a quick win. Each stone in Weiqi functions in exactly the same way, which is to occupy a point on the board. A player is judged by how well he can make his pieces work together as a whole. Taking out an opponent's pieces does not always offer the advantage. It may even be a trap. Weiqi reflects how traditional Chinese people live their lives. A good Weiqi player follows the middle way and is keenly aware of the duality of living.

The first rule of Weiqi is not to be greedy. Like Tai Chi, calmness is essential and excess can invite a deadly response. A player must contemplate each move and its impact on the whole. He must always have the big picture in mind, and be willing to sacrifice the short term for the long term, the individual for the whole.

At the beginning of the game, the board is occupied by only a small number of scattered white and black stones, with no discernable pattern to speak of. As the game progresses, its complexity increases. The pieces are no longer just black and white stones randomly scattered on the board; they now form complex mosaic patterns with ever-changing permutations that vary with every move. A good Weiqi player is someone who can see all the evolving patterns in his head and plan for the future, while moving cautiously with his fingers. One wrong move can cause him to lose the game, while a skillfully placed stone can turn things around for him. Because the focus is on relative advantage, rather than a lopsided win, the best strategy is to be patient and flexible, react to the opponent's moves, and strike where he is weakest.

This is why it can be frustrating for Westerners working with the Chinese. Westerners are accustomed to following clearly defined game plans, with discrete outcomes of winning and losing. While their Chinese counterparts may also share the same objectives, their tactics can be reactive and their focus often shifty. What's more, they like to avoid direct confrontation and only strike when they sense weakness.

The Art of War

War is the ultimate conflict that humans can inflict on other humans. It conjures up images of weary soldiers crawling in combat, to kill or survive. There is plenty of bloodshed, broken families, burnt-out homes and suffering refugees. War always causes a significant loss of life and property, regardless of why it is fought or who wins. In war, each party hopes to extract a certain outcome from the opposite side. If neither side is willing to give in, they may resort to fighting over it. Occasionally there is a ceasefire or truce, but it rarely lasts. However, if the primary objective can be achieved through dialog or other peaceful means, then combat is not always a given.

The modern definition of war can be broadened to include other types of conflict. It is not only fought on the battlefield; it is also fought in conference rooms, on trading floors and anywhere where there are significant differences in expectation of outcomes from different interested parties.

In business, war can be a negotiation between a company and its contractors or distributors, each wanting to cut a better deal. It can be between a tenant and a landlord arguing over a new lease, between workers arguing over assignments, between department heads fighting for mandates and resources, between traders arguing over spreads, between bankers arguing over fees with their clients or between lovers quarrelling over attention. At the end of the day, it is the philosophy of dealing with conflict that determines how it will be handled, with force or not. In this regard, the Chinese and Western views about conflict management can be quite different.

Peace can be achieved either by resolving the fundamental issues behind a conflict or by beating the opponent into submission. In the latter case, peace exists only for the winners. As the losers will hold a grudge and wait to exact their revenge, there can be no lasting peace.

To the Chinese, war is the result of conflict that has gone awry. It is not inevitable, nor should it be the primary objective of those in power, which is to get on with life. The Chinese word for martial is 武, or wushu (and 武术 translates as martial arts). It is made up of two words. The first is to stop and the second is the ancient weapon called a dagger-axe, which looks like a long spear with a sickle attached to one end. Suffice to say, the principle of the traditional Chinese martial spirit is predicated on the avoidance of fights.

The eighteenth-century military theorist Carl von Clausewitz (1780–1831) was an officer in the Prussian army who later became the director of its military academy. He had fought many wars for Prussia and, at one time in his career, also Russia. He is acknowledged to be one of the most influential military thinkers of the Western world. Clausewitz's experience and research allowed him to publish a set of military doctrines appropriately entitled *On War*. The book remains one of the most studied texts in military academies worldwide.

In the first chapter of his magnum opus, Clausewitz lays down his purpose of war, which is to use force to submit the enemy to one's will. He also acknowledges that war should be an integral part of policy and political process, a theme that he repeats several times. However, he doesn't specify that one should exhaust all options before waging war. In this regard, he leaves the triggers to those in charge of policies.

Sun Tzu (孙子, 544 BC–496 BC) was a Chinese general and a military theorist during the Warring States Period. He remains the most influential military theorist in Chinese history. His classic work, *The Art of War*, was written over 2,500 years ago. In the broadest sense, any conflict that requires the yielding of one side to another can benefit from Sun Tzu's work. Also, because war is a violent activity inspired by both fear and greed, emotions that we still possess and will continue to possess, Sun Tzu's ideas will never be out of date.

The Art of War is highly concise and conceptual. It was written with roughly 6,000 classical Chinese characters. One of the reasons it was so compact was that in Sun Tzu's time books were written on thin bamboo slates, so to save space and weight they had to be concise.

In comparison, Clausewitz's *On War* comprises over 650 pages of dense English translated from German. The reason it is so long is because Clausewitz wants to explain his rationales and bring the reader to his point of view. In contrast, Sun Tzu gives his ideas without much elaboration, in fine classical Chinese tradition.

The two military giants also have very different strategies on war. Sun Tzu prefers his battles to be swift and, if at all possible, without bloodshed. He says the best military strategy is to frustrate the enemy's plans; the next is to disrupt his organization; the last is to fight him in actual battles. He also says that to fight 100 battles and win them all is not the best of the best; to break the enemy without fighting is supreme.

Sun Tzu also believes that an enemy's will to fight is more important than his ability to fight. Therefore, if one can break the enemy's will, with diplomacy, deception, intelligence or whatever other non-combat means one can muster, then the military objective can be accomplished without bloodshed.

In contrast, Clausewitz says emphatically that destroying the enemy's armed forces is the most important objective and the only way to succeed in a war. In many respects, the Clausewitzian view on war, which is to use force to impose one's will on the opponent, remains popular in the West.

Despite some similarities, there are major differences between the two military giants. Both Clausewitz and Sun Tzu view war as an instrument of policy and subordinated to it. The main difference is that Sun Tzu's war has a deeper psychological dimension. He considers stratagem, or the ability to outwit the enemy, a better alternative than combat. His collection of stratagems consists of evasion, deception, intelligence, diplomacy, and other psychological and non-combat means. Sun Tzu views these non-combat options as superior to the use of force, especially when the enemy is entrenched.

Today, many of Sun Tzu's non-combat options can be delivered easily via the Internet. Given the proliferation of social media and mass-communication channels, information warfare, including the spreading of misinformation to influence those who are easily swayed, and cyber attack on an enemy's information networks, has been shown to be an effective and low-cost weapon of mass destruction. This further testifies to the genius of Sun Tzu.

In *On War*, Clausewitz articulates a concept called the *center of gravity* to describe where the enemy is most concentrated. According to Newton, all the mass of a solid body can be imagined to be concentrated at a single point inside the body, which he called the *center of mass*. If a person knows where an object's center of gravity (or mass) is, he can spin it or manipulate its motion with ease. Clausewitz's military analogy is just that. If someone could locate the center of gravity of an enemy, then he should be able to engage it in a decisive battle.

However, the Newtonian center-of-mass concept applies only to solid bodies. It doesn't work for a liquids because liquid does not have a fixed center of gravity, as it must conform to the shape of the vessel that holds it. This is where Clausewitz's center-of-gravity concept becomes difficult in practice, especially in the fluidity of guerilla warfare.

When fighters are loosely associated with each other through a set of common beliefs, but not much else, they are by no means a solid organization. Depending on the situation, their movements can be diffused and difficult to pin down. In fact, they can be almost anywhere at any time to cause havoc even without a significant concentration.

In contrast to the Clausewitzian center-of-gravity concept, Sun Tzu's strategy is like water. As water has no fixed shape, war also has no fixed rules. Like water that flows according to the terrain it is in, military tactics must be flexible enough to reflect the actual combat situations. Rather than having a fixed course they should change according to what the enemy does.

Clausewitz also uses the term "cohesion" to describe the state of the enemy. If enemy troops follow strict orders and are disciplined, and if they share strong political beliefs, they are considered to be a cohesive body. If the enemy is cohesive then it is possible to locate its center of gravity and strike hard at it. Otherwise, fighting the enemy is like punching air—a waste of energy.

Sun Tzu's approach to military tactics is quite different. Instead of seeking out where the enemy is most concentrated and striking hard at it, he prefers to strike where the enemy is weakest. He also says that the best formation of an army is no formation at all. That way your enemy will find it difficult to decipher your true intentions.

Skirting direct confrontation with evasion is similar to the parrying move in Tai Chi. It is also how many Chinese people handle conflict.

In the wars between the peasant-dominated communist guerillas and Chiang Kai-shek's US-equipped armed forces in the 1940s, Mao Zedong applied Sun Tzu's tactics masterfully. Because his guerillas were disadvantaged in both size and equipment, Mao had to rely on deception and evasion to survive.

When faced with Chiang's superior forces, Mao's guerillas quickly dispersed and blended into the countryside. They re-emerged to attack where the enemy troops least expected. Like water in a bucket, Mao's guerillas moved away when the enemy attacked and reconstituted to wreak havoc after it had left. After a few years of this mobile warfare, Mao's guerillas became so battle hardened and cohesive that they felt confident waging larger and more decisive battles against Chiang's troops. In the end they prevailed.

During the Vietnam War, the US and its allies were constantly searching for the main body of North Vietnamese army troops, hoping to pound them into oblivion with their superior firepower. But the enemy was evasive like water. Its fighters dispersed and hid in the countryside among villagers during the day, and came out to attack the allies in the dark of night. They hit and ran, and they didn't stay anywhere long enough to be engaged in serious battle.

The guerrillas behaved like water flowing down a hill. They avoided the allies (big rocks) by flowing round them. After they had regrouped and regained their strength, they struck the allies at their weakest points.

During Xi Jinping's visit with Obama in California in 2013, the US team had wanted to engage Xi and his team in a decisive battle regarding several important issues. However, the Chinese delegation was like water at its evasive best. In the end, the visit was downgraded to a photo opportunity for the two presidents.

Evasion vs. Head On

The penchant of Chinese commanders for using evasive tactics may be effective in guerilla warfare but is not so in business operations. Instead of tackling operational issues head on, Chinese managers often choose clever ideas and guanxi to get round them. These evasive tactics may work in the short term but they end up creating bigger problems down the road.

The following is an example of how expediency can hurt in the long run.

In 1998 I was visiting a Lehman client in Zhengzhou, the capital of Henan province in the central part of China. After a couple of days of meetings there, a young man from the Holiday Inn Crown Plaza drove us to the airport to catch our flights.

At that time, Zhengzhou didn't have many nice roads and we were stuck in traffic for quite a while. I started chatting with the young driver and found out that he had worked for a government-owned hotel before his current job. I decided to ask him how he liked working for a US hotel. He told us enthusiastically that he liked it far better because the rules were much clearer.

When the government inspectors came to inspect the US hotel and noted deficiencies, the management team would insist on remedying them fully. They would do it over and over again until the problems were all fixed. Compared with this, his old Chinese hotel managers were more likely to work their guanxi to get past tough inspections. As a result, the state-owned hotel became so dilapidated that it would require substantial investment to bring it back to standard. In the end it had to be sold. This kind of situation occurs quite often in Chinese-run companies.

In comparison, most Western managers would use the Clausewitzian approach, applying critical analysis to identify and solve business problems. Attacking core problems with the best available resources is the most efficient way of running a business operation. While managers may be able to avoid making tough decisions by evading them, they will not have gained the necessary insights to achieve significant breakthroughs. When there is no pain, any gain is only illusory.

Bibliography

R.L. Wing, *The Tao of Power, Lao Tzu's Classic Guide to Leadership, Influence and Excellence*, Ch. 36 and 40, Doubleday & Company, Inc., 1986.
Vincelombardi.com, reviewed Mar 2014.

Sun Tzu, *The Art of War*, translated by Lin Wusun, Long River Press, Ch. 1, P. 11, 2003a.
Vietnam War, Encyclopaedia Britannica, reviewed Apr 2014.
Flora Lewis, *Vietnam Peace Pacts Signed America's Longest War Halts*, The New York Times, Jan 27, 1973.
Eastern Front (World War II), Wikipedia, reviewed Apr 2014.
Abraham Lincoln, Brainy Quote, reviewed Jan 2016.
Congressional Budget Office, *The Budget and Economic Outlook: Fiscal Years 2013 to 2023*, P. 10, Feb 5 2013.
Sun Tzu, *The Art of War*, translated by Lin Wusun, Long River Press, Ch. 7, P. 66, 2003b.
United States debt ceiling crisis of 2013, Wikipedia, reviewed May 2014.
Ashley Parker and Jonathan Weisman, *G.O.P. Senate Leaders Avert Debt Ceiling Crisis*, The New York Times, Feb 12, 2014.
Sun Tzu, *The Art of War*, translated by Lin Wusun, Long River Press, Ch. 7, P. 65, 2003c.
Henry Kissinger, *On China*, P. 23, Penguin Books, 2012.
Michael I. Handel, *Sun Tzu and Clausewitz: The Art of War and On War Compared*, Professional Readings in Military Strategy No. 2, P. 24–30, Strategic Studies Institute, U.S. Naval War College, 1991.
Carl von Clausewitz, *On War,* Edited and Translated by Michael Howard and Peter Paret, P. 485–487, Princeton University Press, 1976.
Sun Tzu, *The Art of War*, translated by Lin Wusun, Long River Press, Ch. 6, P. 55, 2003d.
Sun Tzu, *The Art of War*, translated by Lin Wusun, Long River Press, Ch. 11, P. 55, 2003e.
The Economist, *BREXIT: THE AFTER SHOCKS*, Last updated Jun 24, 2016.
CBSNEWS, *5 ways U.S. and global markets are rethinking Brexit*, Jul 4, 2016.

4
Geography of Management

Geography of Culture

In this book I put Asians into one big camp and Westerners, primarily those of European descent, into another for the purpose of comparing management and leadership styles. Although this approach may seem overly simplistic, I do have reasons.

There are 1.36 billion Chinese people living in Mainland China today, almost a fifth of the world's population. They are all brought up with some kind of Confucian influence either from school or family. If we include the populations from Korea, Japan and Vietnam, who were also influenced by a similar culture, and the vast overseas Chinese diaspora, the total population influenced by Confucianism reaches almost 2 Billion.

There are about a Billion people in the world with European descent, if we count those living in Europe and North America, and a smaller number from Oceania and South and Central America. These Westerners may be citizens of different countries, speak different languages and practice different customs and religions, but they can all trace their cultural heritage and their modern ways of life to the early Greeks.

Together, these two main cultural camps account for about 40 percent of the world's population and over 80 percent of its GDP. Needless to say, their political powers are also immense.

How do people from these two different cultures reason and make decisions? Behavioral scientists have an answer: they classify people into two broad cognitive categories—wholistic and analytic.

A person's cognitive style, which affects how he perceives problems, thinks and makes decisions, is heavily influenced by the culture he is brought up in. In this regard, Asians are traditionally more wholistic because of their Confucian influence, and Westerners are more analytic because of their Greek heritage.

A wholistic manager likes to solve problems in the most comprehensive manner possible. He first grasps the big picture, before reviewing a problem's components and their relationships. He then connects all these different components to form a mental picture of interconnected dots. In this picture, every dot is connected to every other dot through some multi-dimensional contextual links, such as guanxi (relationships), shared interests, personal affinity, history and culture. Also in this picture, every dot is influenced by every other dot in some manner or another. Their relationships are fluid, and very often situation dependent. The picture is comprehensive but lacks precision.

Context is very important to the wholistic manager because solutions to a particular problem can be context dependent.

On the other hand, the analytical manager uses his powerful left-brain to deploy logic to solve problems. He first segregates a problem into its critical components, then attempts to decipher their relationships. He then devises a robust plan of execution and carries it out in a neat, linear fashion. Context is less important to the analytical manager.

Because of the Greeks and their influence in education, Westerners are brought up to think logically. Also, because of their success in science, there is a tendency for Westerners to think their solutions in other realms of human endeavor, such as economics, business and politics, should also follow scientific principles. Just as Newton's Laws have successfully described the motion of celestial bodies, the Western viewpoint assumes human endeavors can be subjected to the same universal laws. However, depending on the subject matter, and the context they are in, this may or may not be true.

In his fascinating book *The Geography of Thought: How Asians and Westerners Think Differently … and Why*, Michigan's Richard Nisbett has shown that Asians and Westerners perceive situations and make decisions quite differently.

He shows that Asian students, who were born either in the US or overseas, including those with Chinese, Korean or Japanese heritage, react similarly to certain questions as a group but quite differently from their Western counterparts. He also shows that Asians perceive objects and their relationships quite differently from Westerners.

Nisbett attributes this to their common Confucian heritage, with its emphasis on relationship, group identity and conformity. Even though the study samples were limited to college students, his conclusions about different cognitive styles are quite insightful.

At the other end of the cognitive spectrum is how Westerners perceive objects and relationships. They like to seek the objective truth and, if possible, independent of the context it is in. This critical approach to problem-solving is courtesy of the Greeks.

The Socratic method, where professors ask questions and challenge students to come up with answers, is taught in many of the world's leading law and business schools. After students graduate and enter the world of business or politics, they bring this critical skill set with them. As businessmen, lawyers or politicians they continue to use the Socratic method to practice their chosen professions.

When these two different cognitive camps meet each other there are bound to be misunderstandings.

In Whole or in Parts?

When Chinese people and many other Asians look at the world, they like to integrate their experiences rather than divide them. They don't like to analyze them independently in the way that Westerners like to. Traditional Chinese paintings and music are examples of this tradition. These are usually harmonious in appearance and feel, without the bold dissonances often seen in Western music or art.

Because of this, Asians can accept matters that may appear ambiguous or contradictory to Westerners. Take good and bad, for example. To Asians, good and bad are the two opposite but inseparable parts of the whole. Something good has always something bad imbedded in it, and something bad always has something good within it. It's neither good nor bad, but both good and bad. It's not right or wrong, but we are in it together. One cannot exist without the other.

This concept of co-existing opposites was first described in *I Ching* (*The Book of Changes*), which appeared in the Zhou Dynasty over 2,800 years ago. Original fragments of the text were said to have existed even before then.

What we observe in nature is the result of different forces constantly contesting with each other to make changes. The Chinese concepts of yin and yang, and the five elements of metal, wood, water, fire and earth, were all created in ancient times to describe different elements, or forces, in nature that must compete and co-exist with each other. These forces cannot be analyzed separately because they exist only in the context of their opposites. Taking them apart would render them meaningless.

This nature-inspired concept of balance and co-existence can also be applied to activities in business, the political arena and personal relationships.

To the Chinese, good and bad are just the same phenomena viewed from different perspectives. For example, the Chinese word for crisis is 危机, which consists of two words, 危 and 机. The first means danger and the second means opportunity. One cannot exist without the other. So why focus only on problems? Why not look for opportunities instead?

We can take pictures with a telephoto lens or a wide-angle lens. These lenses provide us with different perspectives, and that in turn affects how we perceive reality.

The Western analytical mindset is like a telephoto lens. With it we can see details such as tree branches very clearly but not the whole forest. On the other hand, the Asian wholistic mindset is like a wide-angle lens. With it we can see lots of trees but not much detail of each tree. A complete picture requires us to have both perspectives.

Having a complete picture can offer health benefits as well. If we view ourselves through the eyes of others, we can have a more complete picture of ourselves. As a result, we may be less stressed out by what we don't know or don't have. When we are more relaxed, we can uncover opportunities in the most unlikely places.

Depending on where we stand, a glass of water can be either half full or half empty. If we stand up and look down at the glass from above, we will see mostly empty space. We may say that the glass is half empty. If we look at the glass from the bottom up, we may say that the glass is mostly full.

In fact, the glass is neither full nor empty. It is both full and empty. The amount of water in the glass hasn't changed but our perception of it has.

Similarly, if we go outside to shovel snow on a cold winter's morning, we will feel cold. However, when we come back into the house after we have finished shoveling, we will feel warm. The temperature inside or outside the house hasn't changed but our perception of comfort has. Therefore it goes without saying that context can affect our conclusions.

In weather forecasting, we use the term "high-pressure system" to describe an area that has a higher air density than its neighboring area with a lower air density. While the absolute barometric readings may be of interest to some people, it is the relative magnitudes of the high- and low-pressure systems, and the movement of the air masses between them, that make for weather changes. If the difference is large, we can expect severe changes in weather. It can tell us whether we should play golf or carry an umbrella.

While only one attribute—air density—distinguishes the two atmospheric systems, it is the relative strengths and movements of these opposites that are of importance to us. Similarly, in many endeavors where change is a constant, such as the financial market, the more assets are over-valued, the greater the chances of a severe correction, and vice versa.

This opposites-driven movement is what the ancient Chinese referred to as the Tao, or nature's way.

The same analysis can also be applied to social phenomena, such as the widening wealth gap. While everybody has some money, the super rich have a lot more than everyone else. If the gap between them and everyone else is too wide, there is tension. This may manifest in violent social change, just like the weather system.

So there are at least two ways of looking at any phenomenon: the absolute and the relative. Both are valid.

Crossing the River

A Western manager may use all the analytical tools he has at his disposal to solve a problem. A Chinese manager may solve the same problem gradually and intuitively by feeling his way around.

The Chinese have their own way of dealing with complex problems. This is often referred to as crossing a river by feeling the stones underneath.

In the river crossing analogy, someone must take small steps, test the situation between steps, and move slowly from one step to the next. Each new step depends on what was done at the previous step, as well as how he feels about his current step at that moment in time. In this approach, a problem is solved incrementally and creatively at each juncture, but not necessarily according to any detailed analysis or planning.

At each and every step, the river crosser must feel with his feet to assess the conditions of the river bottom, current and swell, before he takes his next step. If he feels he is about to step into a deep recess, he can go sideways or retrace his steps and start over. On the other hand, if he feels sure-footed and comfortable, he can take a bigger step forward.

To deal with the unexpected requires management flexibility and ingenuity. Solving a problem slowly in a piecemeal manner allows a manager to preserve available options to deal with the unexpected. This method may seem amateurish to Westerners but it has been shown to work well in the Chinese context.

This is one of the reasons why China will unlikely adopt many established Western practices in a wholesale manner. Instead, it will find its own path slowly and deliberately, like crossing the river while feeling the stones underneath.

This is also why it is so difficult for outsiders to decipher Chinese policy intentions. It is rare for Chinese officials to communicate their intentions to the public in real time, as their Western counterparts often do. Because of the incremental nature of their approach, it is not easy for them to articulate a succinct near-term vision to the public, even though their strategy may be quite clear. Plus, most officials are used to communicating upwards and not to the public. Therefore they often appear wooden and unconvincing.

The recent regulatory mishaps in the Chinese stock market, and confusions regarding its currency exchange intentions, highlight the deficiencies of this approach and what officials must improve in the new market economy.

A Western manager crossing the same river may do it differently. He may first survey the river and put stakes on the riverbed to mark its depth, and to show his troops where to cross and where to avoid. This methodical approach calls for research and analysis to identify the best solution to a problem before executing it. Once a method is identified and fully vetted, it can be used over and over again, and from project to project.

Compared with this the Chinese approach is more intuitive and situational dependent. Depending on who leads the river crossing exercise and where he starts, there can be as many different solutions, but not necessarily any optimum solution. It is also more time-consuming because decisions have to be made at each and every step along the way. However, in complex situations where there are no clear precedents, the Chinese approach may avoid major pitfalls.

Soup or Salad?

In many respects, the ways in which the Chinese and Americans manage are as different as soup and salad.

The US is often called a melting pot for its racial and cultural diversity, as people from all around the world move to the US to start new lives.

In a melting pot, different metals would melt under high heat. The resultant alloy can be stronger or have better performance characteristics than the individual components. However, once the heat is removed, individual metals may separate out again – their unique molecular structures often render them immiscible at room temperatures.

So a melting pot analogy suggests that American people would come together only under extenuating circumstances, such as wars that threaten the entire nation; otherwise they would just be themselves and mind their own business.

A salad bowl is perhaps a better descriptor for the US. In Europe, a salad is a simple side dish, usually consisting of a few leaves of lettuce and other fresh local produce, topped with a light dressing, such as vinaigrette. The dish is meant to provide some acidity to ready the palette for the main course that follows.

In the US the huge salad selection can serve as the main event. It can consist of all kinds of fresh ingredients, such as lettuces with different flavors and textures, red or white onions, spongy white button or chewy grilled Portobello mushrooms, crunchy radishes, red and green peppers, salty olives, anchovies, crispy celery and sweet carrot sticks. To top it off, one can also have grilled chicken or salmon. With such a large variety of ingredients to choose from, the possibilities are endless.

In a salad, the individual ingredients retain their distinct flavors and textures. They complement each other and are enhanced by the dressing. The beauty of the dish is that someone can choose which ingredients he wants in his salad and which salad dressing to top it off with, including the all-powerful blue cheese.

The US is like that: each person is both distinct and different. People are free to express themselves. They can be loud or they can be quiet. They can be hip or they can be square. They can also choose to associate or not to associate with others of their own volition. That is the beauty of diversity.

Diversity is created when different people come together voluntarily. They complement each other while maintaining their own individual characteristics. A good manager enhances the capabilities of his team much like a good salad dressing can enhance the flavors of the different ingredients. A good manager also makes sure his people work together but doesn't overwhelm them in the way too much dressing can ruin a salad.

Diversity is good for business. By putting different talents together, managers can get the best of what each individual has to offer, and even more from their synergies. In the US, strength comes from diversity.

Tech managers know the power of diversity well. They often work alongside their employees, treating them as equals instead of subordinates. When employees are appreciated and treated with respect, they become energized and flourish.

To Chinese managers, the way Americans manage young tech companies is disorderly and a bit odd. For how can the chief executive officer

(CEO) of a major company such as Facebook sit in an open office with other employees conducting hackathons? Where is his dignity if he sits in the same area with everybody else? And without that, how can he manage his subordinates?

Soup is an important part of the Chinese meal. It is my analogy for Chinese management.

A Chinese soup has to simmer for at least two hours on a low heat. A double-boiled soup is placed inside a container in boiling water and cooked slowly for four hours. The gentle double boiling preserves the integrity of the nutrients so that they can serve their intended purpose, which is to nourish the body.

A typical Chinese soup has only a few ingredients, consisting of some fresh meat, say chicken or pork, and some vegetables and herbs. Unlike US soups, such as clam chowder, split peas and turkey noodles, which are really thin stews in disguise, the Chinese soup is much less thick and chunky. It is the clear broth that gourmets enjoy. That is why Americans say "eat soup" and the Chinese say "drink soup".

Soup can also serve important medicinal purposes. Depending on the season, a soup may include different ingredients and herbs to help balance the body's qi, or energy flow.

For example, in winter, it is important to have ingredients that exhibit heat in the Chinese medical vernacular, and ingredients that exhibit coolness in the summer months. This may include turnips, dates, dried alligator meat and pears for the fall and winter, or watercress and lychee for the spring and summer. When someone drinks a good Chinese soup, he gets the essence of all the good ingredients in the broth and becomes in tune with nature. The leftover soup ingredients are usually discarded.

After simmering for at least two hours, the hot soup is ready for consumption. Its delicate flavors should be just right and balanced. One should be able to taste hints of chicken, sliced ginger, pears and perhaps ginseng, all blended together harmoniously. Seasoning is the chef's job, so no salt or pepper is ever needed.

But unlike a salad, where a person can choose what to eat or not to eat, Chinese soup drinkers must take in everything or nothing at all. One has to have faith in the chef and hope he isn't having an off day.

In many respects, managing the Chinese way is like soup-making. Senior management carefully strategizes and puts together an action plan, before revealing it to the subordinates. The subordinates dutifully wait for their orders, like diners eagerly awaiting the chef's creation. Once they get the order (soup), they eagerly drink it. Their job is to execute orders but not to add value. They have to have diligence but not necessarily passion.

This is because their superiors have already done the exciting value-creation part. Like expert chefs, the experienced senior managers do all the necessary hard work before revealing their decisions to the subordinates. So what else is there for an employee to do except to follow orders?

Unlike a salad, the flavors of the ingredients in a Chinese soup are blended together. Unlike a salad, the soup ingredients can be tasted but not separated. Unlike in Western companies, members of a Chinese organization must accept everything it has in store for them and take it all in. They are not encouraged to change anything, or to add value their own way–just like a Chinese soup.

What Motivates Chinese Managers?

As humans, people everywhere desire safety and wellbeing. However, they may have different ideas about what constitutes safety and wellbeing or, for that matter, success. Unlike in science or medicine, universality doesn't always apply to how people feel about fulfillment.

Asians and Westerners can have very different ideas about what makes them happy. For example, most Asians would feel comfortable if they lived around their family, relatives and close friends. These support groups empower them, and make them feel safe and secure.

In the US, safety could mean having financial security with lots of money, and living in a big house in a safe neighborhood. It could also mean having physical security, such as owning firearms that would allow a man to protect his family. In China, even though people also desire big houses and other material trappings, as in the West, their safety also stems from the power of the group they belong to, in addition to the size of their bank accounts or the hardware they own.

A young Chinese graduate may decide to give up a higher-paying job in a faraway city so he can be closer to his family and friends. Or he may choose to spend a few years in Beijing, Shanghai or Shenzhen to establish his career but then eventually decide to go back to live closer to his family.

The Chinese saying "Falling leaves drop back to their roots" reflects a general desire that people like to eventually go back to where they come from, after they have done what they have to do elsewhere. In the US, young people are more like free spirits. They would most likely opt for opportunities and lifestyles that best suit their individual values and tastes.

Traditional Chinese culture venerates frugality and downplays wealth, especially the accumulation of wealth for wealth's sake. In the Confucian value totem pole, wealth is ranked below academics. Children are taught always to study hard, and to make a contribution to society, potentially through government service.

Getting rich is not something young people should think too much about. They should devote their energy to improving themselves—period. Likewise, having a part-time job while going to school is not something parents would encourage. Most would consider it a distraction and a waste of time.

In old China, after someone had excelled at academic study, he was in a position to consider a government post, and vice versa. This two-way academic to government career transition was favored by one of Confucius' students, Zi-Xia. No wonder government jobs continue to be so desirable today.

Granted, government jobs are both secure and prestigious in a society that venerates officialdom. But academic credentials are also important, even for senior government officials. An advanced degree immediately elevates an official's status above his peers. This explains why so many Chinese government officials spend the extra effort getting an additional degree while working at their regular jobs, and they have "PhD" or "Professor" printed on their name cards.

Even rich tycoons, who made their fortunes in the soaring Chinese property market, wish to appear scholarly. They like to have a scholarly achievement, such as a PhD, to go along with their wealth. They hope that it will help to dilute the unsavory images that successful businessmen may project.

In today's China, the economy is creating opportunities previously undreamed of for the younger generation. As the Chinese saying goes, when going against the tide, those who don't progress will be left behind. And surely no one wants to be stranded on the side of the Chinese economic superhighway, watching others speed by. Rather, they all want to be in the driving seat and leading the charge forwards. If they fall behind they may never catch up.

Now the priority is less about self-improvement and more about learning the correct skills, cultivating the right guanxi and getting rich the quickest way possible. The path is now straight and narrow for China's bright young graduates.

School becomes a place where students learn to apply all kinds of finished products, instead of where they discover their passions and identities, and where they develop tools personalized for their own future. When students graduate and go to work, they bring with them the same cutting and pasting mentality they acquired at school. If they don't have any ready-made solutions to suit the problems they face, they will improvise. There is nothing wrong with improvising, except that most students lack the experience of doing something unfamiliar, such as taking risks and learning from their mistakes.

As a result, some Chinese managers can come up with such outlandish ideas that they resemble almost nothing in existence. While this aggressiveness may be disguised as innovation and is itself not a big issue, it can lead to execution hiccups that diminish the value of their business case.

In China, rapid economic growth can camouflage mistakes, and bold initiatives can often become spectacularly successful. Because of that, they inspire even more aggressive risks. As a result, projects keep getting bigger and more spectacular all the time. Every manager thinks he is better than his peers, and the way to show that is by running bigger and more spectacular projects. Size drives passion; not the other way around.

In the US the view about education is a little different. Learning is a lifelong process and school is not the only place to learn. In fact, society offers a fuller spectrum of learning experiences, so it ought to be tapped into earlier. Academics are important, but so are sports and work experience.

Having a part-time job while going to school helps students to develop a good work ethic. It also generates self-worth, which young people achieve by serving a need with their own labor and getting paid for it. And true to the Western work ethic, it doesn't matter whether the job is delivering newspapers door to door, organizing files in an office or serving burgers at a fast-food restaurant. Work is work—period.

And as long as the work is done honestly with one's own labor, it is also sacred. The added bonus is that young people will get to be judged by their customers and peers at work, and not just by their teachers and parents. For many young Americans, having part-time jobs while going to school is not only a financial necessity but also a path towards eventual independence.

Working familiarizes young people with the real world, its rhythm and its hidden rules. It shows them how to compete and, at the same time, get along with those they compete with. Most importantly, it shows them how they can create tangible value outside of the cloistered environments of school and family. In the West, providing others with what they need creates value.

Through work, young people learn how to assess opportunities and risks, and how to develop a financial discipline. Warren Buffett once sold chewing gum, Coca-Cola, and magazines while he was at school, even though his father was a respectable US Congressman. Later he invested in the Coca-Cola Company and a newspaper publisher, *The Washington Post*, presumably because he was already familiar with their products.

In China it would be unthinkable for the son of a representative to the People's Congress to be selling anything, let alone door to door. It speaks poorly of the family and would surely cause the parents to lose face.

So if Chinese managers do not have the tradition of working while they are young, what motivates them to achieve later on in the business world? Is it wealth, status or power?

Even though every manager wants to get rich, and do so quickly, making a huge amount of money for the company and themselves has never been the only motivator for the traditional Chinese manager.

The long history of China makes people think of themselves and their place in the world in a historical context. It inspires them to dream big and be remembered in posterity. Therefore they often fancy themselves as historical figures, making important decisions that help to shape events in the country and the world. How better can one accomplish this than by running big projects?

It is also quite important for Chinese managers to leave a positive legacy for their children and future generations to remember them by. On the other hand, a heinous crime committed against the innocent can linger in the public mind for a long time, and shame their offspring.

Also, because China has suffered at the hands of foreigners in the past, every Chinese manager wants to support the Chinese Dream and see a stronger China.

Two Different Approaches

In general, Westerners respect business rules and play by the book. It is important that they follow a clearly laid out process. Chinese managers are less constrained by business conventions. It is important to them that they get results.

Western managers, who are used to looking at spreadsheets and financial statements to help guide their decisions, don't quite understand how Chinese managers approach problems. Chinese managers also don't understand why Western managers seem to always focus on the details rather than the higher-level issues, such as politics and guanxi.

The two very different management approaches are illustrated in Fig. 4.1.

Here, the further one goes from the center, the more qualitative and hence riskier the factors become. The fundamental or more quantitative factors, such as strategy and operations, are placed in the middle, and the more qualitative factors, such as guanxi and politics, in the outer layer. While these factors all contribute to the success or failure of a business, Chinese and Western managers have different preferences.

Chinese executives often approach from the outside in (or top down), and Westerners often drive their processes from the inside out (or bottom up.) Culture and the business environment have something to do with this difference.

4 Geography of Management 57

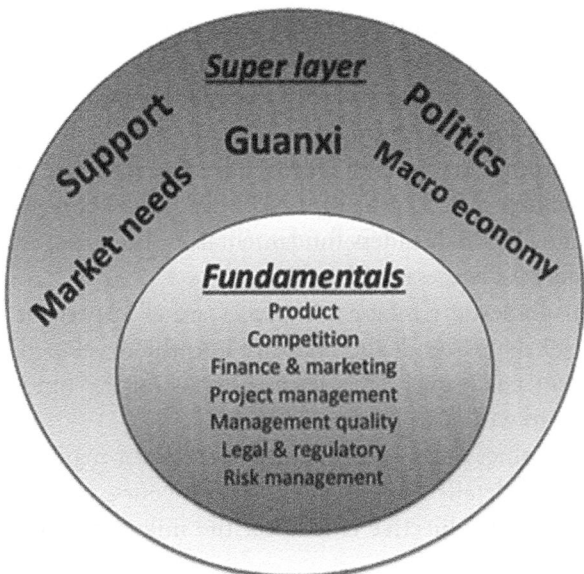

Fig. 4.1 Business success factors

Western managers tend to first focus on the fundamentals of a business, such as product performance, competition, finance and marketing, and legal and risk management, before considering the extraneous factors, such as politics and relationships. This is because they play a game where the playing field is relatively flat and the rules are similar for every player.

Only after they are satisfied with their performance within the fundamentals space do they consider factors in the super layer. These super layer factors should affect every player the same way, who have limited control of them. Players should focus their energy on factors where they can have an influence and not on those that they have little ability to change. Their approach is fundamental or, as Figure 4.1 shows, inside out.

Chinese managers are also concerned about the fundamental success factors. However, in a high-context society with a rapidly developing economy, they have to deal with rules and regulations that are constantly in flux, and their interpretations are often ambiguous and people dependent.

As a result, business fundamentals are often overshadowed by the need to read politics correctly and have the right guanxi to get things done. Plus, they have to contend with the paternal bureaucrats who hold immense power and discretion.

In this environment, the best approach is to go from the outside in, or top down, making sure that the super layer factors are being taken care of while dealing with the business fundamentals. Otherwise, even with the best fundamentals, success can be elusive.

Successful domestic Chinese companies are all experts at navigating the super layer. However, if they venture into the developed world they find a different ball game. They have to focus on the fundamentals of their business to win, just like everyone else.

Once the business plan is concluded, a Western manager will focus on the execution details. He will rarely change course midstream, except in emergencies. His objective is to meet the milestones and deliver his bottom-line numbers.

A Chinese manager is also concerned about his bottom-line performance, but profitability is not the only issue. Other intangible factors are just as important. These may include having a good relationship with his employees and officials, and creating a harmonious workplace. While these factors are also important to Western managers, they are secondary to delivering the numbers.

Another interesting aspect about Chinese managers is that they love to be creative. Many of them are dealmakers at heart who believe their clever ideas can make a real difference.

Chinese managers don't like to fix other people's problems because it does nothing to highlight their own brilliance. Therefore they often throw out the existing process, even in the midst of its execution, and start from scratch. This is especially so if a project has run into difficulties or if a new manager has just taken over. The new boss will want to make his own mark and not be burdened by the mistakes of the previous management.

In the Western legal tradition, a contract is a legal agreement binding the company and its counterparties. It must be honored regardless of who is in charge, and enforced as long as the company stays in business.

The Chinese manager thinks differently. He reasons that because a contract bears the signature of his predecessor, not his own, he is not responsible.

To some Chinese managers, signed contracts, contracts that are legally binding, are more agreements that are legally binding, are more like a memorandum of understanding. Contracts are to be followed when the conditions are right, as in normal operating conditions, and flouted when the going gets tough, as in a global recession. When times are tough, all parties are supposed to come together to modify their contracts and make things work.

To seek legal redress as they do in the West is not the best option in China. Lawsuits can disrupt harmony and cause people to lose face. It also means those involved are not sophisticated enough to solve problems discreetly, the Chinese way. The party who sues will be remembered for being inflexible, and castigated as a pariah in the industry, for the simple reason that he just doesn't quite understand how the game is played in China.

If the counter-party is a Western company, it may indeed choose to go to court and sue. Raising a lawsuit diminishes the possibility of doing business with the company in future. While laws and regulations are supposed to be unbiased, lawsuits raised by foreign companies can rekindle nationalistic sentiments that can affect the judicial outcome.

Again, to seek legal redress is not the best option, especially if the counter-party is a well-known Chinese company. A more culturally amenable approach is to seek compensation in kind. For example, the aggrieved party can ask for guaranteed future business or favors to compensate for losses, while holding the legal card for possible future use in case the promise isn't fulfilled.

At a higher level, the Chinese love clever strategists who win by outmaneuvering their opponents. Winning with the least amount of effort is considered the epitome of military strategy.

According to Sun Tzu, the best way to win a war is not to engage the enemy directly but to make them capitulate and lose the will to fight. By analogy, the best way to win in business is not to go head to head with a competitor but to frustrate him, causing him to lose focus and give up. Winning is much easier when your enemy is confused and disoriented, or his support is diminished.

So instead of competing head on with your competitor in the marketplace, why not massage your guanxi to delay or even deny your competitor the necessary permits to do its job? Why not go from the super layer in and checkmate your competitor before he even notices what has hit him? When we look Figure 4.1 and the business reality that exists today, Chinese business behaviors become much easier to interpret.

However, when the enemy is within, such as a problem encountered in a company's own operations, this approach can lead to procrastination and lost opportunities. No manager can avoid making decisions indefinitely by going around them. This doesn't mean he has to be strong and decisive like John Wayne, and knock out every opponent with a devastating right hook. But if business is at stake, making timely decisions is the only management option.

On management decisiveness, Lao Tzu says one should govern the nation as if frying a small fish. He says that you should be decisive and not change course too often when managing the affairs of a country. This statement is equally applicable to running a business, especially for the Chinese manger who likes to feel his way around. A manager should not change his mind too often without having a solid reason. Just like frying a small fish, if you turn it over too many times the fish will fall apart. Nothing is achieved but a mess.

The Chinese Relationship

A long-term, mutually beneficial relationship is what the Chinese prefer. Relationships connect businessmen, politicians, family members, colleagues, church members and fellow students via their common interests. They have both quantitative and qualitative aspects. The quantitative aspects include written contracts, such as marriage certificates and business contracts that compel the signatories to perform what they have agreed to do.

Equally important are the qualitative aspects of relationships. They may not be legally binding, but they are morally or customarily so, including the contextual obligations that each party is expected to fulfill. This kind of relationship is very important to the high-context Chinese.

A man living in another city is supposed to host his niece whenever she decides to visit. Because he is an older relative and a more established one, he is supposed to accommodate the young lady any time she shows up.

A father is expected to help his son pay for his wedding and the down payment for his apartment because that's what Chinese fathers customarily do. An uncle who is an executive in a large company is expected to recommend his niece for a job opening because that's what a prominent relative does. Someone in need can expect his relatives and close friends to pool their resources to help because that's what relatives and friends are for.

An American host is supposed to greet his Chinese visitors at the airport and pack their itinerary tightly. After business meetings, he is supposed to take them to New York or Las Vegas for some rest and recreation because that's what a good local host is supposed to do. A banker taking his Chinese clients for roadshows in Europe is expected to provide them with spending money because that's what they do in China. And so on.

A good relationship should be mutually beneficial and stand the test of time. Because China is a high-context society with a long history, Chinese people don't mind spending the time and effort to get to know their partners well and to develop their relationships slowly. This may include countless dinners, drinks and rounds of golf, or doing all kinds of small favors over a long period of time. In China a patient relationship is a good relationship.

Western executives are more businesslike in this respect. They are motivated by clearly defined objectives and driven to achieve speedy results. They often measure what they invest in a relationship against what they can get out in a reasonable amount of time. As such, they often find the Chinese relationship-building exercise frustrating and bordering on a waste of time.

Their eagerness often plays to the advantage of the Chinese, who might draw out the process to shake off the weaker parties. Doing a project in China is like running a marathon: those who have the stamina to cross the finish line are the ones the Chinese like to partner with.

All in a Name

Many Westerners are comfortable about being called by their first names or nicknames. In the US, everyone is either a Bob or Jim or Kathy or Michelle, and not a Mr Spencer or a Dr Lee. A person's name is just a form of identification and not much else.

Many Westerners believe that a person is the creation of God, and a human being first and foremost. His title or what he does for a living is secondary. He can be a CEO or a gardener; neither makes him a better person.

The Chinese and many Asians attach a great deal of importance to their names. For example, Chinese people put their family names ahead of their given names. This shows the importance of where a person is from and what his family lineage is. In comparison, Westerners put their given names before their family names to show they are individuals first and foremost.

An American worker may greet his boss in the hallway at work by saying, "Bob, how's it going?" A Chinese employee will never do that. Chinese tradition calls for addressing someone by his title and surname. This practice is also quite common in Korea and Japan. A Chinese worker would say, "Zao, Chen Zong" (Good morning, Manager Chen), not address him by his given name. A proper title instantly reveals the person's social status and authority. With that, others would know how to behave.

Like parents everywhere, Chinese parents want the best for their children, including the perfect names. According to traditional beliefs, there are three things that affect a person's life: fortune, luck and feng shui, in that order. Some traditional Chinese people even live their lives according to a lunar calendar version of *Farmers' Almanac*. It tells them which days are good for planting or harvest, and what to do and not to do, such as house cleaning, moving and even getting married.

According to Chinese astrology, fortune is derived from the position of the stars at the year, month, date and hour of a person's birth. Because of that, a person is born with a certain fortune; so there isn't much he can do about it, except perhaps plan to have a child in a good fortune year, such as the year of the dragon or horse. Like their Chinese zodiac namesakes, children born in these years are supposed to have extraordinary power and vitality.

Luck is also derived from the calendar, so there isn't much one can do about that either, except perhaps get closer to someone who has plenty of it.

Feng shui, on the other hand, has to do with how someone's environment interacts with his fortune, his luck and his health. It is something you have some control of. For example, you can choose a house that has a good feng shui location and layout. You can further manipulate its feng shui by arranging the furniture, or by carefully placing mirrors, jade ornaments or copper coins in strategic locations. You can enhance your own feng shui by wearing jade or gold, or different-colored cloths, or by carrying some old coins in your pocket.

A baby's name is very important to Chinese parents because it carries their hopes for him for the rest of his life. A good name should be both noble and auspicious, and reflect a proper balance of the five elements of metal, wood, water, fire and earth. If a child is born on a certain date that makes his fortune too heavily concentrated on a certain element, such as wood or metal, then the parents will find a name that carries the complementary elements to strike a proper balance. Achieving the proper balance is very important to the Chinese.

Therefore, Chinese parents can spend a lot of time picking out the perfect name for their baby. In the old days, baby names were obtained from a clan registry in the family temple. Each generation would take a character from the clan registry and use it as their middle name. By looking at the middle name, one knew exactly where he belonged in the clan hierarchy. Today, this practice is no longer followed.

A person's name also reflects the prevailing national sentiment. Many Chinese parents named their children Wei Dong (伟东, Great East) or Jian Guo (建国, Building Nation) during the early days of the Peoples' Republic when they had aspirations for their children and the new regime. In Korea, parents name their children with virtuous-sounding names, such as Ji-hoon (智訓, Wisdom and Discipline), or Geon-u (建宇, Builder of Universe).

Few English names have direct meanings, apart from obvious ones, such as Rose, Lily or Tiger. The meanings behind most common English names have Greek or biblical origins, such as Alexander for bravery (after Alexander the Great) and Stephen for wisdom (after the Christian martyr.)

Americans are less concerned about how they name their children. They may take a name from the baby's parents or grandparents, or from their beliefs, or they may choose from whatever names are popular at the time. American parents believe it is what their children do that will affect them later in life, not their names.

Confucius was very strict about the use of names. He believed that if the name or description of an endeavor is not properly established then its success will be in doubt.

Although Confucius did not elaborate on how he arrived at this belief, the Chinese have taken his words for granted. Therefore it is quite important for a person to have a proper title in an organization because it defines where he is in the organizational hierarchy and what power he has.

Similarly, a company's mission statement or its corporate purpose must be both solemn and grand. It should project a solid sense of purpose and legitimacy, both of which are prerequisites for success.

Confucius said that before a person embarks on a mission he should make sure his motives are noble and proper. If they are not then he will not be able to describe them confidently and forcefully. If he can't speak confidently and forcefully about what he wants to accomplish, then success will be elusive. In other words, unless one believes he is in the right and is vocal about it, he will not be able to carry out his intended mission successfully.

The inverse is that if a person believes he is in the right and is vocal about it, his success will be assured. This kind of logic places a huge emphasis on having the proper justifications, and chest-thumping antics before embarking on any major endeavor. This approach is front heavy and generates a lot of enthusiasm at the beginning, but it lacks the proper feedback mechanism to be called a truly scientific process.

If the rationale for undertaking a major project is sound from both historical and financial points of view, but for some unforeseen reasons the project gets into trouble halfway through, what should you do? Should you press on or re-examine the original premise and make adjustments to the plan?

Most Chinese managers would be reluctant to make changes, for doing so would suggest that some of the original justifications were flawed. It would also imply that someone higher up the organization had made mistakes since he was responsible for making the original decision.

Therefore a manager will reason, if the original objective was sound and reasonable, even though the facts are telling him otherwise, that he must press on. Being steadfast should allow him to overcome any obstacles that may lie ahead. This kind of thinking has resulted in several spectacular failures in modern China.

In 1958, China embarked on an ambitious social experiment called the Great Leap Forward, a movement designed to rapidly advance socialism and close the industrial production gaps with Britain and the US.

Chinese people responded enthusiastically. In the countryside, farmers relinquished their private plots and organized themselves into people's communes. They worked in production brigades and ate together at a communal mess. As a result, there were plenty of incentives to consume because it was communal property, and there was little incentive to produce because no individual was rewarded directly for the fruits of his labor. In the end the communes failed to raise farm productivity as envisioned by the planners.

In cities, folks were asked to make steel in the so-called backyard furnaces that were popping up all over the place by using whatever metallic objects they could find. Of course, these homemade furnaces were never powerful enough to make quality steel. Instead they produced plenty of worthless pig iron. The ambitious experiment turned into disaster very quickly.

There were many reasons behind the failure, some of which had to do with culture.

China felt confident in the early 1950s, after liberating itself from the corrupt Kuomintang regime and imperial powers. It fought Americans to a stalemate in the Korean War, and it showed promise in its efforts to build socialism. Thus the Great Leap Forward, which relied on Chinese people's ingenuity and sweat, was positioned as a continuation of that historical trend, and therefore justified.

Since this strategy had been shown to work before, it could not fail. Furthermore, it was Mao, China's paramount leader, who had called for the movement. In Chinese culture, if the name of an endeavor is appropriate, and someone with authority called for it, then it cannot be challenged. Also, for someone to be hailed with such high esteem, he couldn't possibly do anything wrong. Besides, who would dare to challenge him and get shot down?

Of course, it was Mao's policies that were at fault, not his personality or past accomplishments. But it was difficult to separate the two in Chinese culture. Another reason was extremism. By pushing for rapid industrialization without due consideration of China's realities, the Chinese leadership lost its balance and veered off the middle way.

The Chinese Dream

Chinese people love slogans for their high-context messages that say a lot with very little. Traditionally, once the motives are justified and the slogans begin to sound, then everything is set to go. The rest will take care of itself in due course.

Very often, Chinese organizations go through elaborate efforts to show that they are on the right side of history and to justify what they plan to do. You see this often in Chinese government announcements. In the past, an emperor would proclaim that he was following the Mandate of Heaven and grand dynastic traditions so as to act for the good of his subjects. Today the Chinese government positions itself as the custodian of a grand historical tradition, which is its solemn duty to uphold. In fact, this has become a popular vision called the Chinese Dream.

Chinese President Xi Jinping first unveiled the Chinese Dream in late 2012, and it has become a runaway hit in China. It may be difficult for Westerners to appreciate the significance of this slogan. To them, people are all individuals and dreaming is an involuntary activity that no one has much control of. One may indeed wish to have pleasant dreams but there is no obligation for everyone to share the same dream.

The American Dream has to do with traditional US values, such as having a good job, a house and two cars; and being able to go on vacations and send the kids to college. The freedom to pursue opportunities is the spirit of the American Dream. The job of the government is to make sure this option is available for all those who wish to pursue it. However, there is no requirement for everyone to share the same dream.

The Chinese Dream is different. In fact, it may be better translated as "The Dream of the Chinese". Implicit in the phrase is that all Chinese people would want to see their nation, consisting of all who share the common cultural heritage, rise up again.

This sentiment comes from a cultural pride and a residual reaction to China's two centuries of humiliation suffered under foreign powers. That unpleasant memory will linger in the Chinese psyche for a while longer until it has become comfortable with being a great nation again.

Similar but Different

The Chinese prefer a convivial atmosphere even during tough negotiations. However, it doesn't mean they will acquiesce easily to demands. Their negotiation style is also quite different from what most Westerners practice.

On 7 June 2013, Chinese President Xi Jinping met with US President Barack Obama for two days of informal meetings at Rancho Mirage in Southern California. It was Xi's first US trip since he became the president. The meeting was hailed as a historical relationship-building exercise for two of the world's most powerful leaders.

True to his form as the leader of low-context America, Obama started the first day of meetings with several specific items he wished to discuss with Xi. The list included nuclear North Korea, human rights, greenhouse gases, territorial issues in the South China Sea and cyber security.

His counterpart, Xi, parried the list away. Instead he spoke of big picture themes affecting both China and the US, and how the two of them should forge a new strategic relationship. Obama was employing a typical Western negotiation tactic—throwing out all the cards to see which ones stick. He highlighted their differences and attempted to pin Xi down for some serious negotiations.

Instead Xi preferred to build a personal relationship with the US president rather than talk shop. He was more interested in identifying their common interests rather than addressing their differences.

One president dealt with specifics; the other talked generalities. One wanted a discussion; the other preferred a dialogue. One wanted to talk business; the other desired a relationship. It was as if the two leaders were still holding discussions from their own respective time zones.

Public posturing might have something to do with it. Obama wanted to let Americans know that he was not slacking on China, while Xi wanted to look presidential and display a senior posture on his maiden visit to the US. as head of the world's second largest economic power.

The format of the meeting was also too casual. It was held in a resort in the middle of the California desert, without the trappings and protocols that the Chinese deemed necessary to have important state-to-state-level discussions.

At the end of the historic visit, except for an agreement to continue to discuss ways to phase out hydrofluorocarbons (greenhouse gases) and a common understanding on a non-nuclear Korean peninsula, nothing more substantive was accomplished. However, a nascent relationship between the two world leaders has emerged, and both Obama and Xi declared the meetings a success.

This relationship-building trip went exactly the way Xi had planned. He wanted to identify long-term interests common to both countries and establish a senior rapport with Obama, but not to tackle important issues at their first meeting in a desert. In the end, he accomplished what he set out to do.

The two presidents met again in 2015 in Washington on Xi Jinping's official state visit. This time the proper protocols were provided, including a state dinner hosted by Obama at the White House, and the two presidents were able to reach more substantive agreements.

To search for commonalities while agreeing to disagree is an important Chinese cultural trait. Confucius said that a gentleman should be able to get along with others without also agreeing with them on everything. This sums up succinctly the traditional Chinese attitude towards tolerance.

Positive about Negatives

Like an army, hierarchical organizations can be extremely effective and powerful, provided that their strategy is correct. However, without effective feedback they can also veer towards extremes. A common managerial problem specific to this type of organization is the lack of a robust mechanism for generating checks and balances, and the means to obtain important feedback.

Running a business is like the discipline of control engineering, where engineers employ negative feedback loops to stabilize a system, such as maintaining the set temperature for a vat of liquid, or keeping a satellite in a designated orbit. Going about business without considering what can go wrong (negatives) and planning for contingencies (feedback) can throw the business plan out of its intended orbit.

Everyone in the organization pulling together in the same direction is like a system with no negative feedback or, worse, only positive feedback. While this type of management process can generate actions rapidly, it is inherently unstable and can lead to spectacular blowouts. When this happens, the process has to be jettisoned and started all over, often after huge losses.

This was the political situation in China before the Reform and Opening Up era that began in 1978. From 1949 to 1978, China had gone through several major political campaigns, including the Great Leap Forward and the Cultural Revolution. Both were disasters.

These political movements saw the country united under the banner of revolution. However, because there were little or no offsetting forces within the government (moderates or opposition groups were all beaten down, and some eliminated as class enemies), these movements careened out of control. Campaigns that were intended to advance the Chinese economy ended up pulling it back hugely.

While these mass movements testified to the purpose of the Chinese people, in reality they were hugely disruptive. Since the current reformist agenda was adopted in 1978, China has not embarked on any major political movement and the economy has grown unabated.

Over-heating is a potential problem affecting organizations without built-in offsets. However, the Chinese have developed an alternative means to stabilize their organizations. The secret lies in the relationship between leaders and their working teams. These two are symbiotically connected via a web of counter-balancing relationships, with each having a stake in the other. Even though the leader has the stature and authority, he has to rely on his working team to get things done.

In Chinese government circles, senior officials stay in their posts for only a few years. If they perform well, they may move on to other more important assignments. Members of the working team, however, will remain in place much longer, sometimes for their entire careers. Because they are familiar with the organization and history, and its strengths and weaknesses, they provide a healthy counter-balance to the eagerness of newly appointed leaders.

Similarly, in Western governments, elected politicians come and go but the working team provides the needed continuity and stability. So if the working team disagrees with the new leader's ideas, they can tactfully steer him towards more workable options. If the boss is astute enough, he will consider them.

The offsetting balance provided by the working team dilutes the absolute power of the headmen. This is one of the reasons why, even though China is not a democracy in the Western sense, it has been able to maintain political stability over the past 35 years. Having said that, in an entrepreneurial setting, an owner has no such working team to provide him with the important offset. His performance is therefore also more volatile.

Chinese Efficiency

Why is China so good at building massive infrastructure, such as airports, subways and skyscrapers, seemingly much faster and cheaper than the West can? The culture has something to do with it.

In the West, different interest groups, each armed with its own agenda, always try to frustrate long-term infrastructure projects. In the contentious atmosphere, each group fights only for the interest it represents; none care much about mutual benefits.

Take a new highway, for example. The environmentalists want to make sure a rare species of frog will not be harmed by the new highway, so they demand the highway to change course or not be built at all. Local residents don't like the noise from the new highway, so they want it to go through a different neighborhood instead.

Everyone wants something but no one is willing to give up anything. The common good is effectively subordinated to minority interests. Since it is impossible to satisfy all the different constituents at once, serious negotiations must take place and the process can slow like molasses in the winter, while costs keep piling up.

At this point in China, economic development is still a popular consensus. It is both an explicit demand of most of the population and an implicit mandate of the government. To most Chinese people, without a means of making a living and a place to live and raise their families, everything else is just empty talk. Of course, the government must balance development with the public good and plan for the long term, or else the environment will be irreversibly damaged before long.

While city folk may complain about traffic congestion and pollution, and dream of moving somewhere with cleaner air, they don't necessarily want to leave their high-paying careers. Country folks, who account for about half the population in China, can't wait to move into cities, where there exist better opportunities for themselves and their families.

With the average commuting time approaching two hours each way in major cities such as Beijing and Shanghai, new trains and subways can make the dreaded commute more tolerable. They can also take people out of congested city centers into the newly developed satellite towns. For these reasons, new infrastructure developments are still very much welcomed.

There are at least two reasons why the same thorny issues are more manageable in China. One is flexibility and the other is group consensus.

Once the new highway gets the go-ahead, the construction crew will relocate the rare frogs, if there are any, to their new habitat somewhere else. Local townsfolk will welcome the new highway with both arms. They have no problem with the added traffic or noise because it will bring them prosperity.

The construction company will act quickly, with or without all the necessary permits. In a society where the bureaucracy is maddening, rules are constantly in flux and interpretations often subjective. There is never enough time to nail down all the details: one must seize the time and act fast.

In the end, all parties must be flexible and improvise along the way. The ability to tolerate exceptions is an important part of doing business in China.

In China, project sponsors, management, contractors, suppliers, bankers and regulators all have multiple relationships with each other and their fortunes are deeply intertwined. However, they all share the same objective, which is to get on with development. Once they are sold on the project's importance, they will work together to get it completed.

An associated construction company will make its workers put in massive overtime hours at crunch time. Workers won't complain because they will be getting more pay. Suppliers will add additional shifts to clear any backlogs. They want to complete the project in time so that they can be paid. Bankers will provide additional financing for the final push. If they don't, they will be looking at potential bad loans and lost businesses in the future. At this stage of the game, regulators are unwilling to spoil the party and be blamed for impeding progress.

Everyone comes together for the sake of development. As a result, activity levels in large Chinese projects often go up exponentially towards the finish. All parties will set aside their differences and work together at this critical juncture, and the highway will be completed on time.

All in the Context

According to cultural anthropologist Edward T. Hall, Westerners are brought up to believe that logic equals truth, and that truth will lead to reality. In other words, because Westerners think logically, they assume that their versions of reality, or how things work, must be correct.

However, in practice this may or may not be the case. This is because even though logic is a powerful tool, not everything that matters in our lives—most notably our feelings and emotions—is logical. Trying to figure out emotions with logic is an exercise in futility. Likewise, trying to analyze our feelings to death, or how the stock market works, can frustrate the smartest minds.

Hall believes that because of their reliance on logic, it is impossible for those in power to think comprehensively and consider the common good.

He also says that Westerners have alienated themselves from nature due to the power of their logic. As a result they suffer from a number of delusions, such as that life makes sense and that they are sane.

Hall pioneered the use of context to describe different cultures. In his work he breaks the world down into high- and low-context societies. China, India and Brazil belong to the high-context societies, while the US, Germany and Scandinavian countries belong to the low-context societies.

People from low-context cultures tend to be logical, individualistic and linear thinkers. People from high-context cultures tend to be wholistic thinkers who prefer groups.

Context is the frame of reference we use to make decisions. Over time, context becomes enmeshed with our instincts by which we judge events and others.

When we see something unfamiliar, we interpret it by placing the facts we discern in a context we choose. Which context we choose to recall depends on our own experiences. There is a Chinese saying that a person who has seen a ghost will always be afraid of the dark. So such a person will avoid going out at night, because it will trigger his memory of the ghost. In his mind he has equated darkness with ghosts.

Unlike logic, which is linear and precise, context is amorphous and diffused. If we use the proper context we can make more appropriate decisions. If we take things out of context we can be frustrated by the "unreasonable" outcomes.

Our previous experiences affect how we view current events by placing them in a historical context. Our developmental history affects how we see the future in a political context. Our training allows us to view unknown phenomena in a scientific context. Our beliefs affect how we view events in a religious context.

Culture heavily influences our choice of context. If we were brought up in a certain culture, we are accustomed to using only the contexts we are familiar with. It would be difficult for us to put ourselves in the context of a foreign culture. Because of that, we may wonder why people there don't always do the things we normally do.

If we take things out of context and use only logic to reason, we can get mired in the cultural quicksand. On the other hand, if we rely on context and experience, ignoring logic, we can navigate endlessly in fuzzy relationships and go around in circles. We need both to strike a proper balance.

Many Asians, and Chinese in particular, are certifiably high-context people. One sees this in their languages, customs and behavior.

The Chinese language is very rich in context. A word can be pronounced in many different ways and have different meanings. In Chinese culture, people can say very little but it can mean a lot. This is because the associated context encapsulates a huge amount of relevant information. Chinese people have little problem understanding each other because they know which context to use.

Chinese idioms and proverbs, which are usually four-character phrases packed with ancient wisdom that transcends both space and time, are still popular today, even though most of them originated over 2,000 years ago. Chinese people use these phrases all the time in conversation if they wish to emphasize something. Writers love to sprinkle their work with these ancient phrases, thus saying a lot with very little. The reason these phrases are being used today is because human nature hasn't really changed all that much over time. We are essentially the same human beings with the same kind of issues as people in ancient times.

Chinese customs are also rich in context. There are many ways in which an older relative can be addressed. Instead of just an uncle or aunt, an older relative is addressed differently depending on whether he or she comes from the side of the father or the mother, and whether he or she is older or younger than your parents. The salutation immediately identifies where the relative sits within the clan hierarchy and how much respect he or she is due.

Even though context can add color to Chinese culture, it can also cause confusion. The reliance on context to label a person can make it difficult to clearly separate what a person is on the surface from who he really is inside.

According to the historian Fung Yu-lan, Chinese thinkers stress *what he is*, a person's observables, and not *what he has*, the substance in him.

When a person is labeled a certain way in the Chinese world, there is pressure for him to act according to the label he wears. When a person is placed in the context of a teacher or a parent, he must appear stern and authoritative. Others have to deal with him not as the person he really is but as the role he plays. Because of this there is often a rigid formalism in the way Chinese people do things. It also explains why it is so difficult for the Chinese to do something out of character. For example, it is difficult for a Chinese father to horse around with his kid, or dress up as a clown to entertain at his child's birthday party, as many Westerners would gladly do. Doing so would tarnish his image as a stern parent, which makes it hard to discipline his child afterwards.

Similarly, it is difficult for government officials to appear non-official-like, or display private personas on top of the public facades they wear. Doing so would hurt their image as serious public servants, and cause them to lose respect with the people they are charged to govern.

Labels and formalism are also why it is so difficult to promote innovation in Chinese companies. True innovation should come from genuinely good ideas, regardless of where they come from or who initiates them. However, when workers are typecast for specific roles in a hierarchical organization, they are often afraid to think outside of their designated boxes, and when they can't do so, routine work passes for innovation.

In the Confucian world, labels are often used in place of clarity and precision.

In the *Analects*, Confucius often used "gentleman" and "petty person" to distinguish between those men with desirable personality traits and those without. In Confucius' time, a gentleman literally meant the son of a nobleman, or a prince. The original English word for gentleman describes a man from the lower landowners class. Today, "gentleman" describes a man who possesses refined personal qualities, such as politeness, chivalry and kindness to others. If a gentleman behaves exemplarily most of the time but transgresses once in a while, it is quite acceptable in the Western world.

Many well-known Western politicians are known to have extramarital affairs. However, they still get lots of respect from voters and perform their duties with authority. What they do in private and what they do at work are two separate matters.

However, it is difficult to characterize such a person in the Confucian world. There is simply nothing to describe someone who fits in between a gentleman and a petty person. So would the lecherous politician be not quite a full gentleman or should he be called a hybrid gentleman/petty person?

The habit of labeling a person according to what his position is also why revelations about Chinese official corruption and sex scandals always seem to pop up so abruptly. Very often an official is hailed as a public role model one day, but after his misdeeds are carefully revealed to the public the following day he is treated as a scoundrel. In addition to secrecy, culture is mainly responsible for this kind of image flip-flop.

To most Chinese people, a person is characterized by his background and social status. If someone is from a certain social class, such as a merchant, government official or teacher, then he is supposed to behave according to the norms of that social class. If the person is a young foreigner then he is expected to behave like a stereotypical young foreigner—loud and inconsiderate.

If a person doesn't behave the way he is supposed to, others won't know how to deal with him. If too many people step out of their social norms, there will be disorder. Confucius said, let the ruler be a ruler, the subject a subject, the father a father, the son a son. So each person must play his role dutifully in the Confucian world. If everyone does what he is supposed to do, society will be fine. While this is good for stability and governance, it does little for individual development or cross-fertilization.

In a traditional Chinese company, the boss has to always act like a boss, with sternness and authority, and be an expert on everything. If he jokes around too much with his subordinates, they won't quite know how to deal with him. A subordinate is supposed to follow orders and be quietly subservient. If he tries to do something different, such as innovating, his colleagues will shun him as a troublemaker.

A son must always be obedient to his parents. If not, his parents and relatives will chastise him for being disrespectful.

So a person is a son to his father, a student to his teachers, a subordinate to his boss, a husband to his wife and a father to his son, and so on in his many other relationships. Each of his different roles requires him to behave differently. He must be extremely well aware of his surroundings and be ready to jump from one role to another like flipping a switch. This incessant role-switching is a great source of stress and frustration for many in Confucian societies.

It is also a popular theme in many Asian books, movies and soap operas, and a major source of South Korea's soft power export. Korean television dramas and movies are popular with many Asians. The genre resonates with them because they must also role-play in their society to please others, but in the process they have become confused about their own identity and priorities.

What if a wife is also the boss of the company her husband works for? How can she be subservient to her husband and be his boss at the same time? How can her husband behave obediently at work but bossily at home?

What if a mother-in-law decides to move in with a young couple struggling to raise a family and make ends meet, and the same time the mother-in-law demands to be properly catered for in the traditional fashion? How can the daughter-in-law juggle all the chores, placate her mother-in-law and hold down a job at the same time?

If a brilliant young staffer is promoted ahead of his boss, how can his boss, who trained the young staffer, live that one down? What about a father who has brought up his son dutifully but has run foul of the law? Who is the son supposed to support: his father or the authorities?

What about a younger sister whose older sister likes someone, but this young man likes her instead? Should she bow out, play the role of a nice younger sister and let her sister have his undivided attention, or should she follow her heart and let the young man pursue her?

There are endless such variations on the same theme, which is how traditions can co-exist with modernity in the rapidly modernizing Confucian world.

This kind of role-playing can cause a huge amount of stress and frustration, but those who have managed to make the breakthrough can offer tremendous insight and be extremely successful. Ang Lee, the Taiwan-born movie director who won two Oscars, is an excellent example of an Asian who has managed to make the cultural breakthrough. Lee's father was a traditional Chinese scholar, who wanted his son to become a professor, a traditionally esteemed profession. But Lee liked the arts more than academia, so he enrolled in New York University's film school after he finished his college studies in Taiwan. His earlier films, the so-called *Father Knows Best* trilogy, explored the conflicts between traditional Chinese culture and modernizing Taiwan. They brought him initial success and opened up opportunities for him later in the US.

This is quite different from the US, where a person is considered a human being first and foremost. His self-worth is unrelated to where he comes from or what he does for a living. She can be an auto mechanic during the day but a budding country singer in clubs on weekends. He can be an office worker during the day but write romance novels in her spare time. Their professions are just means for them to make a living to allow them to pursue their true passions, and they have less to do with how they feel about themselves. In other words, although they are professional about what they do for a living, their passions may be something else.

It is also acceptable for a Westerner to be out of character sometimes. So a person can be a boss in the office and be a friend outside. He can play golf with his subordinates on weekends and be beaten by them. He has authority in the office only on matters pertaining to his professional responsibilities. Other than that, he is just a regular Joe like everyone else. In China a boss is always a boss. He is in that character 24/7, wherever he is.

For Westerners who are accustomed to speaking their minds and separating issues from personalities, they may inadvertently step on some sensitive Asian nerves. They should first consider the cultural context before they open their mouths.

It All Depends!

When people from low-context cultures interact with people from high-context cultures, confusions abound. This is also where many Western executives have problems dealing with Asians.

Low-context people tend to think high-context people are intentionally unclear or, worse, downright dishonest. On the other hand, high-context people may think their low-context counterparts are too narrowly focused so they must have a hidden agenda.

Some Asian mannerisms can be confusing to Westerners. Many Asians have the habit of nodding when speaking with an authority figure. In this situation, nodding merely acknowledges that the person has heard what the other person has said. It doesn't signal agreement.

When an Asian person says no to a question but nods his head at the same time, is he agreeing or disagreeing with the question? Why is he giving out contradictory signals? In fact, this person is just letting the questioner know that he also agrees that the answer is wrong. However, since the Westerner is focused only on getting a right or wrong answer in a narrower context, he is often baffled by this typical Asian response.

Chinese people live in a complex world where many things are interrelated. Like yin and yang, not everything can be isolated and analyzed precisely, and not every question has a clear black or white answer. It all depends on how and in which context the question is raised.

Limiting the answer to a definitive choice of one or the other can gloss over factors that are important in the broader context but excluded simply because of the way the question is raised. For example, if someone asks a simple question about whether an object is a square or not, a high-context person may not give you a straight answer. However, he may give you a calculated answer. He may say, "It is difficult to say." He may point out that if you look at the object from above, it does look like a square, but not a perfect square in the sense that, if you measure it with a ruler, its edges may not be absolutely equal in length. What's more, if you turn the object to its side and look at it that way, it may resemble a rectangle, or a flat line if the object is really thin.

If someone asks a high-context person whether an apple is red or not, he may get a response like "It all depends." For if you look at an apple under strong sunlight it does look bright red, but if you look at it in a dark room it may even appear greyish. So the common Asian response to many questions is often prefaced with "Its difficult to say" or "It all depends".

If a ball rolls off a table it will hit the ground. No one can dispute the effect of gravity. But if the ball is in a space shuttle where gravitational force is insignificant, the answer may not be obvious. The reason we all think the ball should fall to the ground is because we implicitly assume that we all share the same location context—that is, around sea level. But for complex cross-cultural issues, assuming people all share the same context a priori can lead to misunderstandings.

Depending on the context, the Chinese yes could mean different things. When a Chinese person says yes, it can mean an unequivocal yes, a conditional yes, or that he agrees with you in general and that he will do his best, but no guarantees. Or it could simply mean maybe. The Chinese habit of expanding the contextual elements in discussions can be frustrating for Westerners.

Accepting ambivalence is a price to pay for doing business in China. Many Western business executives believe answers given by the Chinese are intentionally unclear. The Western notion of right or wrong is very clear, while the Chinese notion lacks clarity.

Not being explicit on issues helps to preserve options. It is a common way of dealing with uncertainties in complex, fast-moving environments. Anyone who has to deal with uncertainties for a living knows how to proceed cautiously and hedge his bets. Politicians are famous for doing this. One minute they can be against something; the next minute they can be all for it without even changing their tone. How many stock analysts have correctly called the market demise before it fell off the cliff? How many of them have strong opinions about a call without also attaching an avalanche of qualifiers?

To be sure, politics and the economy are complex matters influenced by many factors, not all of which, especially sentiment, are easily quantifiable. Few analysts are right all of the time so they have to hedge their bets. In this respect the high-context Asians are not that different.

Leader or Manager?

Chinese and Western managers have very different notions about what their roles are. Chinese managers prefer to roll up their sleeves and lead their troop down in the trenches; American managers manage corporate resources.

American managers, in particular, are more problem-solvers than emotional builders. To them, time is money and emotion is subordinated to results. To the Chinese, achieving harmony is just as important as obtaining results.

The rational method that American managers use to solve business problems does not take into account human emotions. To the Chinese, this is way too harsh and not at all engaging. If their manager only asks questions and gives opinions but doesn't get his hands dirty, employees wonder why is he there?

The Chinese prefer to use the word "leader" to describe their bosses. The Chinese word for leader actually consists of two words: to lead and to guide. As leaders they must stay prominently in front of their troops and guide them.

Chinese managers view contributing ideas and leading their teams in problem-solving as their main responsibility. They don't like being observers, sitting in their offices analyzing numbers and critiquing the efforts of others. Their subordinates also want their senior management to be closely engaged in whatever they do.

American managers view managing company resources, including fixed assets, capital and human resources, as their primary responsibility. They are judged by how fast and how much they can generate from the resources they are allocated. And although people are always considered to be the most important asset of a company, the American manager doesn't feel he has to hover over his team. His team members are there because they choose to be there. Therefore they should be self-motivated and do their jobs professionally, regardless of whether their boss is around or not.

Chinese managers prefer to use a more appreciative style of management, where team members work together to tackle problems. If management is too critical, members would feel demoralized. If management is not around, they would feel unsure.

Issues and Personalities

The analytical Western manager is trained to separate issues from personalities. The wholistic Chinese manager has a tendency to mix them up. When an American manager challenges his subordinates, he is often just trying to get to the bottom of the facts and to help find solutions. The American manager may sound harsh but he is usually focused only on issues and not personality. His upbringing has something to do with this.

Many American parents practice positive reinforcement with their children. They often heap praise on a child when he does something well, like taking part in the school band or getting a good grade in a math class. Sometimes this praise is overly dramatized to encourage the child. If he has done something wrong he will also be reprimanded.

American parents tend to focus on the child's behavior and less so on his personality. A mother may say to her child, "Johnny: You should not have taken that toy away from Billy without asking for his permission first. That was not nice! And if you do that again we will have to leave and go home." It is Johnny's behavior and not his personality his mother focuses on. Every child wants to please his parents. No child likes to hear from someone that he loves berating him.

In contrast, the emphasis of *what a person is* from *what he has* makes it difficult to clearly separate issues from personalities in the Chinese context. In the above situation, some Chinese parents may scold their child as a bad boy for taking the toy away from his friend, instead of telling him that he is a good boy but he has done something unacceptable this time around. This behavior is also seen in Chinese corporate arenas. A manager who has performed poorly is often reprimanded for being a bad manager but not because his work was substandard. This makes it hard for the bad manager to make substantive improvements because his boss has used a personal opinion rather than objective measures to judge his performance. So instead of doing a better job next time he may look for more direct means to please his boss, including carrying his bags everywhere he goes and tending to his every need. Hopefully, one day his boss will feel good enough to redesignate him as a *good* manager. This kind of practice where issues and personality are co-mingled confuses personality with accountability. It can also slow progress.

Whose Responsibility Is It?

John D. Rockefeller, the founder of Standard Oil, at one time the largest oil company in the US before the government broke it up, had the following inscribed on a plaque in the New York City plaza bearing his name: "Every right implies a responsibility; Every opportunity, an obligation; Every possession, a duty." It is obvious from one of the most successful businessmen in US history that duality exists in what we do.

Rights and responsibilities are like the two sides of a coin—inseparable. Breaking them apart renders the coin worthless. By the same token, no one has absolute rights, unless he is a baby. In business, a clear relationship between the right to manage and the responsibility behind one's decisions is necessary to hold management accountable.

However, in a deeply hierarchical organization, such accountability is often difficult to establish. When a manager's authority comes from the top, he feels he is only obligated to the person who gives it to him. If the manager performs poorly but his boss is fine with it, then he will be all right. However, in a market economy, the users of products and services (i.e. the customers) and providers of capital (i.e. the investors) should be the judges of how the management team has performed. They will implement brutal benchmarking to determine which company is successful and how its management has fared.

This is a dilemma for China's still substantial SOE sector. Who is responsible for the SOEs: the managers or the state? Some of the SOEs are such behemoths that they are literally their own fiefdoms, answerable to neither the market nor Beijing. Executives in these large companies often play the market against the state and vice versa. They use the market to get experience and paid well, and yet, when something goes wrong, they hide behind the state for support. They consume a huge amount of resources yet they chronically underperform in the market.

At the moment the Chinese government is debating how to transform this underperforming sector. It is an old problem that requires some fresh thinking.

Assigning responsibility is a perennial problem with the Chinese style of management. Who is actually responsible: the headman or his subordinates?

When everyone works together to solve problems there is plenty of teamwork and camaraderie. However, there is also little distinction between the individual objective and the group mandate.

In a US company, each manager is given a specific set of responsibilities he is held accountable for. If he meets his target, he may get a raise and a bonus. If he exceeds his target, he may get promoted to a position with more responsibilities. If he doesn't meet his target, he may get a warning and no raise or bonus. If this happens a few more times, he may even get a pink slip.

The reward for talent in well-run US companies also follows market practices. If a trader calls the market correctly and makes lots of money for the firm, he can make more than the CEO. However, this type of compensation scheme is unimaginable in Chinese companies. That is because the top manager (i.e. the executive chairman or CEO) must always be the highest-paid executive.

Because the headman has to make so many decisions, he is always overwhelmed. But if he delegates more, he will miss the power that comes with having a say in all major decisions. There is also another important reason for not delegating: the headman reasons that if he is the person bearing overall responsibility, he should be involved in making all the decisions. For how can someone take responsibility for decisions he did not make? Assigning responsibility in Chinese organizations remains a challenging proposition.

It's Difficult to Be Silly!

Innovation occurs when people pursue their passions and don't mind doing silly things. Culturally, this is rather difficult for the Chinese because not too many of them like doing silly things.

In Chinese culture, a person is often influenced by how others perceive him, or what he calls himself. According to Fung Yu-lan, if a Chinese person is a sage, then whatever he does cannot be challenged. On the other hand, if a person is considered a bad person, whatever he does is no good.

This kind of stereotyping is quite common in Chinese society. Besides confusing a matter's substance with the superficial, it has also created some interesting phenomena at work.

A person who has a desk job looks down on workers who labor outdoors, as if sweat is demeaning. College graduates all want to start work as managers in clean, air-conditioned offices, even though factory jobs may pay more. In restaurants, customers regularly yell at waitresses as if they are lowly servants.

A non-college-educated person will always be looked down upon as being unsophisticated, regardless of how much he knows or has accomplished. By the same token, a person with a PhD will get automatic respect, regardless of what his field of expertise is or what he has done with the degree. As a result, people stuff their resumés with all kinds of phony academic credentials to gain respect.

A non-Chinese person will always be a foreigner to the locals, even if he has lived in the country for decades, speaks perfect Mandarin and has made significant contributions there. The fact that he is not Chinese by blood means that he will never think or behave like a real Chinese person. What's more, his allegiance is always in doubt and he will never be fully trusted.

Not willing to do things out of the ordinary, or silly things, is one of the reasons the Chinese have not been as innovative as they should have. Their studious attitude and practical approach to life means they prefer to learn the secrets of success quickly without going through trials and tribulations to get there.

There are lots of books on the shelves in Chinese bookstores with engaging titles such as, *Bill Gates' Secret Formula of Success* and *How Warren Buffet Made His Billions*. Some of them were translated from foreign titles but the rest were written by Chinese management gurus. To be sure, these inspirational titles are popular wherever there are ambitious people—in New York, London or Mumbai, in addition to Beijing and Shanghai—but the Chinese interest in them seems more intense, judging from the crowds gathering around them in bookstores and the intensity they display. These self-help books are big hits in a nation obsessed with learning and getting rich. The tantalizing titles suggest that one can become a billionaire, a Chinese version of the Microsoft founder, by reading the book and following its get-rich secrets. But they are missing an important point.

The fact that Bill Gates is successful is because he did things that only Bill Gates wanted to do. The personal computer industry as we know it did not exist in the early 1970s. In fact, no one at the time had any idea that the personal computer was going to take off the way it did. Gates took significant personal risks when he dropped out of Harvard to pursue his passion of developing the operating system software that popularized personal computers. The rest is history. Most significant inventions come from the passions of the inventors. Making a fortune is a side benefit of doing something they really love.

In his Stanford commencement address, Steve Jobs said, "Life is short, so don't waste time living someone else's life." Such a sentiment calls on young people to follow their passions and do their own thing, regardless how silly they may seem at the time. Jobs' statement was also his personal philosophy of life. Jobs dropped out of college after just one semester. Afterwards he lived a bohemian life for several years until he met up with Apple Computer co-founder Steve Wozniak in California. The two began building computers for hobbyists in Jobs' parents' garage. Their first product, the Apple I, garnered rave receptions from the techies. The duo followed with an improved version they called the Apple II, which ushered in the era of personal computing.

To many Chinese people, dropping out of college and becoming a bum is silly and a real waste of time. Most parents would seriously discourage it. However, taking classes in art and calligraphy, and immersing himself in alternative lifestyles, gave Jobs a sense of aesthetics and helped him develop his lateral thinking skills. He later channeled his love for simplicity and aesthetics into the design of Apple products, to the delight of fans all over the world.

Mark Zuckerberg, the founder of Facebook, started off building a website for students in his Harvard dorm room. Now the company he founded in 2004 has become the social media phenomenon connecting over 1.59 billion monthly active users (as of December 31, 2015) all over the world. In the process he has also become a multi-billionaire.

Chinese Management Styles

In *On China*, Kissinger opines that the Chinese are meticulous in analyzing long-term trends but show detachment in operating details. Although he is talking about the Chinese government, the statement is also applicable to Chinese businesses.

In general, Chinese management emphasizes long-term, big-picture ideas over details and execution. Because long-term issues have mostly been identified and studied exhaustively by experts, it is easier to forge a consensus on them. Long-term thinking is also a traditional Chinese trait that comes from the country's agrarian heritage and long history.

More recently, long-term thinking has been attracting more attention in Western management circles, in part because of the financial crisis of 2008 that cast doubt on the Western free-market system, and the subsequent inability of the market to mend societal ills.

The typical Chinese business plan is a weighty and top-heavy document. It has the appearance of a solemn declaration of intent rather than a well-articulated roadmap for business navigations. The plan is usually loaded with indisputable facts that place the undertaking in a favorable historical context. It spills a lot of ink on the question why but relatively little on the question how. As such, it leaves plenty of room for creative implementation.

This is just the opposite of the Western-style business plan where much of it is divided into sections on detailed milestones, assumptions and scenarios, and risk and financial analysis.

If a manufacturing company targeting export markets wants to know what its next product lineup should look like, it studies the latest trends by reading trade journals, visiting customers and attending trade shows. But where does a company whose market is mostly domestic get its inspiration? It would consult China's prestigious government think tank, the National Development and Reform Commission (NDRC). Among other things, including approving key construction projects and setting energy prices, the NDRC's function is to provide economic policy forecast and research, and to coordinate China's ongoing economic restructuring efforts. Every five years, industry players anxiously await a new development blueprint from this prestigious organization.

If a company's investment in a certain industry has been endorsed by the NDRC, such as solar energy or environmental protection, then no one will ask too many questions. Since the authoritative NDRC has spoken, management would not hesitate to kickstart a project and get in the hot sectors while the going is good. It would just refer to the five-year plan for the rationale and justification instead of doing its own in-depth industry due diligence.

Most Western companies in the same industry would do it differently. They might consult industry reports by major consulting firms or think tanks, but they would still conduct their own market and industry due diligence and debate the merits of an investment over and over before taking the plunge.

At the end of the day, it is the management's responsibility to get the company's strategy right. Think tanks are an important resource but they are not the decision-makers, nor are they responsible for management outcomes. Besides, these experts usually only opine on business strategies, while management has to deal with the grunt work of day-to-day execution.

So with an undisputed strategy, hard-working employees and a clear chain of command, Chinese companies should do no wrong. However, that is often not the case.

For starters, the strategy may be out of date when the project finally gets going, or critical details mishandled. As always, the devil is in the detail.

The Chinese manager's propensity to focus on strategic issues often renders details to a lower priority. Hence the phrase "Grab big and release small" is often heard. Managers believe that details can be dispensed with quickly, and very often at the last minute. In contrast, the high-level strategy requires senior managers using their brains to deal with difficult clients, bankers and government officials.

But details are always more complicated than they appear, and the consequences of ignoring them are not always dismissible. In fact, some details are so important that not dealing with them promptly can lead to costly consequences.

The lack of a key part of a major piece of machinery that has a long backlog from the supplier can delay the completion of a major project for months. The lost productivity can be significantly greater than the cost of the missing part. A malfunctioning car component that was not discovered in time can result in fatalities and massive lawsuits. A piece of software in an IT project that has not been tested thoroughly can require costly reverse engineering to rectify the problem.

Ultimately the focus on detail, detail and more detail is what makes Western companies productive in the long run.

The Chinese work relationship is also quite different from that practiced by Westerners.

According to the Chinese philosopher Liang Shuming (梁漱溟), the governing morals of the Chinese and Westerners are quite different. Liang believes that Western morals differ from Chinese morals in two major ways: (1) Westerners emphasize public morals while the Chinese are concerned about personal morals; and (2) Westerners talk about their responsibility to the family, society, the country and the world because what's important in their lives is not just personal relationships but also relationships with society and the other people in it. The Chinese are more concerned about morals among different people, such as between friends, a worker and his superior, a father and son, and a husband and wife.

What Liang describes are the Confucian reciprocal relationships expressed in the modern context. A Chinese person's life is full of these person-to-person relationships. His relationship with the company he works for and, for that matter, society at large is less tangible to him.

So at work the most important thing a worker can do is be loyal to his boss. His allegiance to the company is not as important since it doesn't have any direct impact on him, but his boss does. In fact, his boss can make his life pleasant or miserable because he can either grant or deny what the employee needs for work or pleasure. Therefore it is quite important for Chinese employees to behave as subservient team players. Western-styled lone rangers who are brilliant but unapproachable are rarely welcome because they often make other people nervous.

The Western workplace is different. Each employee is there to fulfill a professional function, regardless of whether he is a manager, a salesman or a janitor. His work ethic is part of his own personal ethics. If he wants to stay late or do something extra for the company, few would object. An employee's allegiance is to the company he works for. His manager is just someone he reports to for his work; he is responsible for his own output. His professional obligations go away after he leaves work. Thereafter his time is his to spend with his family and friends, or by himself.

The Confucian Manager

The Confucian management style is the traditional Chinese management style. It is derived from the family model. Most Confucian organizations have very clearly defined hierarchical structures. They are usually well organized and can move swiftly with a single command from the top.

Like a well-trained army, this type of organization can deliver speedy results, provided that the strategy is correct.

For Westerners dealing with Chinese companies, such as SOEs or family-owned businesses, they should assume that they are run by Confucian managers. Understanding their organizational hierarchy, and their command and control structures, can allow an outsider to apply subtle influences in the right places.

In traditional Chinese families, parents don't feel they need to praise their children much because they are lower in the patriarchal order. Most of the time the Tiger Moms only scold their children for doing poorly at school, such as not getting straight As, and lagging behind their cousins. Similarly, Chinese managers rarely praise their employees for doing good work. Most of the time they admonish them for doing poorly.

The Confucian headman is usually an elderly person. He is highly educated and morally upright. He exudes an aura of wisdom and dignity, and he has a regal persona to match. As the top man in the organization, he must always appear authoritative and knowledgeable, which in the Confucian world also implies that he must be stern and erudite.

The Confucian manager works for the common good. He is highly visible in the public eye and has a big entourage who carefully foster his image as a VIP. His authority is derived from his intelligence and accomplishments, and his solid guanxi with the other senior staff. His effectiveness comes from knowing what's best for the organization, and his ability to command a team that reveres smart leadership.

In addition to delivering his business mandates, a Confucian manager's principal objective is to maintain order. This is because without it there is chaos, and nothing substantive can be accomplished.

Since the Confucian boss has to always appear authoritative, even if he doesn't know it all, he becomes an expert at dictating lofty directives to his subordinates. Over time the employees learn how to decipher these cryptic messages. Knowing how to read your boss and give him plenty of respect is a requisite skill in Chinese organizations.

If a lower-level employee has a good idea, he is often reluctant to propose it for fear that his boss might be offended, having not coming up with it first. And if an idea is really good and the big boss really likes it, he may not want to endorse it openly because that may imply his immediate managers are not capable of ferreting out good ideas from their charges. It then becomes a tricky problem and a minefield to navigate. As the risk is high and the payoff remote, most employees just don't bother coming up with new ideas, so over time the organization becomes stagnant.

In US companies, particularly those heavily relying on creativity, such as technology and media enterprises, the boss's job can be more that of a coach and resource manager than an individual contributor. He may be the smart one who knows the products and the industry inside out, but he prefers to let his team members do the heavy lifting. He may have some ideas about how best to do the job but he will let his subordinates decide what to propose. His job is to set goals and to challenge his team to accomplish them. It is less about contributing ideas. The ideal American boss is a coach, a cheerleader and a referee all rolled into one.

The Tao Manager

The Tao manager is the natural manager. On the surface his organization appears disorderly but it bubbles with creativity beneath the surface. Tao is the order of nature. Anything that evolves, including a business, has its own Tao. The job of a good manager is to understand the Tao of his business and guide its flow properly.

The Tao manager doesn't covet the limelight. He works behind the scenes, gets his job done and lets others take the credit. His power comes from following the Tao. His authority is predicated on his ability to facilitate teamwork, not from where he sits in the organizational hierarchy. Tao managers are a rarity in any organization. For those interested in ferreting out innovative Chinese companies, they should look for their Tao characteristics.

Tao suggests a leader should take actions when appropriate and not be overly passive. He should go with the flow but not behind it. He should not be impulsive and he must maintain a proper balance at all times. The difficulty is how to determine what is important and what is not; which decisions should be made now and which can wait; and, in general, how to read the flow.

According to Lao Tzu, you must tackle a problem before it becomes too difficult. Also, if you aspire to do something big, you should start small. Taking these together, it suggests that the Tao manager should have the big picture in mind but be able to start small and be diligent with the detail. If we deal with detail diligently, nothing will surprise us. If we treat everything we do as difficult, then at the end there will be nothing difficult left. This humble attitude allows us to approach any problem with confidence. It is a tried and true management technique, and very much a part of Tao management.

Chinese food is like that. Unlike Western dishes that often require knives and forks to cut up the meat and potato in public, Chinese dishes are made with bite-size pieces of ingredients meticulously put together to tempt the palate. There is nothing to do except to eat and enjoy. The ability to visualize the end product, cut fresh ingredients into manageable bite-size pieces, and cook them skillfully in sequence to make a hot and tasty dish is a chef's high art.

The art of being a good manager is similar. To be able to diagnose a problem and segregate it into manageable components, plan a rigorous process and execute it is what a good manager should be able to do. If he is able to do that, his clients and his boss can all sit back, relax and enjoy the results.

Like Zhuangzi's story of the dexterous butcher who could slice through an entire ox carcass with just a small blade, a Tao manager should be able to visualize the key business issues, prioritize them and solve them skillfully with a minimum amount of fuss.

Also, we need to keep in mind that management is part of the flow and not independent of it. Management actions can cause the flow to change course, and the result will be different than if no action is taken at all. The analogy is Heisenberg's Uncertainty Principle in quantum mechanics, which states that if we strive to be too precise with one variable we will inevitably create uncertainty in another. In other words, the act of observation can change the value of the observable.

If a person stands in the middle of a stream he will feel the water gushing against him, but he will also cause the water to deviate from its original path. Depending on the size of the steam, such a change of course can be significant. The stream is no longer the one that the person observed on shore because he is now part of the flow. The Greek philosopher Heraclitus described a similar observation.

Likewise, if a manager is too domineering his team will feel obligated to adopt his ideas instead of coming up with their own. The manager has imposed himself on his team and therefore is not fully utilizing their talents and potential. On the other hand, if a manager is too passive and only waits for things to happen, his team may become docile and unresponsive. Neither is productive. Knowing how much an action can affect the outcome and taking advantage of it is a management high art and an important part of the Tao management style.

The Tao manager's presence is everywhere but he is hardly noticeable. He has the status but he doesn't flaunt it. He is like water: penetrating yet supportive, bland-tasting yet essential to life. The Tao manager empowers his people so they can carry on by themselves. Over time they will become so successful that they will forget who got them there in the first place. This is perfectly fine with the Tao manager.

In the *Tao Te Ching*, Lao Tzu says that the highest value is like water because it supports all things but doesn't battle with any of them. Plus water flows down to earth. Likewise, a good manager should be both supportive and down to earth. Many Chinese sages, including Lao Tzu and Sun Tzu, used water to describe the important attitudes of being humble and flexible, going with the flow and providing support to others. Even the martial artist Bruce Lee used water to describe the philosophy behind his unique style of martial art.

Management authority comes from either fiat (i.e. a push style) or employees willingly following their leaders (i.e. a pull style). The latter is a kind of management soft power best exemplified by a humble leader in a corporate arena. As the boss has faith in his team members and has their best interests in mind, he inspires them to work harder to reciprocate. As the boss sets an example, he inspires his team to do more. There is no need to let others know who has the authority. In fact, the less a manager boasts about himself, the more authority he gains. The more he does for others, the more power he accumulates.

The US concept of servant leadership echoes this approach. If a CEO does not mind doing menial tasks, such as taking the trash out or turning the lights off at the end of the day, employees will surely follow. Ronald

Reagan was one of the most-loved US presidents. He was revered for his conservatism and down-to-earth manner. He was once seen kneeling on a hospital floor mopping up a glass of water he had spilled. Seeing this, his aides were astonished and they asked him why he was doing that. Reagan replied that it was his own mess and he didn't want to trouble others to clean it up for him. After all, Reagan was the US President and this incident happened just a few days after an assassin had shot and injured him. This further emboldened his image as a sincere, down-to-earth person worthy of respect and emulation.

Jesus is the ultimate example of the servant leader. He served others with love and compassion, regardless of who they were. In the end, he even died for them. Because of that, Jesus is revered as one of the most powerful leaders that has ever lived.

Therefore the Tao manager listens but he doesn't drain his people. He leads his team but he does not interfere. He does not appear outwardly powerful but he has tremendous inner strength. He is self-confident so he is comfortable with his team running with its own ideas. He is encouraging but not suffocating, and supportive but not overbearing. He penetrates problems easily and he brings along his team to solve them. He leads by setting examples, not by barking orders. He is a captain to his team but he acts more like a cheerleader. He is not there to judge his team but to make it better. His influence is essential but he is hardly noticeable, just like water.

It is not easy to be a Tao manager in modern organizations. Tao concepts are vague and difficult to apply. There are also no performance metrics or management guidelines to follow. Most importantly, there is a tendency for the Tao manager to be overly passive, believing that things will right themselves in due course if nothing is done. Procrastination is often disguised as Tao, to the detriment of progress.

Bibliography

Edward T. Hall, *Beyond Culture*, Ch. 1, *The Paradox of Culture*, P. 9–11, Anchor Books, Published by Doubleday, 1976.

The Tao of Power, Lao Tzu's Classic Guide to Leadership, Influence and Excellence, Ch. 42, R.L. Wing, Doubleday & Company, Inc. 1986.

The World Bank.
U.S. Census Bureau.
Wikipedia.
J.V. Luce, *An Introduction to Greek Philosophy*, P. 9, Thames and Hudson, 1992.
Lawrence T. White, *Can a Westerner Think Like an East Asian? Different Cultures, Different Cognitive Styles*, Psychology Today, Jun 20, 2012.
T.M. Luhrmann, *Wheat People vs. Rice People, Why Are Some Cultures More Individualistic Than Others?* The New York Times, Dec 3, 2014.
Ali Reza Rezaei, Larry Katz, *Evolution of the Reliability and Validity of the Cognitive Styles Analysis, Personality and Individual Differences* 36 1317–1327, Pergamon Press, 2004.
Richard E. Nisbett, *The Geography of Thought, How Asians and Westerners Think Differently and ... Why?* Free Press, Simon and Schuster New York, 2003.
Yin Yang and the Five Elements(阴阳五行学说), baike@baidu.com, reviewed Nov 2015 Amanda Briney, *Low and High Pressure, The Basics of Weather and Their Impact on the World's Weather*, About.com, updated Dec 20, 2014.
David A. Garvin *Making the Case, Professional Education for the World of Practice*, Harvard Magazine, Sep–Oct, 2003.
Edward T. Hall, *Beyond Culture, Ch. 1 The Paradox of Culture*, P. 11, Anchor Books, published by Doubleday, 1976.
Edward T. Hall, *Beyond Culture, Ch. 6. Context and Meaning*, P. 85–103, Anchor Books, published by Doubleday, 1976.
Fung Yu-lan, *A History of Chinese Philosophy, Vol.1, p. 3* translated by Derk Bodde, Princeton University Press, 1953.
Great Leap Forward, Encyclopaedia Britannica.
Confucius, *The Analects*, Book 12, translated by D.C. Lau, Plenum Press, 1979.
Ang Lee, Wikipedia, reviewed Jun 2015.
Rong Xiaoqing, *China Making Up for Cultural Deficit*, Global Times, 15 Nov 2012.
Fung Yu-lan, *A History of Chinese Philosophy*, P. 4–5, Vol. 1, translated by Derk Bodde, Princeton University Press, 1953.
Steve Jobs, *Stanford Commencement Address*, Jun 12, 2005, uploaded to Youtube on Oct 6, 2011.
Facebook Reports Fourth Quarter and Full Year 2015 Results, investor.fb.com, reviewed Jan 29, 2016.
Henry Kissinger, *On China*, P. 135, Penguin Books, 2012.
Paul Polman, *Business, Society, and the Future of Capitalism*, McKinsey Quarterly, May 2014.

Liang Shuming, *Cultures and Philosophies of the East and West*, Ch. 2, P. 53, The Commercial Press, Beijing 2012 (translated by the author) (梁漱溟, 东西文化及其哲学, Ch. 2, P. 53, 商务印书馆, 北京, 2012).

The Tao of Power, Lao Tzu's Classic Guide to Leadership, Influence and Excellence, Ch. 17, Ch. 22, Ch. 63 and Ch. 78 R.L. Wing, Doubleday & Company, Inc. 1986.

Zhuangzi, Stanford Encyclopedia of Philosophy, first published Dec 17, 2014.

Heraclitus, Stanford Encyclopedia of Philosophy, Jun 23, 2015.

R.L Wing, *The Tao of Power, Lao Tzu's Classic Guide to Leadership, Influence and Excellence*, Ch. 22, Doubleday & Company, Inc., 1986.

Bruce Lee's Philosophy, youtube, reviewed Jun 2105.

Why Humble Bosses Are Good for Business, The Street, Sep 13, 2014.

Lindsay Terry, *Ronald Reagan, A Man of Kindness*, crossway.org, Jul 1, 2004.

Laurie Beth Jones, *Jesus, CEO, Using Ancient Wisdom for Visionary Leadership*, P. 186–187, P. 198–199, Hyperion 1995.

5

The Power of the Whole

The Lehman Flu

The global financial crisis of 2008 was the most severe world financial crisis since the Great Depression of the 1930s. It exposed the fragility of the global financial system and the danger of contagion risks. It also tarnished the West's reputation as the undisputed leader in economics and finance, and as guardian of global financial stability.

After the collapse of the tech bubble in 2000, financial engineering rose to become the new US creative frontier and the driver behind a thriving export market. Instead of mechanical, electrical or other traditional engineering disciplines, college students flocked to study a new discipline called financial engineering in the hope of an exciting career and faster payback.

All kinds of structured securities, such as commercial mortgage-backed securities and collateralized debt obligations (CDOs), and others with even more esoteric-sounding acronyms, were conjured up by creative financiers and sold to investors worldwide. Unlike a car or a piece of hardware where buyers can see and touch something solid, and test it out before buying it, the new financial products are nothing but fancy theoretical constructs. They consist of thick stacks of legal documents, ostensibly backed by the creditworthiness of the underlying structures, and supported by legal regimes supposedly robust enough to protect the rights of investors. The recession exposed the weaknesses of these assumptions.

After the collapse of Lehman Brothers, investors beat a hasty retreat and left behind a huge funding vacuum. Companies accustomed to managing liquidity through short-term funding found their money taps turned off. The ensuing liquidity dry spell caused borrowers with previously sound credit to struggle to fund their operations. Many collapsed under the debt load that they could no longer refinance. To make matters worse, trading of structured securities spread the US mortgage risks to all corners of the globe and fanned a global recession.

All over the world, traders, institutional investors, treasurers and even individuals bought structured products. Many did so unaware of their underlying risks. In Hong Kong, over thirty thousand individual investors, including a large number of retirees, bought Lehman mini-bonds, so-called because of a swap guarantee provided by Lehman Brothers on a pool of CDOs of other issuers.

Investors were led to believe that the mini-bonds were similar to high-yielding term deposits backed by the creditworthiness of a group of well-known issuers. When Lehman collapsed, the mini-bond investors suffered huge losses. They protested loudly and publicly for months. Finally, the Hong Kong government, under intense public pressure, capitulated and made the banks that sold the original mini-bonds buy them back.

When world economies and financial markets were growing nicely, the watchdogs relaxed and basked in the limelight of the success. Meanwhile, the risks they were charged to oversee festered and grew undetected. The financiers were paid handsomely for their efforts as originators or intermediaries. The risks, however, landed on the laps of the investors, and were later paid for by the general public.

Unbeknownst to many people, structured financial products have become an essential part of our daily lives. If a person takes out a mortgage on a house, the monthly payments most likely go into a pool with other mortgages to form a MBS. If a company takes out a business loan, it probably goes into a pool of collateralized loan obligations. If a person makes payments with his credit cards, or auto or student loans, the proceeds will go to service their respective asset-backed securities. These structured securities have flourished to meet the needs of our credit-crazed society and investors hungry for yield. They form a large part of the investible universe where global investors hunt and trade. They also became problematic when the credit fundamentals deteriorated.

When Lehman collapsed, the regulators were initially in shock and denial. They looked for culprits to blame at a time when their calm assurance was most needed. Most minded their own business and had plenty of excuses. Officials who regularly pontificated about market discipline back-pedaled and claimed they did not have the proper authority to intervene in Lehman's collapse (they did intervene massively later on to save other institutions). This did not bode well for market confidence. In short, the US financial problems exploded into a full-blown global crisis. Its lingering after-effects are still being felt today, even eight years after the Lehman's collapse.

Wall Street's sophisticated models could not predict the stock market crash, and the supposedly rare black swan event occurred, now with alarming frequency. The market's invisible hands had become just that—invisible. The premise of market economics, which stipulates that the free flow of resources and individuals working for their self-interests is best for the society as a whole, had broken down. It seemed that the Western model had failed, so much so that its validity was even being questioned.

What Did China Do Right?

China is a developing country playing catch-up with the developed world. As such, it doesn't have a sophisticated financial supervisory framework or that many trained experts. Somehow it was able to avoid the brunt of the Asian financial crisis of 1997, and it dodged the global financial crisis of 2008. What did China do right?

In 1997 the Thai government devalued its currency, the baht, because it could no longer defend it from attacks from currency traders. The Thai move triggered a devaluation chain reaction, spreading from Indonesia to South Korea. Foreign investors rushed for the exit while short sellers piled in. Asian markets were in free fall and asset values plummeted.

To ensure financial stability, the International Monetary Fund stepped in to bring tough reform agendas along with credit lines to the governments of Thailand, Indonesia and South Korea. These traumatized governments took heed and carried out structural reforms that put their economies on a much firmer footing for future growth.

At that time, many Western observers blamed the Asian financial crisis on crony capitalism, suggesting that it was not pure capitalism but one adulterated with supportive Confucian values that Asians practiced. Pure capitalism, of course, would let the market determine who the winners and losers are. The winners should reap the rewards and the losers should be punished.

Now fast-forward a decade later to 2008, when the world would face an even worse financial crisis. This time it started with the collapse of Lehman Brothers in New York, the center of world finance. Unlike the Asian financial crisis, where most of the damage was limited to a few Asian countries and, to some extent, Russia and Brazil, this time the impact was global.

As with the Great Depression in the 1930s, the global financial crisis began with a crash on Wall Street that spread rapidly to the rest of the world. This begs the question of why, after almost 80 years of financial reforms and technological advances, the West still could not forecast, let alone prevent, a financial crisis of this magnitude from reoccurring?

While the West was reeling from the crisis, China continued with its steady economic development. Its rapid intervention in the domestic economy had not only stabilized it but also provided badly needed stimulus to counter the massive global deflationary headwinds.

To deal with the crisis, Chinese leaders gelled together as a team instead of working in their own individual silos. They did not employ fancy analytical techniques but relied on ancient wisdom instead. An old Chinese saying goes, "When the lips go, the teeth will freeze." This reflects a wholistic conviction that one's self and others are symbiotically related, just as the lips are there to protect the teeth and the teeth are there to acquire nourishment for the body, including the lips. When one goes, the others will follow. Likewise, when individuals fail miserably, their group will suffer. It's only a matter of time.

The Chinese were keenly aware that events occurring elsewhere in the world can affect them intimately. The fates of trading, investment flows and other economic relationships are tied closely together.

Because this time the global headwinds were so vicious, the Chinese leadership sought to safeguard their main objective, which is to maintain social stability and a concept rooted in ancient traditions. However, while investments by the central and local governments had managed to buffer the deflationary blows, the massive debt-fueled asset bubble continues to put a drag on the Chinese economy to this day.

With unoccupied apartment blocks and empty malls littered across the Chinese landscape, a potential housing collapse is indeed alarming. However, it hasn't really happened, and I believe it is unlikely to happen in as dramatic a fashion as many Western analysts have predicted, because of the demographics and the culture. In China the government's primary objective is to ensure social stability. This translates into having the right policies in place to allow people to have jobs, to put food on their tables and roofs above their heads, so they can raise their families peacefully. To this end the government still holds many levers that it can use to stimulate the economy and to achieve this traditional mandate.

In the US the government's priority is to ensure a fair market for participants, but not to pick winners or losers. It is more concerned about the market process and less so about the outcome. The government will intervene from time to time to prevent major market upheavals. Otherwise it will just leave the participants to sort things out by themselves, based on the conviction that fair competition will benefit all of us in the long run.

However, in a game where the interests and liabilities of the players and the spectators are inextricably related and delicately balanced, allowing a select few to become winners can make the rest of us losers. And the question: is what's good for the market always good for the society as a whole? If you look at the global financial crisis, where aggressive people competed fiercely in a game where intelligence was encouraged and handsomely rewarded, and consider the dismal results, the answer may not be that straightforward.

In the *Tao Te Ching*, Lao Tzu says that good fortune resides within misfortune, and vice versa. In other words, nothing is only good or bad. Like yin and yang, there is always something good within the bad, and there is always something bad within the good. By the same token, while competition is good for the economy in general, unfettered competition can bring out the worst.

The duality of nature in Lao Tzu's ancient message is prescient. You should appreciate that things are not always what they appear on the surface, and you should be circumspect about what meets the eye and look beyond the obvious. Within the obvious lie the unknowns, and within the unknowns exist opportunities.

In 2006 I had the chance to accompany Moody's sovereign ratings team to its annual credit review of China. After a full morning's briefings by Ministry of Finance staff in Beijing, we went to a lunch hosted by the then Vice Minister of Finance, Lou Jiwei.

After describing to us some of the issues China was facing and the government's responses, Lou asked for questions from the lunch audience. I took the opportunity to ask him about the housing bubble that was developing in the US and what China would do if such a bubble were deflated. Without hesitation, Lou responded calmly that they were monitoring the situation closely and that they already had a contingency plan in place. As credit professionals trained to focus on the downside, we felt more assured after hearing his remarks.

Judging by the swiftness of the Chinese government's post-Lehman intervention, it would be fair to assume a contingency plan would have been put in place before the crisis. A decision of this magnitude would require the unanimous support of China's powerful ministries and local governments. It could not have been made hastily by a small group of officials in their offices at the last minute.

Long-term thinking and circumspection are both Chinese cultural traits. Chinese people always seem to worry and fidget about their future, as if something bad is about to happen to them at any minute. This attitude is evident in people's lives. A 40 percent personal savings rate and emphasis on education reflect this kind of circumspection and long-term thinking. The saying that you should not go and dig a well only when you are thirsty, or fix the leaks in your windows when it rains, is constantly on the lips of many Chinese people. To think beyond the issues at hand and consider all parts of the whole is wholistic thinking. It is also traditionally Chinese. These cultural traditions go back thousands of years and they remain important Chinese characteristics today.

Bibliography

The Economist, *Lehman's Mini-bonds, The Good Inside the Dud*, March 2011.
Ian Bremmer, Nouriel Roubini, *Paradise Lost: Why Fallen Markets Will Never Be the Same*, Institutional Investor, Vol. 44, Issue 7, Sep. 2, 2010.
Ian Bremmer, *State Capitalism Comes of Age, The End of the Free Market?* Foreign Affairs, May/June 2009.
1997 Asia Financial Crisis, Wikipedia.
R.L. Wing, *The Tao of Power, Lao Tzu's Classic Guide to Leadership, Influence and Excellence*, Ch. 58, Doubleday & Company, Inc., 1986.

6

The Irrationality of Being Rational

As analytical thinkers, Westerners like to view the world with the models they have developed. There are sophisticated models in science and medicine, economy and social sciences. Good models should be robust, stand the test of time and be able to forecast future events fairly well.

Westerners believe that if things work according to their models then they are dealing with the rational. If things don't work out then they must be dealing with the irrational. If governments behave irrationally there will be social discontent. If markets behave irrationally there will be mispricing of assets and market dislocations. If people behave irrationally there will be disputes and fights. All these can be minimized if people behave rationally according to their own rules.

Culturally, Chinese people don't analyze the world as much. However, they appreciate it more. This traditional worldview was derived from their observations of nature and their desire to live in harmony with it. Since nature is always perfect and humans will never know all there is to know about it, we should revere and accept it as it is. We should not analyze it to death, try to explain everything or change it in any way. It would be irrational for us to believe we can do any of that.

As nature epitomizes balance and harmony, men should emulate it and live a balanced and harmonious way of life. They should minimize conflict and avoid fights. They should practice the middle way and avoid extremes. They should balance their physical and mental halves. Their left and right brains should work harmoniously together. Their selves and their groups should be cohesive as one.

The Western analytical approach is logical and works very well in the physical world. For example, an apple will fall to the ground after rolling off a table, because of gravity. It will never float up in the air like we see in science-fiction movies. We will never be able to build a perpetual motion machine because it is against the laws of thermodynamics.

But the Western approach has limits, especially when dealing with complex problems that are inter-related or infused with human emotions. As is often the case, when emotion overwhelms reason, the rational becomes irrational.

Limits of Analysis

The Western analytical method has solved many of our outstanding problems very well. Advances in medicine allow us to live longer and healthier lives. New technologies unleash productivity and raise our living standards. The Internet allows us to connect with anyone at anytime from anywhere. Financial technologies make the world essentially one big market, allowing people to trade any products in real time with anybody, anywhere. However, there is also a limit to what this analytical approach can accomplish for us. Pushing the limit in a narrow area can bring about diminishing, or even negative, total returns.

A person should perform analysis based on the best data he can gather. However, analysis can only evaluate the known risks, and not those that have yet to surface. We also don't have a very good handle on how to deal with non-linear events, where individual events that are logical by themselves can come together to exact a toll on us. Plus no amount of analysis can accurately predict human behavior. Surging emotions can overwhelm reason and torpedo the best logic.

When different risks coalesce to wreak havoc on us, we have the makings of a black swan event. Such an event is supposedly extremely rare, and it is disruptive because no one can see it coming. The occasional stock market collapse is such an example.

Ouch! The Market Freezes

The stock market crash resembles a phenomenon in physics called a phase transition. This occurs when matter goes from one of its phases, say solid or liquid, to a different phase. When this occurs it does so abruptly. When water freezes to become ice at precisely 0 °C it has gone through a phase transition. This critical phenomenon is the result of correlations of the movements of distant water molecules.

When water is in its liquid phase, water molecules exhibit random thermal motion. Their positions are independent of each other and there is little correlation to speak of. But when the temperature approaches freezing point, water molecules begin to form larger and larger clusters. They also exhibit stronger correlation in motion with each other within the cluster. Put another way, they experience forces exerted on them by molecules far away.

When water freezes to become ice, the molecules become affixed in the frozen ice lattice. So when we pick up an ice cube, every water molecule in the cube moves in complete synchrony with the other molecules. In technical terms, they exhibit long-range spatial correlation with each other.

Investor behaviors mimic this kind of spatial correlation when actions from some investors influence the actions of other seemingly unrelated parties. For example, when momentum investors exit their positions and their actions cause contrarian investors to follow suit, their actions are now correlated by one thing in common—the fear of loss. Fundamentally, these two groups of investors have very different mandates. However, in extreme markets, their behaviors can become strongly correlated.

Other more recent examples are the Chinese stock market crashes in 2015 and 2016 that also triggered sell-offs on Wall Street. The Chinese stock market has been around only since the early 1990s so it is not yet a mature market. In fact, it is a punter's paradise and doesn't have a lot to do with the new consumer economy. But fears of US investors from a Chinese financial contagion is enough to cause the Dow to fail.

In another scenario, an investor is affected by his own emotions from past investment losses. Since he dreads repeating the same mistakes again, he pulls the sell trigger the minute he hears some vaguely familiar bad news. When he behaves this way, his action exhibits autocorrelation in time.

The correlation of investor behaviors in space and time destroys randomness, which forms the basis of financial modeling.

At room temperature—normal market conditions—investors make decisions pretty much randomly. But when the market freezes their actions are much more correlated. At the first sign of instability, all investors care about is capital preservation. So they run to sell risks or seek a safe haven in US treasuries. As there are few buyers, prices drop precipitously.

In a more stable market, investors may look at the most recent prices of securities and their outlooks to decide what to do next. But when bad news comes along and the market goes down suddenly, they ignore the fundamentals and sell. When investor behaviors are correlated in this way, the market tanks.

In a normal market, investor's timescale of correlation with their past actions is short. They focus more on the future and their investment decisions behave more like random motion. When volatility sets in, their timescale of correlation lengthens, as they dig deeper and deeper into their past memories to find insights into trade and to avoid losses. When painful memories are evoked and magnified, it is difficult to make decisions based solely on fundamentals. This shifting of investor sentiment is impossible to model analytically.

When the majority of investors become risk averse and run for the hills, the market is a one-way street—going down.

The supply of tea in Sri Lanka may have some bearing on the price of an English breakfast but it has little impact on the fast-food business in the US. These events are independent of each other and are uncorrelated. However, when market panic sets in, investors will become more cautious, and banks and regulators will tighten up. This affects everybody, everywhere. The tea plantation owner in Sri Lanka and the fast-food operator in the US, though thousands of miles apart, are affected by one thing in common—poor market sentiment.

When market sentiment retreats, businesses find it harder to get working capital or loans for refinancing. They may freeze headcounts or consider layoffs. Asset managers will reduce risks and hoard cash. Customers will wait until the last possible moment to place their orders, and then take their time to pay. The potential bankruptcy of well-known companies will now be constantly on the lips of financial commentators, making the already poor sentiment worse. Negativity begets more negativity, until it becomes reality.

There is a popular statistical tool based on historical trading data called value at risk (VaR). Risk and asset managers routinely use it to estimate potential losses in their trading books, from changes in interest rates to foreign exchange rates and security prices. This works fine until volatility sets in. When the market suddenly becomes volatile, VaR can be way off when its precision is most needed. This prompted hedge fund manager David Einhorn to call VaR an airbag that works all the time, except when there is a crash.

In Quants We Trust

The original purpose of using financial derivatives is to offset risks. Over time, derivatives have also become a popular investment vehicle.

A derivative is something that derives its value from changes in the value of something else. For example, acceleration is a derivative of velocity. A stock option is a derivative that derives its value from the changes in value of the underlying stock. Similarly, a credit derivative is designed to reflect changes in the credit quality of a given debt instrument. Like all derivatives, financial derivatives have the effect of amplifying the underlying risks that they are designed to reflect.

Trading redistributes risks but it doesn't make them disappear. The widespread use of derivatives has inadvertently introduced new risks into the world financial system. When market panic sets in, perfect hedges no longer work as intended. The interconnected nature of derivative contracts can set off a contagion chain reaction that ripples through the real economy. This has prompted Warren Buffet to call derivatives financial instruments of mass destruction.

Over the past several decades, faster computers, massive databases and sophisticated trading algorithms created by rocket scientists have allowed the field of quantitative finance to flourish.

One of the objectives of quantitative finance is to take emotions out of investing. With elegant math and impeccable logic, it gives the illusion that one can predict events that are driven as much by human emotions as by economic laws. And as the discipline evolves, our reliance on it increases. After all, the market has validated such an approach. It is therefore certifiably the rational thing to do.

This reliance on quantitative models has resulted in several spectacular failures on Wall Street, including long-term capital management (LTCM), Bear Stearns and Lehman Brothers. Each failure was more spectacular than the one before it.

LTCM was a hedge fund run by a group of successful traders and economists, including two Nobel laureates. In 1998, barely a year after the Asian financial crisis, LTCM collapsed, triggered by the default of Russia on its sovereign debt. At the behest of the Federal Reserve, a group of investment banks rescued LTCM.

Before the Russian default, LTCM was highly successful. It traded on slim mispricing of a large basket of securities, and it boosted returns by hedging and keeping only a minimum amount of capital. Making profits with the least amount of capital is an ideal trading business and an excellent way to reward shareholders.

However, the Russian default threw a monkey wrench into LTCM's otherwise rational methodology. Hedging strategies premised on investors exercising rational behaviors fell apart. Losses mounted and LTCM failed in this volatile environment.

While the LTCM debacle should have caused other trading firms to be more cautious, the brains of Wall Street all thought they could fix trading problems with better models and controls. This same reliance on quantitative models to manage risk would later lead to the collapse of Bear Stearns, and shortly afterwards Lehman Brothers.

These venerable Wall Street firms thought they could maximize the returns of their capital by carefully choosing what they invest in and

6 The Irrationality of Being Rational 111

what they hedge them with. But when the US housing market unraveled, and ratings of structured securities were downgraded by the same rating agencies that gave them higher ratings earlier, losses mounted and these banks struggled to raise new capital in an increasingly hostile market. In Lehman's case the correlation of investor fears sank the market and led to the demise of the oldest US investment bank. The rational market can turn irrational in an instant.

The demise of the US financial system in 2008 was a glaring example of the failure of the Western left-brain centric mentality. After the US financial market began to unravel, many observers pointed a finger at the major credit rating agencies—Moody's, Standard and Poor's, and Fitch—and rightly so.

Credit rating is one of the more quantitative disciplines in finance. Rating has been in use for over 100 years and is now thoroughly ingrained in global financial practices. Investors, traders and regulators all refer to credit ratings routinely. Without them, fixed-income market practitioners would not have a common language to trade, regulators would not have an important tool to manage risk and our financial markets would not have grown to the size they are today.

A bank profits by charging interest and fees on the loans it provides. The faster a bank can make loans the more profit it can generate. In order to raise funds to service more loans, a bank can sell its mortgage loans to a government-sponsored enterprise, such as Freddie Mac, or to an investment bank, which then bundles them together as MBSs. The MBS may have many different segments called tranches that are sold to investors with different risk appetites, and be priced accordingly.

Underwriters can sell the MBS to investors or rebundle some of the weaker tranches to create yet another form of structured securities called CDOs. After a few iterations of slicing and dicing, mixing and remixing, structure finance experts can create completely new debt instruments with a range of credit qualities. The final products are now represented by gigantic spreadsheet exercises that only those skilled in the art can comprehend.

Any intuitive feel for the underlying credit, and the macroeconomic factors supporting it, such as the health of the US housing market, is lost in the translation. The credit is now represented by a group of alphanumeric symbols built upon other alphanumeric symbols. They are supposed to represent something tangible but in fact they are layers away from reality.

Even though investors might have had doubts about the health of the US housing market, they still purchased structured securities, believing that their risks had somehow been magically structured away.

This was also a case of relegating investment decisions to the quants, and letting the left brain dominate the investment process. Eventually the MBS market took a dive when the US housing market hit a speed bump. The vicious rea-estate defaults sank the MBS market and spread the risks to the rest of the investment world like wild fire.

From 2000 to 2006 the median price of a US home doubled, while per capita GDP went up by only 27 percent. To make housing affordable, and more fees for themselves, bankers created new products that required little or no down payment. It didn't feel right and should have raised concerns among investors and regulators, but these folks were overly confident about their rational prowess, and they neglected common sense. The result was an economic disaster.

When investors think they have the market figured out they are often surprised by how irrational it can be. When they feel so sure about something, they drop their guard and take on other risks. When they think they have figured out the other risks, the original risk, which is supposed to be under control, may come back to haunt them.

This kind of psychology has affected many smart people, including certified geniuses. After Sir Isaac Newton had gone broke from investing in the South Sea Bubble, he said, "I can calculate the movement of the stars, but not the madness of men." When we are so sure of something, we drop our guard and make other mistakes. This is human nature at work. We are our own worst enemy.

If we examine a slide under a microscope, we may see lots of stained cells, but there is no telling which species they come from. Important attributes such as size, sex, age, color and appearance are all absent. If we look for more detail we can miss the big picture. If we define something too precisely we can lose important perspectives. If we try to pin something down precisely, such as the stock market, we can neglect the things that are more important to us, such as our family, our health and our sanity.

Similarly, if we rely solely on statistical models to trade securities, we can lose our feel for the market, or see the trees but miss the forest. Nassim Taleb, in *The Black Swan*, makes this point repeatedly.

The more educated we are, the more we think the world should run according to our rules and logic. But the world has always run by its own rules and rhythms. We are no better at understanding how the world works or how people behave today than we were thousands of years ago. If we were we wouldn't have all these wars, pollution, global warming and other man-made disasters. Like the ancient Chinese, we should be humble and appreciate the world as it is, rather than force it to fit into our narrow design.

To Tao or Not to Tao, That Is the Question

In the opening chapter of the *Tao Te Ching*, Lao Tzu lays down his definition of the Tao, or rather what it is not. He says the Tao that can be described is not the true Tao, and the name that can be spoken is not the true name. This concise but confusing passage encapsulates how the ancient Chinese viewed the world. Basically, it says that the more we know about something, the less we know about it. If we try to get a more precise understanding of something, we can lose our perspective. This applies to many things we do in our daily lives.

Why is it that the Tao, which is so powerful, cannot be described? How can we know what we describe is the truth? If it cannot be described or named, how do we know what it is?

We think in a language we are comfortable with. However, what we wish to convey may be much more complex than the vocabulary we have at our disposal. By using words to describe ideas, we can miss important nuances that are beyond our descriptive vocabulary. This is particularly true if what we wish to describe has something to do with emotions.

The mathematician and philosopher Alfred North Whitehead believed that languages are not universally applicable. They are useful only for those people who take part in developing their languages. Therefore if someone is not familiar with the use of our language, we can't expect him to behave in the manner we would normally expect.

Math is a symbolic language. For financial models to work, they assume that all investors will follow the rules and behave rationally. If they don't then the predictive power of such models is questionable. When this happens we often say that the market is irrational. But why do investors have to trade by the rules that others created for them, and why do humans have to be rational?

If we try to analyze people or predict the future, what we think we know may not always be true, and what we don't know can surprise us. Any model we use is by definition incomplete because it is built on known facts and tested on existing data. What's more, the missing information is often more important than the known facts. Whitehead's famous phrase "Seek simplicity and distrust it" echoes what Lao Tzu said over 2,000 years ago.

In whatever we do—even though simplicity is what we seek, and we may be able to find it once in a while—we should always be vigilant and circumspect about what we think we know. Once we think we've got it, we should seek again. We should never be too complacent or stop seeking.

So in trading, once we have arrived at a winning formula, we should start looking for something different because other smart traders will eventually catch up with us and render our winning methodology obsolete. Similarly, in our jobs we should always be on our toes and find ways to improve the way we work. If we become complacent we will become redundant over time. Likewise, we should always try to improve our relationships with our friends and loved ones. We should never take them for granted. Otherwise our relationships will drift apart for lack of attention, if not anything else. What we think we know will not stay true forever, and the Tao that can be described is never the true Tao.

Some things are better experienced than said. Thinking wholistically and using our right brain more often can open up new possibilities.

The phrase "I love you" is probably the most commonly used English expression besides "How are you?" It is literally spoken millions of times a day by people all over the world. This phrase is a reductionist's attempt to distill the very complex feelings a person has for his loved ones into a simple linear expression. But it can mean a lot or it can mean very little. It can also mean different things to different people.

When used too often, "I love you" becomes a greeting rather than an expression of our genuine emotions. By being too simplistic we lose meaning. How many times have we misinterpreted this expression and ended up feeling surprised or frustrated? How often do we say "I love you" to those we care about but still have big fights with them afterwards?

Instead of using words, why don't we just exchange hugs, smiles or knowing glances, or just simply hold hands? These simple gestures involve our senses, which arguably carry more information than plain language. They also leave plenty of room for us to imagine, and they make us fall in love all over again. And again.

In general, Asians are not as expressive as Westerners. There are cultural reasons behind this. Lao Tzu says that those who know do not speak, and those who speak do not know. Confucius says that a gentleman should be diligent at his work but be careful with his words. Since mum is the word, Asians must rely on subtleties to help them express themselves. Some things are also better experienced than said.

Asian languages, such as Chinese or Japanese, are rich in subtleties. The high-context Asian cultures also mean that people have more ways to express themselves than using just plain language.

Of course, if we are dealing with science and matters that can be compartmentalized and reduced, we should strive to be as precise as possible. But when we are dealing with people and their emotions, we should step back, open up our feelings and follow the Tao.

If we are successful at what we do, we should feel elated. We should congratulate ourselves, reload and try again. If we miss, we may blame ourselves for making stupid mistakes and sink to the bottom of our emotional pit. We may go from feeling exuberant one minute to despondent the next, as we let our emotions jerk us up and down like a yo-yo. These emotional excursions exhaust us but they get us nowhere. We would be better off putting our left-brain analytical machine on idle, relaxing and thinking wholistically. That way we can better engage our senses and follow the Tao.

Don't Fight the Fed!

Trading is affected not only by psychology but also by physiology. When traders are stressed out for a long period of time they become timid and unable to trade rationally.

John Coates, the one-time Wall Street trader turned neuroscience researcher, has studied traders' mentality from a physiological perspective. His research shows that when the market is moving along smoothly, traders are full of confidence and willing to take on all kinds of risks. They are motivated by the prospect of making a killing in the market and getting big bonuses at the year-end. When there is a sudden market downturn the same traders may trim their risk-taking a bit, but they will still look for opportunities to put money to work. If the downturn stretches into a prolonged decline, however, previously ebullient traders can become overly risk averse. This sentiment change can elevate the body's stress hormones to such a high level that it can lead to depression.

Stress can also make a trader relive his worst nightmares—the ones he thought he had buried permanently. Under stress, traders may correlate their actions with past mistakes, and cross-correlate them with a fears of others. When a majority of traders act in this way the market becomes irrational.

When the Federal Reserve makes public its interest rate intentions in advance, it underwrites one of the biggest risks in investment—the interest rate movement. However, this assurance has also indirectly encouraged speculation in other asset classes.

When investors think they know where interest rates are heading, they relax and drive up asset prices. Corporate managers are guilty of the same crime. Instead of innovating and running their operations more efficiently, they borrow at low interest rates to buy back shares. This boosts their share prices but does little to improve competitiveness. What's more, because of the increase in debt, these borrowers can face significant refinancing risks if rates go up suddenly.

In the investment world, different economic forces are intricately coupled and delicately balanced. If we minimize a major risk, such as interest rates, we inevitably create new uncertainties, such as asset bubbles. When we think we finally have something figured out, it is time to reconsider that premise and think again. This paradox can best be appreciated if we think in a more wholistic fashion.

Alas, the Tao that can be described is never the true Tao.

Bibliography

Alfred North Whitehead, *The Concept of Nature*: The Tarner Lectures Delivered in Trinity College, Nov 1919.
Darryll Hendricks, *Evaluation of Value-at-Risk Models Using Historical Data* FRBNY ECONOMIC POLICY REVIEW / APRIL, P. 39, 1996.
David Einhorn, *Private Profits and Socialized Risks*, P. 12, Global Association of Risk Professionals, June/July 2008.
Roger L. Lowenstein, *Long-Term Capital Management: It's a Short-Term Memory*, The New York Times Sep 7, 2008.
S&P/Case-Shiller 20-City Composite Home Price Index, reviewed Feb 2015. The World Bank.
Sam Ro, *Isaac Newton's Nightmare—Charted By Marc Faber*, Business Insider, Apr 2, 2013.
Nassim Nicholas Taleb, *The Black Swan, The Impact of the Highly Improbable*, P. 44, 266, 270, The Penguin Group, 2007.
R.L. Wing, *The Tao of Power, Lao Tzu's Classic Guide to Leadership, Influence and Excellence*, Ch. 1, Doubleday $ Company, Inc., 1986.
Edward T. Hall, *Beyond Culture*, Ch. 4, P. 57, Anchor Book Published by Doubleday, 1976.
Alfred North Whitehead, *Religion in the Making*, Harvard University, Mar 13, 1926.
John Coates, *The Hour Between Dog and Wolf, Risk Taking, Gut Feelings and the Biology of Boom and Bust*, P. 213–229, The Penguin press, New York 2012.
John Coates, *The Biology of Risk*, The New York Times, Jun 7, 2014.
Neil Irwin, *Markets Are Less Volatile. Should We Worry?* The New York Times, Jun 10, 2014.

7

Union of Men and Heaven

Traditional Chinese culture was developed with the view that humans, as an integral part of nature, should follow its rules. This is not to say that Chinese culture has always operated on the same set of rules; it has evolved with time but its foundation has remained firmly unchanged.

During the May Fourth Movement in 1919, immediately after the fall of Qing Dynasty and the founding of the Chinese Republic, China's new intelligentsia severely denounced Confucianism. Many of its odious feudal traditions, such as bound feet and the subjugation of women, were attacked and purged. But core aspects of Confucianism, such as scholarship, family and respect for social order, survived.

In the 1970s, during the height of China's tumultuous Cultural Revolution, the Gang of Four—the four officials most associated with the ultra-leftist movement—viciously attacked Confucius and Mencius. They loudly denounced the sages as villains of old China, and they wanted them expunged from the Chinese psyche. Confucian works were banned in schools until the 1980s, when they were slowly reintroduced into the curriculum.

An entire generation of Chinese people did not have the opportunity to study the Chinese classics formally. Although they were able to maintain their Chinese identity through traditions, they were cut off from the roots of their culture.

At the same time as Mainland China was embroiled in the Cultural Revolution, Taiwan countered with its own Chinese Cultural Renaissance Movement. Its objective was to revive traditional Chinese culture in the face of increasing materialistic influences from the West, and the destructive Cultural Revolution from the Mainland. In fact, the main thoroughfares in Taipei are all named after Confucian virtues.

Many modern Asian economies with large Chinese populations, such as Singapore and Hong Kong, also continue to teach traditional Chinese culture.

Now traditional studies are once again being promoted in Mainland China as an important part of Chinese heritage. In 2011 there was even an attempt to put up a giant 9.5 m tall statue of Confucius, right in front of the Beijing National Museum, not far from the mausoleum of Mao Zedong, the communist founder of the People's Republic.

According to Bertrand Russell, Chinese culture may be just what is required to modulate the excesses of the Western way of life, with its attendant strife and exploitation, plus discontent and destruction. In fact, almost 100 years ago, he said that we could all benefit from a Chinese way of life.

Just what is so resilient about the Chinese culture, and in particular Confucianism, that allows it to survive after all these centuries despite repeated attempts to extinguish it? And how relevant is Confucianism in today's world? This is a question that has intrigued many modern scholars, including Tu Wei-Ming of Harvard.

Tu is the champion of the new Confucianism, or Confucian humanism. He argues for a Confucian approach to modernity as an alternative to the concept of modernity defined exclusively in Western terms. He believes that the West's drive to explore and conquer has exhibited unbridled aggressiveness towards humanity, nature and itself. In this respect the humanism aspects of Confucianism should be promoted to offset the extremes of the Western post-enlightenment mentality.

However, the pros and cons of how traditional values affect modern behaviors have never been clearly established. Determining which aspects of Chinese characteristics are resilient and should be promoted, and which should remain in the history bin, has defied scholarly research.

Let's examine the growth of the Chinese economy, which in the past three-and-a-half decades has no historical parallel, as a manifestation of the traditional culture.

In a little over a generation, China has managed to accomplish what the US and Britain have taken many more generations to achieve. As mentioned earlier, the government attributes this success to socialism with Chinese characteristics, a politically correct yet vague phrase. Although this high-context slogan has been around for over three decades and is constantly on the lips of officials, it has never been given an official definition. And in good old Chinese fashion, it is left open to interpretation. To appreciate the importance of this slogan, we need to take an excursion back in time to see how Chinese traditions evolved.

Chinese civilization originated in farming communities located in the middle of the Asian continent, where family clans lived together, tilling ancestral lands. Unlike the ancient Greeks who were surrounded by sea, and were sailors and traders, the ancient Chinese were more land bound, and they didn't travel away from their homeland that much. As farmers, the Chinese revered the higher order in nature that provided them with the fertile soil, rainfall, sunshine and wind. As clan members, they lived and worked closely in self-sufficient extended communities. In order for members to get along, they developed a social order emphasizing harmony among people. Such traditions are still being practiced today.

To look at Chinese traditions, one needs to step back to the Warring States Period (475–221 BC), a most volatile time when independent kingdoms fought incessant battles with one another. The Warring States Period followed the Spring and Autumn Period (770–476 BC), and it formed the latter part of the Zhou Dynasty (Eastern Zhou).

Zhou Dynasty: Origins

The Zhou Dynasty (1122–256 BC) began as a feudal society with its capital located near today's Xi'an in Western China. The early Zhou kings distributed land they captured in battles to the generals and noblemen, according to the patriarchal clan order.

A person's status in the Zhou Dynasty was dependent on his relationship with the headman of the clan. For example, the eldest son was the most important person in the Zhou family, other than the patriarch. He would run the family and receive the inheritance when the patriarch passed away, a tradition that is still practiced in many parts of Asia. A junior member of the clan could only improve his lot by marrying someone higher up in the hierarchy. Similarly, in the Zhou court, an official's status was dependent on how closely he was related to the king.

The relationship between the various classes in Zhou society, from the king to the different noble classes, and between members of the same clan, was codified and rigid. This established the Chinese tradition of associating status with protocols.

In the Zhou Dynasty, each class observed its own rituals and protocols, designed to reinforce the feudal social order. Harsh punishments, including death, were meted out to those who strayed.

For example, at banquets, the king could have nine bronze vessels filled with different meats and fresh fish to entertain his guests, while the lords could have seven vessels of food (all the king's dishes minus the fresh fish and freshly dried meats), and the lower-level officials of the court could have only three vessels, consisting of roasted piglet, dried fish and meat. There was little room for deviation.

In today's China the elaborate nature of a formal banquet also correlates with the status of the guests. The government's attempt to temper official extravagance has run into an ancient practice from the Zhou Dynasty.

Visitors to China are often overwhelmed by the formalities accorded to them. Many of them originated in the Zhou Dynasty. For example, on arrival at an office building, a visitor may find a large red welcoming banner and a red carpet, photographers and a team from the host organization waiting to greet him. Welcoming guests in an elaborate manner is a Zhou tradition. The red carpet and the camera, however, are modern imports.

Humility is behind many of the Zhou rituals that are still being practiced today. For example, a person should never accept a gift from someone outright. It would be considered impolite unless he has declined the offer at least three times. Of course, the presenter will persist, because he knows its part of the ritual, and the gift is left on the table to be collected later on.

When being offered a seat at the dining table, the guest should always reciprocate by asking the host to sit down first. The host will persist, and the offer and decline routine will repeat two or three times, before they all sit down together. The same ritual applies to many common courtesies, such as entering a room, an elevator or a car, toasting each other, and basically any social activity involving different people.

Mandate of Heaven

It was during the Zhou Dynasty that the concept of the king as the Son of Heaven first emerged. Invoking the mystical yet powerful heaven elevated the king's status and gave him implicit authority. The Zhou king further combined this authority with the patriarchal clan order to legitimize succession based on bloodlines, and to make the status permanent for his offspring.

The king's power was secured as long as he was able to pacify his lords, and perform the Mandate of Heaven.

According to John Fairbank, the Mandate of Heaven asserts the ruler's accountability to a supreme moral force that guides the human community. It also defines the moral criteria for those holding power.

Zhou kings believed practicing moral behaviors would allow them to be better rulers. The Chinese word for morality is 道德. It consists of two words, 道(Dao or Tao) and 德 (De). Dao is nature's way, and De means moral behaviors. Intuitively, moral behaviors can be interpreted as human behaviors that are also congruous with nature's way.

The king's job is to behave morally and set a good example for his subjects. If he could do that he would have the Mandate of Heaven to govern. The corollary was that if a king behaved immorally, he would naturally lose the mandate. Back then there were no public opinion polls or media to provide feedback to the ruling class. And even if ordinary people were unhappy about how they were governed, they dared not complain. So how could changes be made?

If a king's performance was really poor, as evidenced by persistent social strife, or if there were hints of disapproval from heaven, such as earthquakes, famines or other natural disasters, then he would be deemed unfit to govern. Heaven would then pass the mandate onto someone else better suited. For centuries in China, a ruler's mandate to rule has been equated with how morally he behaved, and how well his administration could provide stability to the masses.

Later in the Zhou Dynasty the lords became increasingly powerful, and they grew disloyal to the Zhou king. They fought non-stop, at times using the king as a figurehead to support their blatant power grabs. The king's authority had diminished to such a point that he was only in control of an area around the capital. His duties were also reduced to calling meetings of his lords and conducting important rites, such as praying for bumper harvests. The decline of the Zhou king's authority ushered in the Spring and Autumn Period, when the capital was relocated eastward to Luoyang in today's Henan province.

Confucian scholars figured out something interesting over 2,000 years ago. They saw how orderly nature was, with its regular patterns of days and nights and four distinct seasons. Year after year, spring follows winter and summer follows spring, and the sun never fails to rise from the east and set in the west. The almighty nature, which provides everything humans will ever need, has never deviated from these pristine patterns.

What's more, nature is as fair as it is orderly. Regardless of how rich or powerful a person is, he cannot have more hours in the day than another person; or a longer summer than his compatriots. The Chinese call this implicit fairness Heaven's Way. Implicit in the concept of Heaven's Way is that even though things may appear unfair at times, as they often do, nature has a way of rebalancing itself, and Heaven's Way will always prevail.

One must have faith that eventually wrongs will be righted and justice will be served. This is one of the reasons Chinese people could endure so much suffering and hardship, because deep in their hearts they believe that one day Heaven's Way will prevail and whatever injustices they face will be remedied, even though it may take a long time for this to happen.

We should also note that the Chinese concept of heaven does not have the same meaning as the physical universe we study in science classes, nor does it have much to do with religion.

The Chinese heaven is an ideal, comprising the physical universe observable by the naked eye and a metaphysical one premised on a set of common human aspirations. There are no powerful gods sitting atop the Chinese heaven, dispensing justice or telling mortals what they should or should not do. In fact, the few Chinese deities were really just common folk who had lived exemplary lives. To the Chinese, heaven is man's vision of the perfect world, consistent with what is accepted as fair and just by most people.

In comparison with the Western view of the objective universe, which is observable, analyzable and exists independent of men, or heaven, where God resides, the Chinese heaven is a synthesis of men and their ideals. Once these two become miscible as one, you have the union between men and heaven. In this union, Men's way and Heaven's Way are indistinguishable—one and the same. If all men follow Heaven's Way, society will become orderly and fair. When Men's Way and Heaven's Way are as one, the society becomes humane.

Heaven's Way reflects a commonly accepted degree of fairness and justice in a society, which is for ordinary folks to make a living and raise their families peacefully. If they can do that there is heaven on earth.

Chinese people often invoke Heaven's Way in arguments and whenever they wish to appear legitimate. If they wish to be seen as just, they may proclaim to act on behalf of Heaven. In disputes, the Chinese often lean on their concept of justice and fairness, and argue until they are blue in the face, instead of submitting themselves totally to the legal process, which after all is based only on men's laws.

This is because, irrespective of what men's laws have to say, there exists a higher order, Heaven's Way, against which all human behavior is judged. However, there is also built-in arbitrariness, as there are no absolute standards describing what Heaven's Way is, or what is morally right or wrong. As a result, the authorities often end up being the arbiter of both morality and laws.

As nature is regular and harmonious, Confucian scholars argued long ago that humans should also follow a similar social order and live harmoniously with one another. The implication is that actions disrupting social harmony would perforce upset heaven. In the worst case, floods, earthquakes and other natural disasters would occur.

Patriarchal Workplace

The existence of an inviolable order derivable from Heaven's Way is deeply ingrained in the traditional Chinese mindset. This is so whether we are talking about the family, business or government.

In a traditional Chinese family, the man of the house is like heaven. He is the rainmaker and protector of his family. He has the authority to call the shots, but he should also be fair to family members, just like heaven. The wife's job is to nurture the family and provide support to her husband and children, just like the good earth. Within the family, the son should obey the father, the wife should be subservient to her husband, the younger brother should listen to the older brother and so on. All these hierarchical relationships are also reciprocal in nature. So, in return, the father should bestow kindness onto his sons, the husband should be caring to his wife, and the older brother should take care of his younger siblings and set a good example for them. The feelings that family members have for each other are considered innate and part of the natural order. Mencius believes that a person's love for his parents and respect for older brothers are innate qualities, and a manifestation of this natural order.

So, at work, a junior staff member must be deferential to his senior manager, who in turn must show deference to his boss, and so on all the way to the CEO, who must pay heed to the executive chairman. To reciprocate, the boss should show kindness and respect to his staff. And within society, everyone must be deferential to government officials because they occupy the highest rung of the social hierarchy.

This nature-inspired order has allowed the Chinese to live their way of life for thousands of years and it remains important to this day.

The Warring States and Chinese Philosophical Traditions

The Warring States Period (480 BC–221 BC) was a volatile but also defining moment in China's long history. Many of the philosophical traditions from the period are still being practiced today, so it is worth looking into.

When the world is in tumult, ambitious people wish to apply their talents to serve justice and right wrongs. China's Warring States Period was just such a time, when greed, treachery and brutality were commonplace. Life was cheap and power was the only thing that mattered. Partnerships were struck for convenience only and could dissolve overnight.

Against this volatile backdrop, the Warring States Period was also one of the greatest and probably freest times of Chinese intellectual expression. The term "Let a hundred flowers bloom" fairly describes the intellectual fervor that existed then.

During the Warring States Period the different lords were always feuding and trying to get one up on each other, so they were constantly on the lookout for talent to give them an edge over their rivals. This demand brought forth a group of talented people with very different skills and ideas, who traveled to the different kingdoms to preach their ideas to the lords. Some of the lords ended up hosting hundreds of these men in their courts, just in case one day they might be of help.

At this time, China was made up of seven kingdoms. In the end, the kingdom of Qin conquered the other six kingdoms and prevailed in unifying China.

The incessant turmoil and the vicissitudes of life during the Warring States Period raised questions about how best men should conduct themselves and run governments. Two of the greatest Chinese thinkers, Confucius and Lao Tzu, came from this period.

Although Confucius was credited in the West as the founder of Confucianism, the traditions he promoted did not all come from him.

Rather, he preferred to be called a collector and editor of ancient Chinese traditions that pre-dated him for some 1,000 years.

Lao Tzu was the founder of Taoism, the objective of which is for humans to follow the way of nature, which he called the Tao. Besides these indigenous philosophies, the Chinese were also influenced by Buddhism, which was first brought to China from India at around the first century BC.

There were also Islam and Christianity, world religions that have found devotees in China. However, the thoughts that most influenced the Chinese people were Confucianism and Taoism. Buddhism is considered too passive and detached from the real world, thus not very helpful in managing day-to-day affairs. The influences of Islam and Christianity were more limited to believers, as they have never achieved the mainstream status of Confucianism and Taoism.

Confucianism

Confucius (551–479 BC) was born into a poor family during the latter part of the Spring and Autumn Period in the kingdom of Lu in today's Shandong province. The reason this part of history was called the Spring and Autumn Period was to imply that history will always repeat itself, just like spring and autumn will come around year after year.

When Confucius was young he was very inquisitive and had a knack for learning. He loved all kinds of knowledge and was basically self-taught. In this respect, Confucius and the Greek philosopher Socrates had something in common. Socrates also believed that the only valid education is self-education.

Confucius served as a minister in the Lu court. However, he was not all that successful at advancing his own political career and had to go into exile because of palace bickering. Later he travelled to the various kingdoms with his disciples, preaching his ideas of model behavior and governance to those who would listen.

Before Confucius, education was only available to the sons of noblemen. Confucius changed all that. He taught anyone who was willing to learn, including commoners. He also tailored his teaching style to suit each individual student. He was said to have had over 3,000 students over time, and about 70 of them followed him closely.

To Chinese people, Confucius is revered as a person of exemplary character and the greatest teacher of all time. At one time or another in Chinese history, he was considered as a teacher, as a sage and a god. His influence in China and Asia was immense and continues to be so still.

Not long after Emperor Qin had unified China, he banned the teachings of Confucius. He believed Confucianism, with its emphasis on social order and human relationships, had undermined his position as the absolute authority. The emperor was also quite a tyrant. According to the Han Dynasty historian Sima Qian, Emperor Qin was said to have burnt all Confucian books and buried over 400 Confucian scholars—alive.

The Qin Dynasty adopted the legalist tradition and established strict laws for the land. Harsh punishments were routinely meted out to offenders. Minor offenders got beatings, face tattoos or exile. More serious offenders had their noses cut off. The worst offenders got themselves and their families beheaded. As time went on, Qin's tough rules had become too impersonal, and they conflicted with the warm and fuzzy teachings of Confucius that most Chinese people had grown accustomed to. In the end, Qin's severe leadership brought on its own demise.

While most Chinese would agree that Emperor Qin was a brutal dictator, whose style is no longer politically correct, they nonetheless admire his brashness and strong-arm governance. They consider his qualities, which are opposite to what Confucius preached, are what are required to govern a country as large and diverse as China.

Emperor Qin was also noted for his bravado as well as his love for the grandiose. His most important contribution to China was that, under him, the country was united into a single political entity. Since then, China has been ruled by a central administration from the capital for over 2,300 years.

Emperor's Qin's legacy also includes the original Great Wall, an almost 9,000 km-long fortification built to repel nomadic invaders from the north (the present-day wall that tourists visit was rebuilt during the Ming Dynasty). He also constructed his own mausoleum, which is still unevacuated but was said by Sima Qian to have a miniature model of China inside, replete with all the treasures that existed at the time.

On its perimeter stood a large contingent of terracotta warriors, each built to resemble an real person. With weapons at hand, the determined warriors stood ready to repel any intruders who would dare to disturb their emperor. It is incredible that Qin was not only a powerful ruler but also the mastermind behind two of ancient world's greatest wonders.

The emperor's appetite for the grandiose has not been lost with the current crop of Chinese managers. They also love big projects. It is a matter of immense personal pride for a manager to lead a large project and be in a position to be mentioned in the history books. It is also worthy of significant bragging rights to claim the biggest revenue in the industry, or the tallest headquarter building in the city. Not surprisingly, some of the largest corporations are in China. Five of the ten tallest buildings in the world are also there, and the world's largest shopping mall is located in Chengdu in western China. Scale is an important motivator for Chinese managers. This attitude goes all the way back to the Qin Dynasty.

Bibliography

Chinese Cultural Renaissance Movement, Wikipedia, reviewed Jan 2016.
Andrew Jacobs, *Confucius Statue Vanishes Near Tiananmen Square,* The New York Times, Apr 22, 2011.
Tong Zhang and Barry Schwartz, *Confucius and the Cultural Revolution: A Study in Collective Memory,* International Journal of Politics, Culture and Society, Vol. 11, No. 11, 1997.
Tu-Wei Ming, *Beyond the Enlightenment Mentality: A Confucian Perspective on Ethics, Migration and Global Stewardship,* P. 58–59, 64–65, International Migration Review, Vol. 30, No.1 Spring 1996.
Tu-Wei Ming, *Centrality and Commonality, An Essay on Confucian Religiousness,* State University of New York Press, 1989.
Bertrand Russell, *The Problem of China, Chapter One, Questions,* P. 6, London, George Allen & Unwin, 1922.
Zhou Li (周礼), baike.baidu.com, reviewed Jan 2016.
J.A.G Roberts, *A Concise History of China,* P. 7, Harvard University Press, 1999.
Peng Lin, *Yi Li, The Complete Interpretation,* P. 12, Guizhou People's Publisher, 1997 (彭林,仪礼全译, P. 12, 贵州人民出版社, 1997).
Encyclopedia Britannica, reviewed Jan 2016.

John King Fairbank and Merle Goldman, *China, a New History*, second enlarged edition, P. 40, The Belknap Press of Harvard University Press, 2006.

J.A.G Roberts, *A History of China*, P. 10–12, Harvard University Press, 1999.

Gao Shenyang, *A Study of Traditional Chinese Thought Process*, P. 25, Scientific Publishers, 2012 (高晨阳,中国传统 思维方式研究,科学出版社, P. 25, 2012).

Mencius, Ch.13, edited by Zhong Mang, Chung Hua Books, 2012, (孟子,公孙丑, 钟芒主编, 中华书局, 2012).

J.A.G. Roberts, *A History of China*, P. 44–46, Harvard University Press, 1999.

Huston Smith, *Confucianism, The World's Religions,* p. 154, HarperOne, 1991.

Buddhism in China, *Geoff Foy*, Asia Society, asiasociety.org, 2013.

J.A.G Roberts, *A History of China*, P. 14 Harvard University Press, 1999.

*Qin Dynasty (*秦朝*)*, baike.baidu.com, reviewed Jan 2016.

J.V. Luce, *An Introduction to Greek Philosophy,* P. 88, Thames and Hudson 1992.

8

Contemporary Expressions of Tradition

While core Chinese values have remained substantially intact, some have been challenged by modern ways of life. Let's see how they fare below.

Confucianism as the Official School of Thought

The Qin Dynasty fell apart shortly after the emperor died. Although it lasted for only 15 years, it was one of the most spectacular dynasties in Chinese history. In the end, high taxes and brutality led to a peasant revolt that toppled the regime. The new Han Dynasty took its place.

At around 140 BC, Emperor Han Wudi resurrected Confucianism and mandated it as the official school of thought. The new Confucianism attempted to define a perfect social order—one that was derived from nature and existed in harmony with it. It also tied human behavior with Heaven's Way. This implies a basic sense of fairness that is universal and non-violable, regardless of who is in power.

Pillars of Confucianism

Confucianism encapsulates the beliefs of the ancient Chinese. It presupposes that humans possess four basic virtues: *Ren* (仁) for empathy and benevolence; *Yi* (义) for righteousness and justice; *Li* (礼) for etiquette and respect for others; and *Zhi* (智) for wisdom and intellect.

Besides the four virtues, moderation (中庸), frugality (廉) and humility (耻) are considered important qualities. Although these are considered innate qualities, they must be embellished with education.

Confucius holds that the four virtues are the qualities of a gentleman, which in feudal times literally meant a prince. A Confucian gentleman is the polar opposite of the despicable petty person, who has no fine qualities and is selfish, full of self-pity, jealous of others' success and lacking in self-discipline.

Mencius (372–289 BC) also provided significant insights into human nature. Together, the teachings of Confucius and Mencius formed the foundation of Confucianism.

Mencius further elaborated on the four virtues of Ren, Yi, Li and Zhi, and he compared them to the four limbs of a person. Those who possess both arms and legs should be able to work for the good of his fellow men. If a person can make full use of his powerful limbs, he is like a gushing stream or a prairie fire, capable of spreading his influences widely. If he is able to perfect his four virtues, he is in a good position to help others, including potentially running the country. However, if he is not able to exercise the four virtues, he will not even be able to serve his parents. Mencius even went on to say that those who do not possess these virtues should not even be considered as human beings. This puts huge pressure on aspiring leaders to behave virtuously.

A Western Corollary

In ancient Greece, Plato also considered wisdom, courage, moderation, justice and piety as human virtues. Indeed, there were some similarities between the Greeks and the Chinese on the subject. Wisdom is similar to the Confucian virtue of Zhi, and justice is comparable to Yi, while temperance is very similar to the Chinese concept of the Middle Way.

While Confucius considered the four virtues to be innate, Socrates was not so sure. Instead he attributed hese virtues to the divine. According to Socrates, virtues cannot be taught; they can only be attained through divination. On the other hand, Confucians believe that humans are inherently good, and can get even better through hard work and the suppression of selfish desires. If they are able to do that, they should be able to behave virtuously through their own efforts.

Inner Sage and Outer King

According to Fung Yu-lan, Chinese philosophers have never been as preoccupied with knowledge for knowledge's sake like their Western counterparts. Chinese philosophers don't like dealing with abstract concepts. They instead preach practical ideas that can help people to live better lives.

Traditionally, Chinese philosophers have defined two major areas of pursuit: Inner Sage and Outer King, after a concept first described by Zhuangzi.

Inner Sage (内圣) is for the cultivation of morality, which is what a sage possesses. Outer King (外王) is for the provisioning of meritorious services to others, similar to what a king does. If one fails to do either, he could write philosophy, according to Fung.

Since China's Reform and Opening Up, the government has promoted economic development as its top priority, and the only hard truth. Corporate managers have heeded the clarion call by rapidly pursuing growth, leveraging the traditional Chinese work ethic with Western management tools. This has allowed them to approach the Outer King goals, but at the expense of the development of the Inner Sage.

To some executives, providing meritorious service means building the largest factories, employing the most people and having the biggest sales. However, any accomplishment based solely on the achievements of material success, without first satisfying the Inner Sage, is contrary to the Confucian order and therefore without a solid foundation.

The traditional Confucian worldview begins with one's self at the center of a series of concentric circles, and it radiates outwards. The innermost circle is the self, followed by the family and then society at large.

The Book of Great Learning, the traditional course for grooming future leaders, was unequivocal about this order. It stated emphatically that an aspiring leader should first endeavor to develop his self, before he can properly raise his family. And only after he has successfully raised his family should he consider leading others, including potentially running the country and the world. Around the same time, the Greeks described a similar order between a man, his family and society.

In modern terms, this process can be described as management via exemplary behavior from an individual through his family to society. However, because of the radiating nature of the trajectory moving from the self at the center towards society on the outside, a person's efforts usually drop off rapidly after leaving the family.

In the same breath, *The Book of Great Learning* says there were three reasons for undertaking the study: understanding what constitutes true morality; being able to relate that to other people; and not relaxing until the ultimate goodness is reached.

However, the ultimate goodness is difficult to reach, unless one is already a sage. Therefore it goes without saying that an individual should never stop improving himself.

The Inner Sage deals with a person's self-development. This important exercise comprises a critical analysis of facts to achieve true knowledge, and sincerity of thought to control your desires.

To appreciate how all these can be put into practice, you must consider an important Confucian concept called *shendu* (慎独), which roughly translates as "cautious while alone". The closest English word to it is "integrity", which is a person's ability to uphold moral behavior, regardless of what circumstances he is in.

Shendu says that a gentleman must redouble his efforts to behave properly when he is alone. This does not mean that he should cherish his solitude but rather that he should control his desires so that he can behave morally at all times, alone or with others.

Maintaining moral behavior takes effort. Most people relax and drop their guard when no one else is around. Also, the temptation to deviate from moral behavior increases as you become more successful. Wealth and power can give a false sense of security to people. It makes them believe that they can be exempted from the consequences of misbehaving.

The endemic official corruption in China highlights two important causes: the weakness of the legal system and a lack of integrity of individuals. The former is being addressed by putting in place stricter laws and enforcement, while the latter requires a refocus on traditional values.

After a bureaucrat has worked diligently for years to rise to a position of authority, he faces daily temptations from those seeking to buy his favors. At the beginning, he takes only small gifts, in accordance with customary practices. Later, he relaxes and accepts larger and larger bribes. He thinks he can get away with it because no one is watching and, in addition, everyone is doing it. But, in reality, he has violated the law and compromised his own personal integrity because he has forgotten the teachings of Shendu.

In accepting bribes, the corrupt official has traded his most valuable asset—his personal integrity—for mere commodities. Abraham Lincoln once said, "Nearly all men can stand adversity, but if you want to test a man's character, give him power."

The same holds true for the many insider-trading cases in the US, where money and power have lured normally upright individuals into committing illegal insider trading. The offending parties did it because they thought they were cunning enough to skirt the law, and that no one was watching them.

Conformity is an important rule in a Confucian society. Because of that, a person's individual identity is often conflated with the roles he plays and the group identity he assumes. Conformity has the adverse effect of confounding personal responsibility with group objectives, and substituting a group mandate for self-discipline, but it doesn't mean that an individual is not accountable for his own actions.

The key point about Shendu is that a person should not conduct himself for the sole purpose of achieving something or pleasing others. He should do things only because he believes they are the right things to do, regardless of what others may think of him. For example, a person should not say nasty things, curse others or have all kinds of devious thoughts while alone, then put on a smiley face as soon as someone important walks by. He should not cheat or even think about cheating on exams, take bribes or steal from his employers, even if the chances of his getting caught are slim.

Shendu counter-balances much of Chinese culture's emphasis on getting along with others and the practice of reciprocity in relationships. When alone, a person must rely on his own character gauge to make decisions. He cannot count on the familiar social constraints to help him with that.

Shendu has traditionally been responsible for keeping those in power from misbehaving. Today, such self-discipline is sorely lacking in China.

China's successful drive for economic growth and its lack of emphasis on character development have resulted in material wealth and morality flying in opposite directions. The government's solution is to produce more and more guidelines on how people should behave. This has met with mixed results.

A return to traditional Chinese values, especially self-discipline and self-improvement, should be re-emphasized. At the end of the day, a person's character is a better predictor of his future behavior than a set of rules given by others.

No Way but the Middle Way

In China, relationships are often built upon exchanges of favors between parties. Now almost nothing can be done without first bearing gifts. But what is the right gift to give, or the appropriate number of favors to ask for in return? And, in general, what is the action one should take in particular circumstances? In this regard, Confucians believe that Zhong Rong, or the Middle Way, is the answer.

Zhong (中) means center and Rong (庸) means common. Together they represent the Middle Way, or common sense.

While the Middle Way favors moderation of behavior, it doesn't mean that someone should split every decision smack in the middle. Rather, his actions should revert to the appropriate mean over time. So it's fine for a person to have a couple of bottles of wine with friends on an evening out, but it doesn't mean that he should do it every night. Common sense tells us that such behaviour can be bad for our health.

The Middle Way eschews extremes, such as eating too much or too little, feeling too ecstatic or too sad, or working out too much or too little. It suggests that you should do things that are appropriate, but it doesn't mean that you should be non-committal or, worse, wishy-washy. It also does not set limits for proper behavior. So what is missing is the bottom line, below which no actions should be contemplated.

The Greek philosopher Aristotle also discussed a similar doctrine called the Golden Mean in the Nicomachean Ethics. The Golden Mean as a virtue resembles the Middle Way in many respects. Both favor moderation and eschew extreme behavior. Also, proper behavior should be fair and supported by correct reasoning. However, Aristotle stated unequivocally that some behavior, such as adultery, theft and homicide, are so vile that they should never be contemplated. The Golden Mean does not apply to these activities. It does not mean that you should take a numerical average to determine what is in the middle, or what is too much or too little.

For example, committing adultery is strictly forbidden. It doesn't mean that cheating on your wife once is more acceptable than cheating on her ten times; that swiping a pack of cigarettes from a convenience store is fine but stealing millions from a client is not; or that accepting a watch from a business associate is fine but taking an apartment is not. None of these behaviors should ever be considered—period.

Today, the boundary to acceptable behavior is getting fuzzier. Many previously prohibited actions have now become socially acceptable. What might be considered extreme behavior in the past—such as nudity, or same-sex marriage—is acceptable in some quarters today. This presents a real challenge for those who must navigate these ethical domains.

The Middle Way has been practiced for a long, long time in both Asia and the West. Its practice can help to moderate the extremes in our hectic lives, and that in turn should make us more content and productive in the long run.

Ren Is for People

Confucius considers Ren to be the most important of all human virtues. The Chinese character Ren (仁) is actually made up of two characters. The character on the left is 人, which represents a person, and the one on the right is 二, the number two. Intuitively, Ren represents the relationship between two people or, as Confucius says, Ren is about people.

The Confucian focus is on this world, not the afterworld. Ren, or benevolence, is that special kindred spirit that one shares with his fellow human beings, and what distinguishes humans from animals. Accordingly, if a person fails Ren, he is no better than an animal. In many respects, the Chinese concept of Ren is more direct and intimate than in cultures that require people to first go through a higher authority before they can relate to each other.

Ren begins at home with a person's love for his parents and empathy for his neighbors. In terms of its importance, Confucius says that if someone cannot achieve success in life, then self-sacrifice, including death, can also bring about the kind of closeness he seeks with his fellow men.

While Ren is considered innate, it must be expressed through the practice of Li, the elaborate rituals and protocols first developed in the Zhou Dynasty to govern social behavior.

The argument goes like this. If a person has been hungry before, then he knows how unpleasant it is. Because of Ren, he also knows that his fellow human beings will be miserable if they are hungry. So he should be sympathetic and generous towards them. If a person has been cold before, he should commiserate with those who are not properly dressed and freezing. If a person has been poor before, then he should be sympathetic to those who have nothing. His feeling of benevolence should encourage him to share what he has with those in need, in accordance with appropriate Li protocols.

But what if a person was brought up privileged and has never been deprived—how is he able to feel the sufferings of those who are less fortunate? Confucius believes that education is the key. This is because, in practice, self-interest always stands in the way of the greater good.

Most importantly, Ren connotes a sense of basic fairness, which most Chinese people would find acceptable. This basic sense of fairness, or humanism, is also evident in many Chinese management practices today.

Regarding the practice of Ren, Confucius believes that if a benevolent person wishes to become more successful, he should endeavor to bring others along and help them stand on their own feet. If he wishes to become wealthy, he should help others to become better off. In other words, a benevolent person should apply his own standards of wellbeing to those

8 Contemporary Expressions of Tradition 141

who are less fortunate. Mencius embellished on this altruistic idea. This makes Ren arguably one of the most important Chinese characteristics.

While the idea of Ren is noble, it is difficult to put into practice. In reality it is always the family that comes first, and greater society can come afterwards. So the doors for family members are always open. Few Chinese families would turn away their relatives seeking help, regardless of their own circumstances.

And for the same reason, few Chinese companies have gone bankrupt in as spectacular a fashion as Enron or Lehman, where thousands lost their jobs and billons in wealth were wiped out. The reluctance of creditors to enforce their rights to the letter, for fear of triggering massive job losses, has so far prevented this type of large-scale financial panic from occurring in China. Doing so would be so against Ren.

At this point in China's market development, the line between creditor and investor is still fuzzy. The Western concept of the creditor, which has the right to collateral and is senior to shareholders in receiving a fixed rate of return, and the investor, who sits at the bottom of the priority totem pole but has the right to appoint management and receive an upside if the borrower is profitable, is not very clear-cut in China.

In China, lenders often make loans as if they are investors in the borrower. This attitude dates back to the days of China's command economy, when state-owned banks funded industries according to official quota, and there was little distinction between equity and debt capital to speak of.

Heavily indebted Chinese companies rarely go belly up for the simple reason that no one really wants it that way. This is so despite the government's stated objective to promote market discipline and improve corporate governance.

This is also where Western observers often have difficulties when they analyze the Chinese economy. They assume that Chinese creditors would act rationally in their own self-interest to drive the bankruptcy process of failed borrowers, just as they would in the West. If every creditor were to pursue its rights to the letter, China's massive debt-funded asset bubble would burst, and the resulting financial calamity would spread afar. However, the Westerners neglect to factor culture into their analysis.

Trade creditors may chase a customer hard for outstanding receivables, but they would rarely go to court to lodge their claims. Doing so would harm their relationship with the customer and diminish their chances of ever getting paid, not to mention receiving more business in the future.

Chinese lenders who would normally be expected to drive the bankruptcy process are reluctant to pursue deadbeat borrowers in court for fear of causing job losses that would lead to social unrest. They may eventually mark down their loans as non-performing, or go through the legal motions in court, but in the end all parties would just look to the government for guidance.

Most of the time the regulators prefer to act as arbitrators in disputes rather than bureaucrats with the authority to sanction. The courts also drag their feet, preferring to give the parties involved more time to resolve their problems before rendering legal judgments.

Everyone wants to resolve the dispute discreetly, get their job done and move on. In a society still heavily influenced by tradition, it is simply abhorrent to consider putting a company out of business and its employees out of work just because of a moment's economic difficulty. The type of involuntary bankruptcy practiced in the West is anathema to the Chinese simply because it is so against Ren.

While Ren has allowed heavily indebted companies to survive, many have violated it. Chinese manufacturers are notorious for producing all kinds of fake products. Some are cheap replicas of famous brands while others can be harmful.

Adulterated baby formula is one example. By adding the nitrogen-rich chemical melamine to baby formula, unscrupulous manufacturers faked an artificially high protein content to make more profit. The sad fact is that scores of Chinese infants have become ill from drinking these faked formulas and many have died. This egregious act has endangered the welfare of a large number of young Chinese children, the country's future. If the faked formula manufacturers had any real sense of benevolence, they would have treated the infants as their own children and provided them with the best and purest products possible.

Faking a product for the sake of making more money was unthinkable in traditional China. Such a heinous act would have brought scorn from heaven to the perpetrators and shame on their families. Likewise, a senior government official is supposed to be a morally upright person who labors for the public good. His power is there for him to serve the people, not to allow him to engage in self-gratification. The revelations of official corruption and sex scandals in China prove that this traditional supposition is far from correct. The self-disciplined and cultivated individual, a hallmark of traditional Chinese society, is a rarity today.

The Chinese Are Confusing!

Foreigners are often baffled by the seemingly contradictory behavior of the Chinese, who can be both selfish and generous at the same time. The following account may explain some of the reasons behind this confusion.

A few years ago there was an interesting program on the Japanese television network, Nippon Hōsō Kyōkai. It was about the annual Chinese New Year festival (Spring Festival), when several hundred million Chinese journey back to their hometowns to celebrate with family and relatives.

During the program, a young Japanese reporter in his 20s recounted his own experience to a panel of commentators. He chose to travel by train from China's east coast to Sichuan, a province in Western China, where many migrant workers come from. As this was peak travel season and train tickets were notoriously hard to come by, the young reporter went to the train station well ahead of time to get his. While there, he lined up dutifully in a queue at the city's main train station, just as he would in Japan. However, because people kept cutting in front of him, he didn't get very far even after a long and increasingly frustrating wait.

Then all of a sudden he felt a sharp kick to his thigh from behind. The young man was stunned. He turned round and saw an old lady, who seemed annoyed by his tardiness and gesticulated furiously for him to move forward. Given that the assault came from an older person, he swallowed his pride, pushed himself to the ticket counter and finally got his ticket to Sichuan.

When it came time for the reporter to board the train, he went to his car and proceeded to his assigned seat. To his astonishment, another passenger, whose seat was occupied by someone else, had taken it. No one would budge an inch. Not knowing what to do, he stood in the aisle with others in the standing-room-only train. It started to move but none of the illegal occupiers would move.

Feeling being taken advantage of, the young reporter felt lonely in the midst of a train full of Chinese migrant workers and wondered how he could endure the over thirty-hour train ride to Chengdu. But lo and behold, the old lady who had so rudely kicked him before was in the same car. Seeing that the young man was standing alone in the aisle and seemingly lost, she created some space on her seat and offered for him to sit down, which he gladly did.

As the train chugged along China's central plains towards the west, the mood lightened. Passengers swapped food, seats and stories. Songs broke out and the crowded cabin took on a festive atmosphere. All the passengers were just so happy finally to be able to see their families during the Chinese New Year, a time to be joyful and make plans for the coming season after working away from home all year.

As the young man recounted his experience on television, he was still perplexed. No one else on the all-Japanese panel was able to make much sense out of it either. They were baffled by the seemingly contradictory behavior of the Chinese. One minute they were cold and selfish, and the next they were generous and caring. But isn't this just the teaching of Confucius at work? You have to take care of yourself and your family first. Only after that should you strive to spread benevolence to those around you.

The Other Kingdom

Han Confucian scholars revered the idealized nature so much that they championed a nature-inspired social order. Subsequent dynasties all adopted the same order and governed accordingly. But Confucian scholars had neglected another important part of nature—the animal kingdom. In this kingdom, only the fittest survives. Today's business world is still very much like the animal kingdom, except that the jungle rules have been replaced by more sensible market rules.

Investors reward companies that have the best strategy and execution with higher share prices and market access. If large companies don't perform, their more nimble competitors will eliminate them. If smaller companies can innovate, they may turn into big winners. Capital will naturally flow to the winners, and consumers will benefit from great products from these well-run companies.

The cycle of destruction and rebirth, where previously good companies that have become poorly run are eliminated, and poor companies innovate to transform themselves into good ones, is part and parcel of market economics, and a part of the natural order. However, this transformation is contrary to the Confucian belief that something good must always stay that way and something bad has little chance of turning into something good. As a result of support, poorly run companies often stay in business far longer than they should.

The supportive model has the effect of absorbing the responsibility of decision-makers, but it doesn't make them better managers. Similarly, training wheels are useful when a child first learns how to ride a bike, but keeping the wheels on too long makes the child a poor cyclist. Besides pedaling, the child must develop a feel for the ride and, most important, be able to read traffic and be part of the flow. These skills can only be achieved once the training wheels come off. Falling a few times can sharpen a child's awareness of risks. Likewise, having failed and paid the price for it makes a manager into an executive.

Many Asian companies operate their businesses based on mutual support. The dilemma is that too much support can weaken their competitiveness, just as overly protective parents can spoil their children. How to achieve a healthy balance between competition and support remains a challenge for Asian business.

Yi Is for Justice

Yi, an essential quality of a Confucian gentleman, is translated as justice or righteousness. Like the other virtues, Yi also requires education to reinforce it.

Confucius praises those who possess a sense of justice, who protect the weak, and who right wrongs. Mencius says that if he has to choose between life and justice, he would choose justice. However, in practice, Yi often runs up against the hierarchical order.

If a person sees a young child trapped inside a burning house with no one else around, should he go in to rescue him or should he wait for help to arrive? What if the child is his son? What if there are two children inside the building, one of them his son and the other his boss's son, which child should he rescue first? If he saves his own son but his boss's son dies, how can he go back to his office again? If he rescues his boss's son first but his own son dies, how can he face his family and his own guilt?

These are the types of justice questions often raised by Michael Sandel of Harvard. It is not always easy for an individual to do the right thing, especially when he has little time to consider his options. Revisiting the teachings of the ancient sages can help to shore up someone's moral aptitude, such that if he is ever required to respond quickly he can make the right decision.

In October 2011 a two-year old girl in Southern China was run over by a car twice. She was left lying in a pool of blood in an outdoor market and was ignored by scores of passers-by. An old woman who was working as a street cleaner eventually pulled her over to the side of the busy street and called for help. The girl was taken to hospital but eventually died from her injuries.

This incident caused public uproar in China and elsewhere in the world. It also raised serious questions about the state of morality in China. In their rush to get rich, Chinese people have lost their moral compass. People in civil society should not have tolerated such callous behavior, least of all in a country where Confucius is supposedly revered. However, it was also interesting to note that the lowly street lady, perhaps the poorest and least-educated person among the crowd, was the only one who offered to help the stricken girl.

In April 2014, the South Korean ship *Sewol* sank en route to Jeju Island in the southern part of the country. Most of the ship's 476 passengers were students from a high school near Seoul. A large number of them drowned. It was the worst maritime disaster in South Korean history. Koreans were sad and frustrated about the loss of so many innocent young lives, but they were angry as well. As the ship was listing to its side, the crew informed the passengers to stay put and wait for help to arrive. As South Korea is a deeply patriarchal society, students complied and stayed put as they were told. Meanwhile, the 68-year-old captain and several of his crew got on lifeboats and fled to safety by themselves.

When news broke that the captain had abandoned his ship and passengers, the Korean people were outraged. They couldn't believe how such a senior person could flee while those he was charged to care for were in serious distress. Some lamented the loss of honor in a society caught up in the material rat race. Others were plainly frustrated and ashamed.

The President of South Korea, Park Geun-hye, went as far as to say that the captain's actions were tantamount to murder. However, an act of heroism that received little attention was that by a young crewmember in her early 20s who insisted on staying behind to help with the evacuation. She performed her job dutifully and honorably but, in the end, she also perished.

These two tragedies highlight an enigma in Asian societies—the loss of ethics among people in high places. True, there were other captains who committed similar offenses, but such unspeakable acts were not supposed to happen in the Confucian China or South Korea.

The dilemma in Confucian societies is that the higher up people are, the more they are respected and revered. They have more authority and responsibility, but also more temptation. Because of that, they often drift away from the lives of the common folk they are charged to serve. At the same time, their own moral ethics, which are increasingly numbed by their growing status and wealth, fail to properly guide their behavior. As a result, they often fail both Ren and Yi, and unthinkable things happen.

In the case of the Chinese toddler, the driver and the passers-by were all busy with their own lives. They had little time or desire to help others, least of all a little child lying on the street in a pool of blood with no ability to return the favor. The old street cleaner who had tried to help the child was really poor and a nobody. However, she was able to do the right thing.

In the case of the Korean sea captain, we can assume that he was urged by his crew to leave the sinking ship first, in accordance with his status and seniority. It was difficult for the captain to deviate from the routine he had grown accustomed to. Therefore, in a moment of confusion, benevolence and justice were tossed overboard by self-interest.

The virtues that are responsible for keeping Confucian societies moral have unfortunately been relegated to the second priority status behind economic development.

Li Is for Respect

Li refers to the elaborate rituals and protocols meticulously crafted and calibrated to allow Chinese people to interact with each other in social settings. Confucians believe that Li is what allows people to live together in harmony. Its practice can be traced all the way back to the Zhou Dynasty over 3,000 years ago.

As practicing Li can engender goodwill and respect from others, it can also be interpreted as a component of soft power, even without the bearing of gifts.

The essence of Li is a respect for people and the social order. The superficial parts of Li are the formalities.

From the Zhou to Qing Dynasties, the king or emperor was also the Son of Heaven. As such, he held the main communications channel with the almighty Heaven. At the most auspicious moment each year, he solemnly performed the most important Li ritual of all—giving thanks to Heaven and praying for a bumper harvest.

Since the early Han Dynasty, violating Li was equated to an offense against Heaven, and was punished severely. For example, if a person showed disrespect to the emperor by bad-mouthing him, or a son failed to take care of his parents by letting them starve while he was out having a good time, or if a wife had an affair with another man, they all failed Li. Back then, these crimes were punishable by death.

Today's Chinese society is much more liberal and its social norms are more relaxed. Doing something against social norms can be seen as rude, and can run the risk of offending others, but that's about it. However, the essence of Li, which is a respect for others, remains valid.

Confucius believes that one should suppress his own desires and at the same time practice the appropriate rituals and etiquette to show benevolence to others. In the Confucian world, Li is the primary vehicle through which benevolence can be expressed.

Over time, Chinese people have developed sophisticated rituals and etiquette for different social occasions. That is not to say that Li is just a set of context-dependent rules meshed together to dictate how people should behave. Beneath the surface its essence is timeless.

Ancestor worship is one aspect of Li. The Chinese revere their ancestors for many reasons. First, a Chinese person believes that he is a part of a family lineage with a unique tradition, and not an act of God or the result of some random act of passion. If a person's great grandparents had hailed from a certain part of China and they were merchants, scholars or farmers, then there is a certain pride in that and there may even be a desire to continue with the tradition.

The Chinese also believe that spirits of their ancestors are there in the afterlife watching and protecting them. They often pray to their deceased parents or grandparents for guidance and protection, even if they are practicing Christians or Buddhists.

Westerners also study their family genealogy to understand who their ancestors were, what they did and where they came from. However, they are also more individualistic, and have less of a desire to worship their ancestors or continue their family legacy.

When Chinese families visit their ancestors' graves to light incense and pay their respects, they are not only professing their love for the departed, or having a picnic in the countryside, they are also recommitting the values of their ancestors to their own lives and the lives of their children. The gravesite rituals are designed to reinforce important clan values, such as hard work and frugality, and loyalty to family members, all exemplified by the departed and passed on to future generations.

Each year the Chinese celebrate Teacher's Day on Confucius' birthday. Teachers occupy a very important position in the Chinese social hierarchy, just a notch below parents. They are the ones who have the knowledge and are willing to pass it on to the younger generation. The ceremonies on Teacher's Day are designed to show respect for knowledge, and to honor teachers for being an important conduit for its transmission.

In the Chinese culture, Li is like the gears of a machine, whose purpose is to transmit power to do work. Without the proper meshing of gears and a generous helping of grease, a machine cannot run properly, regardless of how powerful the motor is. Without Li, a hierarchical society is like a machine whose gears don't mesh. If Li is not practiced properly, the society will not function smoothly.

Confucius says that one should not speak, hear or do things that are against Li. Since Li is a social exercise involving other people, a person should always be aware of what others are doing. He should be careful of how he behaves in front of others and how they perceive him. He should show proper respect and not express his feelings without first considering how they might affect others.

Li can be viewed as a map for social navigation. With it a person can take shortcuts and get to where he wants to go faster. Without it he can get lost in the social morass. Unlike a modern map with precise coordinates, Li is more like an old Chinese map, fuzzy and symbolic. In the old days, a Chinese skipper would navigate his sea journey by using an old sea map. He would look at the crude ink brush drawings depicting landmasses and oceans, and consult records of old sea captains with times of travel and compass directions. This allowed him to go where he wanted to reasonably well. However, there was no telling how deep the oceans were or how far apart the islands were. Without precision, the skipper had to rely on his experience and judgment. Similarly, in a society governed by fuzzy Li rituals, you must rely on your judgment to navigate properly.

Reciprocity is a basic tenet of Li. The acts of giving and receiving are coupled. The party who gives usually expects something in return. By presenting a gift, a person either fulfills an obligation or expects a favor. The recipient also knows that if he accepts a gift, he has a debt to repay.

In the West, giving is more an act of individual expression and not necessarily tied to receiving something in return. But despite Western influences making inroads into China, the practice of reciprocity in Li will likely remain for a long time.

Guanxi and the Art of Managing Upwards

The Chinese live in a world built on reciprocal relationships. Because there are always many more people desiring the same limited resources, competition is fierce. Since someone else always controls everything of importance that one desires, it is imperative to be on good terms with those who are in control of these important resources. In other words, a person should cultivate good guanxi with those who have power so that he can get what he wants. This is the essence of guanxi.

Guanxi is usually translated as "relationship", and a good guanxi is a beneficial relationship. In China, guanxi is a means of getting things done in a society where human relationships are important, rules and regulations are fuzzy and their interpretations are often people-dependent. In this environment, knowing someone who has good guanxi and can help expedite things is of utmost importance.

In the West, where rules are more transparent and enforcement more stringent, you would still need to maintain good relationships with those around you, especially your boss. This is partly because if you are a nice person that's what you are supposed to do. If you do that, others will reciprocate, and your relationships with them will be fine. But you don't necessarily have to bow down to them, or expect something in return for your efforts at being nice.

In China, guanxi is more than just simple relationships. It can be viewed as a person's relationship with those who have influence, whose power can be accessed from multiple points of leverage. It also has an unmistakable upward bias because almost nothing significant can be accomplished without first developing the proper guanxi with those who have power.

So who are those people whose guanxi you should cultivate? She could be your future mother-in-law whose daughter's hand you desire; they could be the school officials at the distinguished primary school where you wish to enroll your daughter; he could be a famous surgeon at the hospital where you wish to arrange an important operation for your father; she could be your spouse or significant other whose affection you desire; he could be your boss, whose approval is needed for you to go on an overseas training trip; he could be the person who stamps your passport application at the local town office; he could be the official in charge of granting permits for your business; or he could be the head of the department managing a project that you are bidding on. Any time someone has power over something you want, you have to develop your guanxi with him.

Because of Confucian traditions, those in a position of power are expected to help those who are less fortunate. However, reciprocity is also expected. The powers that be will only consider your request for help after you have properly carried out your end of the bargain. In other words, you need to show sincerity and bear gifts to fulfill your part of the guanxi.

Developing guanxi in China involves mostly managing relationships upwards. Only those who have power can offer something you may want. Developing guanxi with your peers is less productive and may even be counter-productive because you are most likely competing for the same resources. Last, there is no need to develop guanxi with people with a lower social status because they most likely don't have much to offer you.

If the person you wish to develop guanxi with is an officer in a company or an official in the government, your gift should appropriately reflect his stature and seniority. Gift giving is not just for cultivating good guanxi; it also acts as an insurance policy. It is not just whether your gift is appropriate or not but also how it stacks up against what your competitors are offering. If your gift doesn't stand out or is much poorer than theirs, the party you wish to influence may decide to go with your competitors just because they appear more sincere.

Giving gifts does not guarantee you'll always get what you wish for, and there is no obligation for the recipient to reciprocate the way you want him to, but it will at least keep you in the running. This is one of the reasons gift giving has reached extreme levels in China, along with rampant official corruption. Yet even though Confucius advocated the practice of Li, he did not condone lavish gift giving because gifts should come from the heart.

Westerners also like to deal with people they feel comfortable with. However, personal relationship is generally subordinated to professional ethics. For example, even though your potential mother-in-law may want her daughter to marry the right man, she is not going to stand in the way if her daughter really loves you, even if you have just graduated from college and have a large student loan to pay back. Who her daughter marries is her business because she has to live with that decision for a very long time. A surgeon's priority is to treat patients, irrespective of whether or not their relatives have brought gifts. School administrators are supposed to admit applicants based on their merits, not according to who the applicants' parents are, unless they are legacy applicants.

In the West, a good relationship also helps, especially at the higher echelons of the government—for example, the professional lobbyists who roar around the Capital Hill in Washington DC, whose job it is to provide information to help influence government decisions. Another example is the relationship between political contributions and election outcomes. While in the US these activities are regulated by law, and there are restrictions on what lobbyists can do, or the amount that donors can contribute to any political candidate for office, there are ways to get around the rules.

The Super Political Action Committee (PAC) was developed to circumvent the legal political contribution limit. While wealthy supporters cannot make large contributions to their preferred candidate directly, they can now form Super PACs to contribute as much as they like to support their candidate's campaigns. As a result, wealthy patrons can have an undue influence on electoral outcomes, especially at the federal level. Presumably reciprocity is also expected.

The Ultimate Guanxi

Today we need to urgently improve our guanxi with a most important power—our environment. Like the traditional Chinese heaven, our environment holds the key to our happiness and that of our children. As with all relationships, our relationship with nature is reciprocal. We should only take from nature what we need to live in a sustainable manner. We should not waste natural resources or cause irrevocable damage to the environment.

Nature is no longer represented by an infinite supply of oil and gas, timber, minerals, sunshine, rainfall or even fresh air. It has limits. If we take too much from it without considering sustainability, one day it will surprise us with its wrath. This is particularly urgent for China, where well-documented damage to the water supply, soil and air testifies to a massive development program gone awry. In fact, nature has already registered its displeasure with us through global warming.

The long-term consequences of climate change are dire, and irreversible. According to NASA and the World Bank, the mean global temperature in 2014 was already 0.8 °C higher than it was prior to industrialization.

What's alarming is that the earth's warming trend has been accelerating, because two-thirds of this warming has occurred since only 1975. If we continue with our current pace of development and spew massive amounts of greenhouse gases into the atmosphere, by the end of 2100 the mean global temperature could rise to 4 °C above the baseline, with dire consequences for humankind.

Rising temperatures will exacerbate already violent weather patterns and traumatize millions. It will cause the arctic icecap to melt, raise sea levels and threaten coastal inhabitants. Rising carbon dioxide levels will increase acidity in the ocean, ruin the coral reefs and devastate the surrounding ecosystems. Warming temperatures will reduce snowfall and make farming more difficult for downstream communities, potentially driving food shortages and massive migrations. Rising sea levels will also in one day render island nations such as the Maldives and Kiribati uninhabitable. Coastal cities such as Boston, Miami and Shanghai could also become partially submerged by 2100.

While climate change affects everyone, everywhere, it disproportionately affects those who have the least to contribute to its cause.

In Bangladesh, a country most vulnerable to rising sea levels, it is expected that 17 percent of the land will be submerged and 18 million people displaced over the next 40 years. Many folk living around the Bangladesh deltas don't drive gas-guzzling cars, use canister shaving creams or even have an electricity service, but they are made to pay a heavy price for the consequences of global warming caused by the industrialized nations. It behooves us to have a better relationship with our environment.

Just like the ancient Chinese, we must both revere and fear nature (or heaven.) We should not look upon it as an inexhaustible storehouse available solely for our exploitation. We must understand that taking too much from our environment will diminish us all, and damaging it will harm us all in the long run. If we go too far and destroy our environment irreversibly, nature will bring us its wrath.

For China, now the second largest economy and the biggest polluter in the world, this means redoubling its efforts to lessen its reliance on fossil fuel, to move away from the Western model of exploitation and consumption, and to return to a more traditional Chinese model of living harmoniously with nature. Failing that, our environment will deteriorate rapidly and our offspring will suffer as a result.

Bertrand Russell saw this coming almost 100 years ago. If China acquires foreign vices that make for success but cause misery to others, he wondered, what would become of all of us?

Clearly if China continues to modernize along the lines of the Western model of exploitation and consumption, all of us will be worse off in the long run.

At the 2015 Paris Climate Conference, representatives from 195 countries came together to formalize an agreement to limit global warming to below 2 °C from the baseline. The agreement will become legally binding after individual nations have ratified it in 2016. Given that the warming trend has been accelerating, not breaching the upper limit will entail a serious consumption mindset shift and test the resolve of the major industrialized nations. However, this development also testifies to the acceptance of the seriousness of global warming and the development of a consensus to tackle it in earnest.

Zhi Is for Wisdom

Confucians believe that wisdom is an innate human virtue, albeit one that must be embellished with education. Scholarship as a Chinese tradition has been around for thousands of years. In the opening chapter of the *Analects*, Confucius comments on how it is a pleasure to learn something new and practice it regularly. For most Chinese students, this is their first lesson from the master. Confucius also says that whenever three people walk together, one of them would be qualified to teach him something. This studious and humble attitude is ingrained in the Chinese mindset, where learning is considered to be a pleasure and not a chore.

What Kind of Education?

Stuffing children with a massive amount of information is commonly practiced in many Asian countries. This kind of passive learning is meaningful only if information is static and it is all that young people are supposed to know. It does little to encourage students to think for themselves or ask questions, let along challenge existing knowledge.

Learning should not only be a mental exercise; physical exercise is also important. Being physical can help to strengthen our bodies and relax our minds, and that can make us more aware. Competition can drive us to do our personal best instead of fulfilling what others have prescribed for us. These two endeavors complement each other and together represent true learning.

The Greeks were the first people to combine sports with academic study to educate their young men. Athletics is an important part of US education, to the extent that it seems that the average US high-school student plays more than he studies. While his Chinese counterpart buries himself in books and homework, the typical American student spends much of his time on the athletic field or in the gym. It is not surprising that American students have not scored as well as their Asian peers in international standardized tests.

In the 2013 *Brown Center Report on American Education*, American fourth and eighth graders scored lower in standardized math and science tests than students from Singapore, Japan, South Korea, Hong Kong and Taiwan (students from China and India had not yet participated in these standardized tests.) It is interesting to note that the East Asian countries where students have done well in these tests are modern economies that have at one time or another been heavily influenced by Confucianism.

This worries American educators, especially in the Internet age where proficiency in math and science is a prerequisite to compete. There is also a concern that China and India, with their vast number of able graduates, will leapfrog the US in the coming economic race.

Judging from the breakneck growth of these two emerging giants, it would be reasonable to assume that their students' strong foundation in math and science might have something to do with it. In the meantime, however, the US, with its substandard math and science scores, continues to churn out not only popular innovations, such as the smartphone and social media, but also hi-tech wizardry, such as nanotechnology, 3D printing and biopharmaceuticals. Why such a dichotomy?

The US also has the largest number of Nobel laureates of all nations. As of the end of 2012, he US had a whopping 39 percent of all Nobel

Prizes ever awarded; and in science, medicine and economics, its share was even higher at 48 percent.

This raises a question about whether achievements in math and science are a reliable predictor for discoveries and innovation. No doubt educators will debate this topic for a long time, and there may never be a straightforward answer. The fact that most modern innovations—the digital computer, microelectronics, the Internet, biotechnology, and many other things that we take for granted—came from the US begs the question why.

But it is not only information that American students learn in schools that is important; the process of active learning is also important.

To raise questions and challenge existing knowledge is a Western intellectual tradition. To be able to take things apart down to their fundamental attributes, visualize new opportunities and come up with new innovations is what creative minds like to do. To work hard on something that one believes in, and defend it passionately, separates the innovator from the follower. In addition, a supportive environment that respects different ideas is crucial for nurturing future talents.

To defend one's position while acknowledging the viewpoints of others familiarizes a child with the routines of the real world. It helps him to build self-confidence and prepares him for leadership. It doesn't really matter if the child is academically gifted or just an average student. I found that most successful American executives exhibit this type of self-confidence, along with a dose of self-deprecating humor acquired when they were young.

Chinese students are typically hard-working and inquisitive about all subjects. What they would benefit most from earlier on in their lives are critical thinking skills, and how to deal with uncertainty and risk.

In Chinese Mainland high schools, students have to study a set of core subjects around the clock. Their goal is to score well in Gaokao, the highly competitive national college entrance examination, and to enter a good college, preferably one with a national reputation. There is little time for extracurricular activities to relax and unwind. When they enter college they have to choose their majors right away. Most students opt for the popular subjecs, such as IT, finance or communications, hoping that these will lead to good jobs after college. So there is little time to explore.

Having said that, in the US, ambitious college students often choose majors that can also lead to lucrative careers, such as pre-med, finance or computer science.

However, most US college students don't have to settle on their majors until they are in their third year of college, so there is plenty of time to explore and discover what they really like before deciding.

Given the sophistication of the US education system and its freedom to experiment, it is not surprising that in 2014 over 330,000 Chinese students were attending colleges and graduate schools in the US. They form the largest foreign student contingent on US college campuses. What's more, the number of Chinese parents sending their children to the US for high-school education is also on the rise.

All Can Be Taught or All Can Learn?

Confucius taught anyone who was willing to learn, and the Chinese revere him as the greatest teacher of all time.

In the *Analects* he opined on a variety of topics ranging from moral behavior to human relationships. He did this in the form of simple dialog, which he conducted either with his students or with officials during his visits to the various kingdoms. After his students had asked their questions, all they could do was listen attentively to his every utterance. There weren't many follow-on discussions about what Confucius had said. His words were definitive and no one ever challenged them.

In Socrates' time of around the fifth century BC in Greece, he entered into extensive dialog with his students. However, there was a major difference between the teaching styles of Socrates and Confucius. Socrates would not provide direct answers to questions raised by his students. Instead he asked them questions and engaged them in lengthy debate. He explored their arguments for weaknesses and challenged them to come up with something more precise. This inevitably raised more questions than the students had originally thought of. Most of the time there were no satisfactory answers and everyone left the session exhausted and with more to think about.

The pursuit of knowledge for knowledge's sake is a Western intellectual tradition. The difference between the Western teaching method, which is bottom-up and self-oriented, and the Chinese teaching method, which is top-down and expert-based, continues to be quite pronounced today.

In traditional China, nothing could be better than what was already established by the sages. Therefore all that students could do was to comprehend and perfect what they were taught. This method may work well for the study of the classics, since they deal mostly with morality and human relationships, which arguably have not changed all that much over the millennia. However, in the more quantitative disciplines, such as science and medicine, this approach is woefully inadequate.

Westerners learn by asking questions and finding the answers by themselves. Asking good questions is actually more difficult than finding the right answers. It requires one to first think about why he is asking a question. If a teacher likes to challenge his students, he must also have some idea of what the answer should be before he opens his mouth. In other words, the student asking a question has to first answer the question in his own head. This, after all, is what learning is all about. If repeating information is what's desired, the Western teaching method is not all that efficient. However, once students have become comfortable with asking questions and finding answers by themselves, they can progress rapidly.

American teachers often ask their primary school students to do research and present their findings in class, and get praised for it. In this way a young student learns to explore on his own and look at issues from many different perspectives. He also learns to propose his own ideas and defend them in front of others, while thinking on his feet. On the other hand, the Chinese schools continue to teach rote learning. Teachers are respected as authorities on knowledge rather than experts at stimulating ideas.

While rote learning helps students to memorize information and facilitates recall, it also assumes that there is only one version of the truth, and knowing that is good enough. After a student graduates from school and goes into the workplace, he can function reasonably well if he remains in a similar environment going through the same routines.

A Chinese student who does well in school may aspire to work for the government, as generations of scholars have done before him. If he is lucky, he may get a nice starting position and spend his entire career there. This person should be able to function quite well because he is already familiar with the system logic, as well as its unwritten rules. What's more, he will be subjected to continuous retraining as he moves up the government ladder.

However, such an individual will find it difficult to lead in China's fast-moving market economy because his education has always come from the authorities, instead of his own investigations. Therefore he may have difficulty in fully appreciating the basic tenet of the market economy, which is the freedom to choose—a bottom-up process.

The purpose of rote learning is to propagate a set of acceptable ideas that serve to box people in. As a person becomes more successful, his box will grow bigger to accommodate his increasing stature. Over time, he will stretch to become part of the box. As part of the box it is difficult for him to think outside of it.

The Chinese and Western views of children are also quite different. The Chinese believe that a child is innocent, like a blank piece of paper. The teacher's job is to help him draw the most beautiful picture and write the most wonderful prose on it. Without proper guidance, the child will make a mess. Whether the child is interested in drawing the same picture the teacher shows him is not important. He is there to learn the proper way to draw.

This is very different than in US schools, where kids are encouraged to draw whatever they like and be praised for their efforts. US schools are where kids can play and learn, have a good time and build up their self-esteem. In Chinese schools, children are taught to study hard because diligence is more important than passion. In fact, the Chinese word for study is xuexi, which consists of two separate words: study (学) and practice (习). And that's what Chinese students do all the time—study from their teachers and practice what they have learned.

There is a Chinese proverb that says, "A piece of jade is nothing unless it is properly chiseled." This implies that a young person is like a piece of raw jade. He may have some natural talents but they are hidden. Unless experts polish him and bring out his talents, he will never shine. His achievements can only be made possible by the recognition and diligence of his parents and teachers.

Westerners consider a child as a gift from God. He has a soul, awareness and innate intelligence. The Western educational approach is to stimulate the child's own innate desire to acquire knowledge. Anyone can succeed, provided that he is willing to try. The teacher is there to assist him in this learning process.

In *Meno*, one of Plato's dialogues, Socrates demonstrates his idea of education with an uneducated slave boy. The subject he wants to talk about with the boy is geometry. However, Socrates doesn't want to just teach the boy geometry; instead he wants the boy to learn geometry by himself by answering his questions. So Socrates asks the boy the same question over and over again, but with a slight variation each time. With each iteration, the boy's understanding of geometry improves. At the end of the questioning, his understanding of geometry is as good as anyone's.

The most iconoclastic figure in the world of modern technology is probably Steve Jobs, the former head of Apple Computers. Jobs is an example of someone who eschewed formal education, challenged authority and succeeded in creating an entirely new industry. He co-founded Apple with Steve Wozniak in 1976. He left in 1985 then returned in 1997 as CEO a second time. In his second stint at Apple, Jobs shepherded it to become the most valuable company in the world, before his untimely passing in 2011.

Jobs had the unique ability to see what lies ahead when others could only fumble in the present. The products he championed at Apple, such as the iPhone and iPad, are ubiquitous in our busy lives. They make information available at our fingertips and mobile Internet a reality. Although Jobs was the head of a technology company, he was not trained as an engineer or in a technical discipline. However, he was able to weave ideas across emerging technology trends while his competitors doggedly pursued their linear development paths.

When Jobs' competitors saw straight lines, Jobs saw dots that he could connect together to form multi-dimensional patterns. When others were making more powerful mobile phones, he created the iPhone, a cross between a phone and a mobile computer. When his competitors were making bigger and more powerful personal computers, he created a new category of device, the iPad. This cross-disciplinary approach to product development could not have come from someone trained strictly in the traditional engineering disciplines.

In Jobs' youth he marveled at the beauty and simplicity of calligraphy. At Apple he championed aesthetics as a product design function, and he drove the development of products that were both technologically advanced and aesthetically pleasing. What's more, he liked basic critical thinking. He once said, "I would trade all my technology for an afternoon with Socrates."

When wholistic and critical thinking work hand in hand, the results can be revolutionary. Steve Jobs was a fine example of this synthesis.

Bibliography

Qin Dynasty (秦朝), baike.baidu.com, reviewed Jan 2016.
Mencius, Ch. 3.1, P. 57–58, edited by Zhong Mang, Chung Hua Books, 2012, (孟子,公孙丑, p. 57–58, 钟芒主编, 中华书局, 2012).
Plato, Complete Works, *Republic*, translated by G.M.A. Grube, rev. C.D.C. Reeve, edited by John M. Cooper, 426–435, P. 1058–1066, Hackett Publishing Company, 1997 (Plato's four virtues).
Plato, Complete Works, *Protagoras*, translated by Stanley Lombardo and Karen Bell, edited by John M. Cooper, 330b–332b, P. 763–765, Hackett Publishing Company, 1997 (included piety as a 5th virtue).
Plato, Complete Works, *On Virtue*, translated by Mark Reuter, edited by John M. Cooper, P. 1698, Hackett Publishing Company, 1997.
Fung Yu-lan, *A History of Chinese Philosophy, Vol.1*, p. 2, translated by Derk Bodde, Princeton University Press, 1953.
The Book of Great Learning, The Four Books, edited by Zhu Xi, (朱熹,大学, 四书集注).
Confucius, *The Analects, Chapter 12*, P. 163, translated by D.C. Lau, Penguin Books, 1979.
Confucius, *The Analects, Chapter 6*, P. 78, translated by D.C Lau, Penguin Books 1979.
Abraham Lincoln, Brainy Quote, reviewed Jan 2016.
Aristotle, *Nicomachean Ethics*, P. 51, Collector's Library of Essential Thinkers, CRW Publishing Limited, 2009.
The Four Books, edited by Zhu Xi, Kwong Chi Books, Hong Kong, 1966.
Sun Tzu, *The Art of War*, translated by Lin Wusun, Long River Press, Ch. 7, P. 65, 2003.
Confucius, *The Analects, Book 15*, English translation by D.C. Lau, Penguin Books 1979.

Edward Wong, *Inquiry on Tinted Milk Powder*, The New York Times, 14 Jan 2011.

Editorial, *Of Power, Sex and Money*, CaixinOnline, Feb 6, 2013.

Michael J. Sandel, *Justice, What's the Right Thing to Do?* Penguin Books 2010.

Keith B. Richburg, *Toddler in China Hit by 2 Vehicles, Then Ignored, Dies*, The Washington Post, Oct 20 2011.

Peter Foster, *Chinese Toddler Ran Over Twice after Being Left on the Street*, The Telegraph, Oct 17 2011.

Choe Sang-hun, Su-hyun Lee and Jiha Ham, *Human Errors Suspected as Hope Fades in Korean Ferry Sinking*, The New York Times, Apr 17, 2014.

Chico Harlan, *South Korean President Says Ferry Captain's Actions 'Tantamount to Murder,'* The Washington Post, Apr 21 2014.

Confucius, *The Analects, Chapter 12*, P. 163, translated by D.C. Lau, Penguin Books, 1979.

Confucius, *The Book of Rites*, Baidu Baike, (孔子,礼记礼器: 礼之以少为贵者, 以其内心者也, 百度), reviewed Jan 2016.

Super PACs, OpenSecret.org, reviewed Jan 2016.

Federal Election Committee, *Quick Answers to PAC Questions*, reviewed Jan 2016.

The World Bank, *Turn Down the Heat: Why a 4°C Warmer World Must Be Avoided*, Nov 2012.

The World Bank: Turn Down the Heat, Confronting the New Climate Normal, 11 Nov, 2014.

NASA, Earth Observatory.

Paul Chapman, *Entire Nation of Kiribati to Be Relocated Over Rising Sea Level Threat*, The Telegraph, 23 Nov 2012.

Coral Davenport, *Rising Seas*, The New York Times, 28 Mar 2014.

Gardiner Harris, Borrowed Time on Disappearing Land, *Facing Rising Seas, Bangladesh Confronts the Consequences of Climate Change*, The New York Times, 28 Mar, 2014.

Bertrand Russell, *The Problem of China, Questions, P. 2, Chapter 1*, George Allen & Unwin Ltd. 1922.

www.cop21paris.org (Dec 18, 2015).

Confucius, *The Analects*, Book 1, translated by D.C. Lau, Plenum Press, 1979.

The 2013 Brown Center of American Report: *How Well Are American Students Learning?* BROWN CENTER on Education Policy at Brookings.

en.wikipedia.org/wiki/List_of_Nobel_laureates

Keith Bradsher, *Next Made-in-China Boom: College Graduates*, The New York Times Jan 18, 2013.
Didi Tang, *Chinese Seek Freedom, Edge at US High Schools*, AP, Aug 13 2014.
Plato, *Meno, Complete Works*, P. 881–886, Edited by John M. Cooper, Associate Editor D.S. Hutchinson, Hackett Publishing Company, Inc. 1997.
Steve Jobs, Wikipedia, reviewed Jan 2016.
Steve Jobs, *in The Classroom of the Future*, Newsweek, Oct 28, 2001.
Walter Isaacson, *Steve Jobs*, p. 118, Little, Brown 2011.

9
Etiquette with Chinese Characteristics

As China modernizes, it imports more and more Western culture and etiquette. The pace at which this is happening is at least as fast as the economy is growing. Over time, Western etiquette has been skillfully assimilated into the Chinese mainstream. It now looks and feels Chinese.

In large meetings, the host usually welcomes the participants by uttering the phrase "Ladies and Gentlemen" in Chinese, similar to what hosts normally do in the West. This may appear as if the Chinese are respecting women more by saluting them ahead of men, but that's where the similarity ends.

In the West, out of courtesy and fairness, it is important to give women priority, such as opening doors for them or giving them seats. This has become a fine social etiquette. However, the spirit remains regarding helping the weak and those who are less fortunate. The same courtesy is given to children, the elderly, people with disabilities and those who can't compete with healthy adult men on equal terms. But despite the adaptation of this imported etiquette, the best of China is still reserved for those with the highest status in the social hierarchy, irrespective of their gender, age or physical condition.

Because culture affects how we organize and work, we can use some common activities, such as food and food service, to compare and contrast Chinese and Western work styles.

Chinese people prefer to sit around large round tables and have a meal together. The round table symbolizes smoothness. It has no sharp corners, which is also how a civilized person should conduct himself. In a formal Chinese banquet, guests are seated round a big round table according to their social status. A guest's age, his relationship with the host, his professional level and his experience determine where he should sit relative to the host, who normally occupies the seat at the table furthest from the door, facing the entrance. Across from the head of the table is his co-host or the person who is handling the evening's program. The seat to his right is the power seat reserved for the evening's honored guest. This is an adaptation of Western dining etiquette. In old China, the seat to the left of the host was reserved for the honored guest.

At the Western table, the guests are arranged according to their common interests, such as professions, hobbies or marital status. Status is less important at the Western table. Affinity is primary.

At a Chinese banquet, alcoholic beverages, including beer, should be consumed only during toasts. Tea, mineral water, soda or juice are the only beverages that one can drink alone. The Chinese believe that drinking is a social activity, so it ought to be shared. Enjoying a cocktail or wine in solitary contemplation is considered to be disrespectful to those around.

Drinking helps to loosen the inhibitions in the protocol-rich Chinese culture. When a group of family, friends and colleagues share drinks and laughter together, the formalities they strive so hard to maintain during the day are subsumed by the alcohol-induced bliss with their fellow beings.

At the dinner table there is often a small bottle of Baijiu (sorghum distillate, or "firewater") and a shot glass in front of each person. Just because it's there doesn't mean that you should drink it. Chinese etiquette stipulates that you should pour drinks for others before you serve yourself. After the glasses are all filled, the guests should raise them to toast each other before they drink.

This ritual, which is designed to show respect for others, is practiced all over Asia. In Korea it goes even further: it is quite common for two old acquaintances to exchange soju (rice liquor) glasses and drink from them as a gesture of friendship and respect. I experienced this when I visited South Korea during the SARS epidemic in 2002. After I drank from my host's glass, I secretly hoped that the spirit was strong enough to render any virus that might be there inoperative.

When a subordinate offers a toast to his seniors, he should circle to where they sit at the table and do it in front of them. He should never raise his glass across the table or, worse, wait for the seniors to come to him. When a subordinate proposes a toast, he should not raise his glass higher than his senior's glass because this would be seen as disrespectful.

A typical Chinese banquet has at least ten courses, usually consisting of a variety of fresh local produce and delicacies, including the must-have chicken and steamed fish. The meal usually begins with soup and appetizers, similar to Western restaurants. Again, this is an adaptation of Western-style table service. In the old days, soup was served at the end of the meal rather than at the beginning. Too much fluid intake before the main meal can slow down digestion.

In a Chinese banquet the dishes are carefully chosen by the host to reflect the season, a contrast of textures, and a balance of color, fragrance and taste. With such a variety to choose from there is bound to be something for everyone.

Sharing food is a fine ritual at the Chinese table, and very different from the more individualistic style of dining in the West. In a Western restaurant, each guest orders his own choice of food from the menu and eats by himself. There is little sharing, with the exception of wine and bread. Dining is less about the sharing of food and more about a culinary experience enhanced by good ambience, conversation and humor.

The service in Chinese and Western restaurants is also organized differently. In a US restaurant, each waitress is assigned a set number of tables. It is her role to take care of these. If she does a good job taking care of her customers, she will make good tips. After deducting a portion for the busboys, she pockets the rest. The waitress is accountable to her own customers and responsible for how much she makes.

In a typical Chinese restaurant, every waiter works with other waiters on all tables. They take orders when the guests come in and serve the dishes when they are ready. They watch out for each other and operate with a keen awareness of what's going on in the entire restaurant at all times. They know what the guests are missing and what the other waiters are working on. They are busy running around but also working smoothly together.

At the end of the evening, all the waiting staff sit down to share a meal and split the tips. In this type of team arrangement, everybody shares the same responsibilities and benefits. Everyone does everyone else's job and feels responsible for the group. There is camaraderie and efficiency, but little personal service.

A Chinese banquet can last for two hours or more, so there is plenty of time for toasting. Red wine is for casual toasting, whereas Baijiu is the heavy weapon after everyone has had a chance to warm up. However, the ritual of having red wine with food is also modified with Chinese characteristics. Here the quintessential Western activity of savoring burgundy slowly is modified to accommodate the Chinese desire for sharing and group affinity. So instead of slowly sipping their red wine, Chinese people walk round the tables and clink their wine glasses to toast each other. They empty the nectar in big gulps, sometimes even downing full glasses. Never mind the ritual of slowly sniffing a burgundy to savor its fine bouquet and swirling it in the mouth to release its complex flavors of fruits and spices. The strong tannin aftertaste of a bottle of regal Bordeaux is now hopelessly comingled with the delicate flavors of a steamed giant grouper.

Despite a slowdown in economic growth, Chinese wine consumption continues to increase. A 2013 CNBC report statee that wine consumption in China is expected to double every five years. So in 2016 China should catch up in wine consumption with the US, which is currently the second largest wine-consuming country after France. With all the bottoms-up wine toasting there is very little risk to this forecast.

In greetings, most Chinese now use the common Western handshake. Young people may say "Hi" or hug each other as they do in the West. In the old days, men never shook hands. Instead they shook their clasped fists at a distance to greet each other. Touching another person was considered rude, and prohibited if the party was from the opposite sex.

However, like many other imports, the handshake has been modified with Chinese characteristics. To greet a senior person, a subordinate should demonstrate subservience by softly squeezing his boss's right hand instead of applying the customary vice grip. It is quite different than what is considered best practice in Western societies, where a crushing handshake and piercing eye contact projects sincerity, irrespective of the other person's status. On the other hand, a dead-fish-like handshake connotes weakness and mendacity. In other words, this person cannot be trusted.

The Chinese No

The Chinese and many Asians don't like to say the word no or give negative answers for fear of offending people. Hence they are masters at saying no without ever uttering the word. To deliver rejections without offending others is humility in practice and an art of getting along with others without appearing negative. However, because a Chinese no may not be a definitive no, one should not take no as an answer.

If a Chinese person is asked a question that requires a negative answer, he will often dance around the subject and not give a straight answer. Sometimes he may even give an ambivalent yes and no answer. To many Westerners, this reeks of dishonesty. However, this high-context answer is not limited to the Chinese; many other Asians use it routinely. The Japanese, for example, often turn silent to difficult questions so as to not embarrass each other.

Sometimes questions are asked and answered in a sort of word game to allow people to interact socially. They are not meant to carry much substance.

In the US, people greet each other by saying, "How's it going?" Such a greeting does not require an elaborate answer. It is just what it is supposed to be, a greeting. No one would really want to stop and listen to the other person's life story every time he asks the question "How are you?" Similarly, Chinese people greet each other by saying "Ni hao?" and then move on.

Another common Chinese greeting is "Have you eaten yet?" This shows just how important food is to the Chinese. The response to this query can be a bit more involved. An old lady in Beijing greets her neighbor by saying, "Have you eaten yet?" If the neighbor answers,

"Yes", she would say, "Too bad, next time come have dinner with us." However, if he answers, "Not yet", she would say, "Then you should hurry home to have dinner with your family. They are waiting for you." Of course, the person who is being asked knows this is just pleasantries and plays along.

People from other high-context cultures are also comfortable with a certain level of looseness and ambiguity when they interact with each other. Westerners who take it too seriously are often baffled by this kind of double talk.

The Chinese have many subtle ways of delivering negative messages, so they must be viewed in the proper context. Silence is a common response to a difficult question. If a Chinese person stays mum for a long time, you should consider other approaches. Many Chinese people also defer answering tough questions by pushing them into the future in the hope that by that time the question will be conveniently forgotten.

The following are some common no responses and their interpretations:

- It's not easy for me to comment on this (这个不好说)—meaning you already know what the answer is but it is difficult for me to say it out loud without incriminating myself.
- It is not convenient for us to discuss it now (现在不方便讨论)—meaning factors outside of my control are standing in the way. Most likely the senior people have not made up their minds yet or there are some changes to the organization coming soon, so no one is in a position to comment. The Chinese like to use the phrase "not convenient" to give an answer when they really don't have any. Encapsulated in the phrase are things that are important but may or may not be directly related to the subject of discussion. There may be technical, financial, personality or political reasons. It is up to you to figure out what they are.

The equivalent English expression is "Our system is down. You will hear from us as soon as the problem is fixed." In other words, we don't have an answer for you now; you should just wait.

- We need to wait for the appropriate moment (等适当时候再说)—meaning let's defer the discussion until I am authorized to talk about it, which may be in a while or never.
- Let's do some more research on this (需要再研究一下)—meaning we need to stew over this some more, or can you do better with the terms? It may also be a delaying tactic because the Chinese love to learn, especially if it's done for them free.
- We should look at this again (要再看一下)—meaning I am not convinced you have the right stuff, or the boss has not indicated his preference, or you have not fully considered our position.
- This matter has some difficulties (这事情有难度)—meaning we can't go on until you understand and do something about the hidden agenda. The ball is now in your court.
- There shouldn't be a fundamental problem (这事情基本上没有问题)—meaning although we agree on the main items, the hidden agenda is holding us up.
- We need to be more diligent (要继续努力)—meaning you need to come up with more concessions or else the answer is a definite no.

Most Chinese people would immediately recognize what these replies stand for. They may work the channels to apply leverage or refocus their attention on something else more productive. Many other Asians also practice the subtle no answers. It's not dishonesty but a contextual-rich way of communicating something negative without ever saying the word no.

Sometimes saying no is actually an indirect way of saying yes. Traditional Chinese culture venerates humility and modesty. A person should never boast about his own achievements to others. When an employee is praised by his boss for doing a good job, he may say something like, "Not really! It is really just average work", even if he has slaved for months to complete the assignment with good results, and he is quite proud of them.

A Chinese parent may humbly say, "My son is just lucky. He is really just an average student", even if the youngster has won an award in the prestigious Intel Science Talent Search or has gained admission to an elite college.

When being presented with a gift of value or an important invitation, the Chinese recipient always appears reluctant to accept it. He politely refuses and pushes the gift back to the presenter, saying something like, "You are too generous. I really can't accept it." The presenter persists and pushes again. This push and parry routine repeats for at least two or three times before the recipient acts reluctantly and says, "Ok, if you really insist, I'll do the safe keeping for you", and leaves the package on the coffee table before he sees the guest off.

When asked to give a speech at a function, a Chinese person may say, "You are too kind. I am really not qualified to give such a speech at your esteemed function." The requester would insist. After a few rounds of this back and forth, the speaker would reluctantly say, "Alright, I'll try my best, but please don't be embarrassed by my meager presentation." This etiquette goes all the way back to the Zhou Dynasty.

To most Westerners, if someone insists on not accepting something then he must have some legitimate reasons. The person proffering a gift should respect that and try some other way to show respect. However, if they understand this part of the Chinese culture, they should definitely consider the indirect Chinese no as a possible maybe.

A Coinish Way of Living

The old Chinese copper coin, which is round and has a square hole in the middle, symbolizes just how a civilized person should conduct himself. He should be smooth and forgiving on the outside but a square on the inside. In other words, a man should be tough and principled on himself and his family but forgiving towards others.

Many Asians behave this way. Beneath their genteel appearances, there is toughness and resiliency. Westerners often interpret this kind of manner as meek, and push hard. If they venture too far into an Asian's comfort zone, they will inevitably be surprised by the ferocious response.

Most Asians have a reserved manner. Unlike Westerners, who often speak their mind and wear their emotions on their face, Asians rarely display their emotions openly. They also don't like to openly challenge others, or appreciate being challenged in the open. If they have to argue with someone they would rather do it in private.

The Chinese believe that challenging others exposes a person's rough edges. It destroys harmony and doesn't bode well for their cultivation. Westerners often interpret this as being passive or unsure.

Westerners are more comfortable speaking up at big meetings, where they often fight to make their point. To be able to state and defend one's position clearly and forcefully when everybody else is speaking at the same time is the art of advanced verbal combat. Western politicians, in particular, are experts at hurling insults at their opponents to score political brownie points. This type of confrontational behavior is at odds with most Asians.

Because of the virtue of humility, many Asians are hesitant to speak up and be noticed, especially when there are senior people around. In traditional Asian culture, no one wants to be seen as the nail that sticks up, for doing so would invite a painful hammer strike. This is opposite from the West, where squeaky wheels would get the grease. So when Asians do speak, they often don't make their point loud enough or fast enough, even though they may have a good idea. As a result, the fast-talking Westerners simply talk over them.

The ability to speak up is an important skill to have in today's corporate arenas. In the fast-paced business environment, it is not enough to have good academic credentials and brilliant ideas; it is as important to leverage people and resources to turn your good ideas into reality. To do that, you must speak up, bring others to your cause, and lead with purpose and integrity. This salesmanship aspect of success is often lacking in Asians, who were brought up to be humble.

When I was managing Moody's financial institutions ratings team in Asia, I had to modify a practice in our Japanese office. Moody's had a team of very talented analysts in the Tokyo office covering major Japanese banks and insurance companies. When I was there, the team was led by a couple of very capable senior analysts who knew the Japanese financial system inside out and had great respect from institutional clients and issuers. Given that this was Japan, they often dominated the internal discussions and the junior analysts rarely said anything. However, I knew from their written work that the juniors were strong analysts with interesting ideas, and we could benefit from their participation at meetings.

This was very different from my experience at the Moody's New York office, where analysts were not only good at credit analysis but also were opinionated and outspoken. As Moody's is an organization that prides itself on diversity and the free flow of opinions, I needed to find a way to reconcile these two different work cultures.

I instituted a practice in the Tokyo office where every one of our analysts had to express an opinion at meetings, regardless of his rank. One by one, starting from the lowest-ranking analyst, each was asked for his opinion and rationale regarding the credit issues being discussed. In the end, the lead analyst would make his rating recommendations and the votes were tallied. After we had done this for a few awkward meetings, the junior members, including several women, became more vocal and confident at expressing themselves. The resultant analysis also became richer.

Managers in hierarchical organizations should find practical means to encourage their team members to contribute freely and professionally to the organizational cause.

As a Matter of Face

Face is an important facet of Asian life and a major component of its social etiquette. It is much more than just what you see in the mirror; it is how Asians view themselves through the eyes of others. For an Asian person, face is positively related to his self-esteem, and his ability to function effectively in a society that depends on mutual acceptance and support.

A person's face should be firm and radiant, without too many imperfections. If it is blemished, he will feel self-conscious in front of others. His productivity and relationships will suffer as a result.

To the Chinese, if other people respect them, they gain face; if others compliment them, their faces glow; if others challenge them openly, they lose face.

Losing face is akin to losing power and influence in a society that thrives on mutual support. If a person of authority loses face, he is damaged goods. His acquaintances will stop coming by to visit him, and it will be difficult for him to seek favors from them ever again. If one person has caused another to lose face, it will be remembered as a terrible insult and the resentment will not go away easily.

How much face a person is entitled to is directly correlated with his social status. Therefore the higher up a person is in the social hierarchy, the more face he is entitled to.

In Chinese temples, devotees often paste gold foils on their idols' faces. That is because, as deities, they deserve the best face. Therefore when a person compliments another person, it is often referred to as pasting gold on that person's face. On the other hand, people at the lower end of the social strata are not given much face.

When the US Secretary of State John Foster Dulles, a staunch anti-communist, refused to greet Chinese Premier Zhou Enlai in Geneva in 1954, it caused Zhou to lose face badly in public. This famous cold war episode angered the Chinese so much that it helped to fan their resentment towards Americans. It was not until 1972, when President Nixon visited China, that the Sino-American relationship began to thaw from the deep freeze.

Nixon understood perfectly how important face was to the Chinese. When *Air Force One* touched down in Beijing for his historic visit, Nixon made sure that his entourage stayed inside the plane when he and his wife, Pat, walked down to greet the awaiting Chinese Premier Zhou Enlai. The two then shook hands warmly as if they were long-lost friends who hadn't seen each other for ages (they had never met before).

Nixon wanted to make sure that he, as the US President and leader of the free world, showed Zhou the proper respect and gave him plenty of face in front of his Chinese audience. That would make Zhou's job of convincing his party colleagues easier, and that in turn would help to make Nixon's China trip more successful. A simple gesture by Nixon went a long way towards repairing the delicate relationship.

Because of humility, blowing your own horn is frowned upon in much of Asia. In contrast, Westerners, especially Americans, do not hesitate to trumpet their own accomplishments. After all, if a person does not blow his own horn in a society where everyone's primary objective is to look after number one, who else is going to do it?

Because a Chinese person cannot give himself face, he must get it from someone else, preferably from someone more powerful than he is.

When a foreign dignitary praises a project or development, he gives tremendous face to the Chinese host, irrespective of how perfunctory his comments may be. Photos taken with dignitaries instantly give face to a person, notwithstanding they are routinely taken at large gatherings for a small fee.

Strategic possessions can also bolster a person's face. An executive may dress shabbily, yet his office shelves are stacked with massive volumes of bound technical manuals and important literary works. The impressive book collection bodes well for his intellect and enhances his face, even though they may never have been opened.

Because face is so important to the Chinese, they can be either its biggest promoter or its biggest abuser. When Chinese managers want to promote a project, they often hold a big ceremony, sometimes called a swearing-in ceremony, and invite all kinds of senior officials and dignitaries to participate. The bigger the crowd of luminaries, the more face it gives to the organizers and the greater the likelihood that the project will be completed successfully.

At the gathering, attendees all give flowery speeches, heaping praise on the project and its team members. There is plenty of backslapping and camaraderie to go round. This ritual raises the project profile, bolsters the face of team members and makes them feel that they are part of an important undertaking. However, there is also another important function.

This kind of ritual also serves as an unwritten social contract that binds the attendees together for the same goal. This is essential for the Chinese world, for no participant would want to default on his commitment and, as a result, lose face in front of his peers.

Western companies also have big kickoff meetings before launching important projects. However, these are usually reserved for team members only, unless it is for a major product launch, where all sales people would gather to share battle cries. Even so, it doesn't quite have the same significance as the Chinese swearing-in ceremonies.

Because face is so important to Chinese managers, they are masters at using it both as a tool to motivate and as a weapon to punish. Like parents, Chinese bosses don't praise their employees much. So on the rare occasions when they do, it gives plenty of face to those receiving it.

A common management trick is to give employees plenty of face in front of their colleagues, such as giving them all kinds of small rewards or by praising them in public gatherings. In a typical awards ceremony, the honored recipients, with red boutonnières pinned on their lapels, proudly march up to the stage to collect their awards from the headman, amid thunderous applauses form their colleagues. The ceremony gives them face in front of their peers, which fosters their loyalty as employees.

On the other hand, managers with ill intentions often use face to humiliate those they wish to discredit. In this situation, face can become a deadly psychological weapon.

Tarnishing the face of a Chinese person is akin to stripping him of his dignity or, worse, denying him of his raison d'être.

Because of cultural reasons, Chinese managers are often reluctant to engage in direct confrontation. Therefore they are masters at applying indirect means of influence, including face and group pressure, to achieve their management objectives. Often, large crowds are directed to do the management's dirty work, such as killing someone with a borrowed knife.

During the Cultural Revolution, a decade-long self-inflicted calamity that lasted from 1966 to 1976, youthful Chinese Red Guards often staged large rallies to humiliate Mao's political opponents. The Red Guards, who were mainly young students, would normally not have commanded much respect in patriarchal Chinese society. However, in large crowds and incited by loyalists, the dynamics reversed and they became ruthless tormentors.

Chinese intellectuals, including many prominent teachers and professors, writers and artists, and other so-called class enemies, were denounced and persecuted in this way during the Cultural Revolution. The Red Guards often dragged these undesirables on stage and accused them of all kinds of misdeeds, while inciting the crowds to go along. To add insult to injury, they made the denounced individuals parade through the streets wearing degrading placards and dunce's caps.

The seniority and reputation these fine folk assiduously accumulated over decades of hard work and sacrifices were instantly removed by this humiliating exercise. Worse, it was done at the hands of teenagers, who at more normal times would have bedn studying hard to emulate those they persecuted. Many could not endure the humiliation and serious loss of face, and some committed suicide. It was a national tragedy.

Comparatively speaking, Westerners judge themselves by who they are and what they have accomplished, and less by how others view them. Therefore they may find it difficult to appreciate the Chinese (and Asian) obsession with face. Americans are brought up as individuals. Many of them also possess a self-deprecating sense of humor. They are able to smear mud on their own faces and joke about it. It's a part of the culture.

It is important for Western managers to find out ahead of time where the Chinese person they deal with sits in the corporate hierarchy so as to provide face-appropriate treatments for him. For example, it is imperative that whatever the guests are being offered, such as a reception and banquet, rest and relaxation trips, and souvenirs, is at least equal to, and preferably better than, what their peers are given.

It would be a serious loss of face for the guest and a faux pas for the host if a Chinese executive was feted at a restaurant in a four-star hotel while his competitor dined at a five-star establishment. While these issues may seem trivial to Westerners, they are hugely important to the Chinese because of face.

Regardless of how fast China is modernizing, face will always remain an important part of people's lives. Understanding the importance of face can help foreigners to appreciate the broader context of the country's culture and navigate its befuddling ritual landscapes. For those Chinese venturing overseas, it behooves them to understand that locals may not be as sensitive as they are about face. Therefore they should be less concerned about their own face, and strive to take things more at face value.

Bibliography

Holliday, K. *Is China Causing a Global Wine Shortage?* CNBC, Oct 31, 2013.
Doward, J., *Chinese move up from snapping up fine wines, to buying up the whole vineyards*, The Observer, 11 May 2013.
Dulles ignores Chou En-Lai at Geneva, United Press, Apr 28, 1954.
Joe Gromelski, *Chinese Premier Zhou Enlai at Geneva, 1954*, Stars and Stripes, Jun 10, 2010.
Nixon in China (The film), Richard Nixon Presidential Library, Youtube, Feb 22, 2012.

10

The Chinese Model

The Practical Chinese

According to Fung Yu-lan, Chinese philosophers are more pragmatic in their pursuit of knowledge than their Western counterparts, who prefer to unravel mysteries of the universe and men's relationship with it. Chinese philosophers are mainly interested in practical ideas that can help people live better lives, with a conviction that doing so will lead to contentment.

This practical attitude permeates Chinese life. For example, many Chinese people go regularly to their temples or churches to worship, but they also have shrines at home to pay respect to their ancestors or deities. They may go to churches at Easter and Christmas, but they also burn incense at home to ward off evil spirits, or pray at Buddhist shrines during major holidays. They perform these different religious rituals to play it safe and to cover all bases. They gladly take the parts of different religions that are mutually agreeable, such as peace and salvation, and ignore the parts that conflict, such as exclusivity.

Likewise, many Chinese people go to their Western-trained doctors for shots and medicines when they get sick, but also visit their Chinese doctors to get herbs or to have acupuncture. To them, they are getting the best of both worlds. There are no conflicts; it is the practical thing to do. The Chinese focus is on getting results, and less about the process or what it takes to get there.

China's paramount leader, Deng Xiaoping, once said that it doesn't matter if a cat is black or white, as long as it catches mice. This famous saying sums up succinctly the pragmatic Chinese attitude. With this, a cat is reduced to the practical function it performs—catching mice. Nothing else matters much. A cat is no longer a pet, capable of providing affection and companionship to its owner. It is now a superior mouse-catching machine.

Because of this, Westerners and Chinese people often approach problem-solving differently.

Most Western managers use the analytical method and approach problems in a rational manner from the bottom up. They first collect all the facts, identify the issues, prioritize them, and test the hypotheses. Then they formulate a plan to tackle the issues one by one.

Chinese managers use a more intuitive approach and don't always adhere to a step-by-step, rigidly laid-out process. They may jump from point A to C, skipping point B entirely, if they believe they can get the job done faster. On the other hand, most Western managers would methodically go from solving one objective to another in a neat linear fashion. It is important to them that they follow the process diligently so they don't miss any important details.

A Western manager in charge of a new product launch will study the detailed financial model, from volume forecast to cost analysis, to marketing and financing plans. He will review the benchmarking study, comparing his product with those that are already out or rumored to be out there in the marketplace. He will look at the focus group results to finetune his marketing plan. He will review the safety profile of the new product against regulatory requirements, making sure that it won't cause injury to customers and harm his company's reputation.

Once the Western manager is satisfied with the information he has, he will push for approvals to launch the new product. The way he deals with the unknown, such as customer acceptance and likely competitive responses, is to find out as much as he can beforehand to assess the risks, and he factors these into his business model to see how they might affect his bottom line. If at the end he still doesn't have all the information he likes, he will have to make a decision about whether or not to go ahead based on his company's appetite for risk. A Western manager's job is to control the process as thoroughly as possible to reduce the risk down to an acceptable level.

Compared to his Western counterpart, a Chinese manager is more aggressive in his approach and less concerned about details. A Chinese manager can study a similar set of data on the project but come out with a different approach. Instead of following a detailed action plan, he is willing to go ahead quickly and take on risk much earlier in the process. For the practical Chinese manager, getting a product to the market quickly is more important than slogging through a detailed business plan. To him, expediency trumps precision. The market will determine who the real winners and losers are, not a detailed business plan. Unlike many Western managers who believe that the devil is in the detail, Chinese managers believe that details are not what make or break projects. Of the 3 Ss in business—*strategy, speed and steadfastness*—strategy and steadfastness are also traditional Chinese traits.

There is an old Chinese saying that a boat will naturally align with the river current when it gets closer to a bridge. This implies that there is no need for the boatman to steer his boat so carefully when it comes to a bridge because the river current will do the alignment for him. In other words, why waste energy on matters that no one has control of? Why not wait until a problem has become more visible before taking action? By then the problem may either be easy to handle or have ceased to be important.

Because the end result is more important than the process, management often favors clever shortcuts to do the right thing, but not necessarily to do things right. This attitude of always looking for shortcuts and waiting to do the right thing is also the standard excuse of procrastinators:

they are always waiting for that perfect moment to act, but that moment may never come.

The Chinese Government Model

The traditional Chinese government model is meritocratic.

Lucien Pye first describes China as a civilization pretending to be a state. Zhang Weiwei and Martin Jacques attribute China's rise to the development of a new civilization state. Zhang further argues that China's large size and unique culture will sustain its current revival. On the other hand, Francis Fukuyama opines that the current model continues the centuries-old Chinese dynastic tradition, except that it is now operating under a different name in a slightly different format.

A civilization state should be run by officials chosen for their requisite skills, track record, and knowledge of the country's history, culture and civilization. The Chinese Mandarins have done this for centuries. The selection process for Chinese civil servants is quite thorough. First, aspiring candidates must pass stringent civil exams to enter government service. In the dynasty days, candidates had to pass a series of local exams before they could even sit the national exam in Beijing. Today they can take the highly competitive public service exam every year.

After passing the exam, ambitious cadre must show what they are made of by volunteering to work in a difficult environment, such as a poor village somewhere in an underdeveloped part of China. They must demonstrate that they are both tough and capable, and can handle personal sacrifice. After a few years of this hardship duty, successful cadre will be promoted to positions with increased responsibility. There they must gain the confidence of those who are higher up by helping them tackle a long string of economic and political objectives. For example, they might be tasked to find ways to meet their region's growth targets from sustainable industries, or surpass poverty alleviation and pollution targets, or maintain social stability, and so on.

By the time they have reached a really senior position, such as a vice provincial governor, the cadre are all battle-hardened and politically savvy.

Most will have long strings of accomplishments under their belts. They will also have demonstrated strong management and leadership skills, and established important guanxi with the powers that be in Beijing.

Because officials are promoted based on their track record and how well they work with others, the Chinese selection process is no different than what any well-managed Western company does with its senior management team. To be promoted, a Western manager must also demonstrate strong performance and leadership qualities.

There are qualitative criteria as well, including whether an official is from a solid background with important relationships, and whether he fits the profile of a future China. If the official is well educated with a degree from a well-known foreign university, and well connected with important members of the elite, he will be given priority and groomed.

By the time an official has reached a certain level of professional competence, such as a department head or vice governor of a major bank, he will have spent years working diligently on different assignments and cultivating important relationships. His circles, which are now getting smaller and tighter, are also filled with like-minded career bureaucrats with similar accomplishments and ambitions.

Members of this selected group work on projects and attend training together, but also compete for future promotions. They are a fraternity of tenacious individuals dedicated to the advancement of their careers under the banner of the Chinese Dream.

Important policies are the result of research carried out by study groups that is validated by feasibility studies. The research phase involves serious brainstorming and a free flow of ideas. The atmosphere is cordial but not necessarily consensual. However, over time, by focusing and working hard, team members gradually coalesce towards a consensus. By the time a policy is ready for public consumption, all the hard work has been done and major disagreements have been resolved.

To Westerners who are used to a more transparent political process, the apparently uniform outcomes suggest that they must be manipulated by a select few behind closed doors. In fact, what they see is the end result of a long process of debates and negotiations involving many participants.

The Chinese believe that it is important to have consensus on major decision because strength comes from unity.

The US Government Model

The US model is democratic.

Every two or more years, American voters elect their representatives or local officials. Because the terms are short, campaigning is an ongoing affair, and politicians have all become adept showmen comfortable performing at the political theater. To win, a politician must be strong and vocal on issues. Mr Smith will not go to Washington but Mr Cantankerous might.

Not surprisingly, a large number of American lawmakers are trained as lawyers. In 2012 some 55 of the 100 American senators (55 percent) and 167 of the 435 members of the House of Representatives (38 percent) had law degrees. In comparison, there were only three scientists (one physicist, one chemist and one microbiologist) and six engineers in the house and none in the Senate. In roughly equal numbers to the group of scientists and engineers were four radio talkshow hosts, three radio or television broadcasters, one sportswriter and one television commentator.

No wonder American politicians love to argue—they were trained that way. In comparison, only 16 percent of the 25 members of the all-powerful Politburo of the Chinese Communist Party have law experience, most acquired on the job. The rest were evenly distributed with 20 percent each in economics, engineering and political science. Two had a military background. One was trained as a physicist and another one in agriculture.

In the US a lawyer is an advocate for his clients, or causes he believes in. On any single issue, he must choose only one of the binary positions—for or against, but not both. Otherwise he risks appearing disingenuous, which is a fate worse than death in a profession where personal integrity is of utmost importance. His job as a Socratic-trained lawyer is to examine the available evidence and ferret out inconsistencies in his opponent's arguments. He strives to raise doubts about their validity, develop a strong case for his client and argue for him vociferously in court or in front of the television camera.

On any contentious issue there is therefore very little middle ground. Compromise can only be made after drawn-out court battles, with the media happily supplying all the juicy bits. To the average Chinese person, American politicians and the media are far too negative. They seem always to be digging for dirt as well as competing for sensation. Most politicians complain a lot and rarely have anything good to say about anybody, except perhaps at weddings and funerals. This is, of course, very different than how most Americans behave normally.

If a lawyer is convinced that a serious injustice has occurred to someone, he may take the case pro bono. His client can win if he can convince the judge or jury with his arguments. This is the beauty of the US system, where the little guy has equal rights under the law, and he can win with good legal help.

In the US the underdogs can win if they fight hard. And when they do, they often change history. The Minutemen who fought the British colonial forces led to the founding of the US. The Civil Rights Movement that began with the black minority protesting against unfair treatment was later broadened to include other minorities, and it culminated in the signing of the Civil Rights Act in 1964, which forbids employment discrimination due to race, color, religion or country of origin.

Rev. Martin Luther King Jr. fought for equal rights and paved the way for a more just and harmonious society. Michael Dell, who fought the established tech giants, succeeded in bringing personal computers to millions of households. When underdogs win in the US they often bring new ideas, and the entire society can benefit.

In China, the system always funnels the power upwards. As a result, the little guys rarely have any direct say on matters that are important to them. Instead, they have to rely on the judgment and goodwill of those who are higher up.

In the US an official could have been a lawyer, a businessman or a movie star before entering politics. He must win elections, but prior government experience is not a must. In fact, voters may prefer candidates with no such prior experience because they may bring fresh ideas to the job. Unlike established politicians, a newly elected official is not beholden to the vested interests and is therefore, in theory, free to act as a change agent. In the US, strength comes from diversity.

In an election, voters choose a candidate for his platform, or what he promises to do if elected. They have to decide, based on his track record and personality, whether such an extrapolation is warranted. In addition to his ideas, a candidate's touch and feel qualities also figure prominently in his electability because voters don't necessarily want someone who is brilliant but doesn't have much in common with them.

Campaign marketing is a persuasive high art in a market economy. Potential voters are targeted with the same type of sophisticated campaigns designed to sell consumer products, with messages to either promote their candidates or instill fear about their opponents. They serve up simple solutions for complex problems, often with fanciful claims that sound fantastic but are difficult to verify. The difference is that in an election, voters have to live with their choices for at least two more years, whereas consumers can return the products they purchased and receive a refund immediately. Here lie the major differences between the Western style of democracy and what China practices.

In a democracy, voters are the boss. They have needs and elected officials are there to serve them. However, voters often pin their hopes on those politicians who are more polarizing than unifying, or those who promise quick fixes. As a result, longer-term problems such as infrastructure gaps and global warming, which require a unified approach, are often relegated to the back burner. Also, because of the adversarial nature of US politics, policy stalemate or vacillation occurs all too frequently. This makes execution a nightmare.

In China the government acts like the boss. It is massive, well organized and can accomplish a lot for the public in a short period of time. In this system, power goes to the paternalistic bureaucrats, who often behave like parents to their children rather than servants to the public. This all works well if officials perform diligently at what they are supposed to do. If they don't perform, people may grumble and complain but they have no means of replacing the officials directly.

This is what Fukuyama refers to as the Bad Emperor Syndrome, where a bad leader can stay for a long time in the Chinese system and there isn't much that people can do about it. This situation can go on for some time until the government has become so insensitive and corrupt that it completely fails Ren and violates Heaven's Way. When this happens, the regime is doomed and a new, and supposedly more responsive, one will replace it—often abruptly. It has been like this for thousands of years in China.

The Family Model

Many Chinese businesses operate like extended families.

In the old days, Chinese families had their clan values enshrined in the registry of their temples. Typically, the solemn document extols the descendants to be righteous and diligent, hardworking and honest. They should be respectful to their parents, live harmoniously with each other and be loyal to the family clan. If they could do that, the clan would be prosperous and perpetuate forever. These high-level messages are not too different in tone from the mission statements prominently displayed on the altars of today's major Western corporations.

The headman of the family is often a stern and fatherly figure. He is advanced in age and wise in worldly matters. He has to always appear humble, but without being humbling to others, for no one dares to challenge his authority.

Per Confucian traditions, the headman leads an exemplary life and tends to the family business in meticulous detail with the other elders. He dishes out orders to members and enforces family rules, which can be more terrifying to than the laws outside.

Irrespective of their differences, it is imperative that family members stay united to face the outside, for unity is virtue and fractiousness is vice.

Family unity is also a popular theme in many other cultures. The famous five arrows sign of the House of Rothschild carries a similar message of unity. Many Chinese children learn of the importance of unity from the Mongolian parable of the five arrows. According to the Mongolian legend, Alan Goa, the mythical ancestor of Genghis Khan, gave one arrow to each of her five feuding sons and asked them to break it. They did it easily. She then gave a bundle of five arrows for each to break, but no one could do it. Thus unity is strength and the family always looms larger than any individual.

A member feels he is obligated to consult with his extended family on important matters. His family is only too happy to oblige. After a while, their interests and concerns are so closely entwined that it is impossible to set them apart. This kind of mutual dependency and liability sharing is also quite common in Chinese companies.

As in a family, Chinese employees expect their company to show concern for their wellbeing. In return, the company expects its employees to show loyalty and dedication. It is not uncommon to see the CEO of a large Chinese company visit an injured lower-level employee in hospital. The boss usually brings flowers, fruit baskets and treats, and an envelope stuffed with cash. With cameras flashing, the CEO grabs the injured employee with both hands and warmly wishes him a speedy recovery. Pictures of his hospital visit will be plastered all over the company cafeteria and newsletter to showcase the benevolence of the headman, and to foster a familial working environment.

Family ownership is a common corporate structure in many Asian economies. Cross-shareholding among members ties their fates intimately together. They are protective of their own kind but compete ferociously with outsiders.

In China, the state remains the largest shareholder in the economy through its ownership of the large number of SOEs. South Korea has its own version of the corporate family called *chaebols*. Japan has its equivalent corporate family, *Keiretsus*. Southeast Asian countries such as Thailand, Malaysia and Indonesia all have large corporate conglomerates run by ethnic Chinese families. Because these corporate families are so large and pervasive in their economies, they also form significant systemic risks.

Parents Know Best?

Asian and Western parents bring up their children differently, and this affects them later in life.

From a very young age an American child is encouraged to think for himself. He is always asked for his opinions on matters and to defend them, regardless of how insignificant they may seem. For example, an American boy of around 10 years old wants to wear his new red hoodie to school, but the weather has taken a turn overnight and it has become much colder. In the morning when he takes the school bus, the temperature is below freezing. His mother says to him, "Johnny, why don't you wear the blue parka instead? Today is really cold and you will be warmer with the parka." Johnny replies, "Mom, I am fine. I want to choose what I want to wear. It's my life!"

Upon hearing this, his mother relents and thinks little Johnny should learn a lesson from this, so she says, "Ok, you can wear what you want, but don't blame me if you get sick." Sure enough, that afternoon when Johnny comes home he has a fever. Because of that he has to stay home for a few days, which he doesn't really mind, but he will also miss his best friend's sleepover party that weekend, which means a lot more to him.

So next time when it's cold outside, Johnny may think of wearing something warm instead of something that just looks nice. But he will still argue with his mom about making his own choices. The important thing is that the child is now making decisions based on his own experience and not simply from what he was told. With repeated lessons like this, when Johnny leaves home he will be in a good position to be independent.

Most Asian parents would think that a kid like Johnny is too unruly and ill-mannered. He doesn't listen to his mother's advice and, worse, he talks back to her. They may also think that asking for a child's opinion is a waste of time. Asian children may agree. Why argue with your parents if what they are doing is for your own good? Parents know best because they have been there and done it. Why experiment with something new if the answer is already out there in front of you? Why make the same mistakes someone else has already made?

If little Johnny lives in China, his parents will bundle him up like a little Michelin man when it gets cold outside. They will give him antibiotics the minute he sneezes, thinking it will prevent him from getting sick. So when he does get sick, common antibiotics may no longer work and he may become really sick.

Most Chinese children continue to obey their parents even when they have become adults and left home. Likewise, parents remain closely involved with the lives of their children. Without their children, Chinese parents' lives have little meaning.

This is also one of the reasons why many Chinese managers love to micromanage and give all kinds of directions to their subordinates all the time. Their subordinates also look up to them as authority figures, rather than just co-workers with a different professional function. Like parents, they just can't let go.

The Family Economic Unit

The traditional Confucian world has five categories of reciprocal relationships: between the emperor and his officials; between parents and children; between husband and wife; between siblings; and between friends. Each relationship has its own codes of conduct. The first relationship no longer exists. Three of the five relationships have to do with the family.

The strong family bond has been the bedrock of stability in China, allowing the people to weather numerous regime changes, natural disasters and foreign invasions.

The Westerner's view of children can be a little different. Children are gifts from God, and the parents' job is to raise them until they are adults. Thereafter they should leave home and be off on their own. Their relationships will become more cordial and less intimate. They may get together for major holidays, such as Thanksgiving and Christmas, or they may not. Compared with this, traditional Chinese parents think they have the responsibility to care for their children for as long as they are parents, which is as long as they live. It is quite acceptable today for the parents of the groom-to-be to purchase (or assist in a serious manner in the purchase of) a starter home for him. Otherwise it will be difficult for their only son to get married in today's hypermaterialistic society and the parents' job will never be done. Given how much property prices have gone up in China, this is a tremendous outlay for most families. The children also don't mind receiving such generous assistance from their parents. They think that because their parents are better off, theyshould continue to support them. When they have children of their own, they will repeat the same routine.

This practice is not as common in the US, where adult children are supposed to be independent and fend for themselves. Many would not even accept family assistance if it was offered. However, this attitude is slowly changing because of rising home prices and stagnant wages.

The practice of assisting sons to get started is also quite common in other parts of Asia, such as South Korea. Property prices in Shanghai and Seoul have seemingly defied gravity, but most parents just grin and bear it. Piecing together life savings towards helping a son to get started is a time-honored tradition and a natural part of Asian parenting.

In a Confucian society, mutual support allows family members to endure economic tough times so as not to be held hostage by the vicissitudes of the market. This strong family bond also doubles as a hidden yet substantial economic block. This makes it difficult for financial analysts using traditional metrics based on individuals to gauge Chinese consumer behavior. As a result, their conclusions about the Chinese economy, especially its housing collapse, can be off the mark.

The SOE Family

China's giant SOEs were the instrument of the state during the era of planned economy, when they were charged to allocate scarce resources to advance national objectives.

Today's SOEs have taken on the role of change agents. They lead the charge to restructure industry sectors where they were once privileged. In so doing, some have become fierce competitors.

Many SOEs are listed in the NYSE, HKSE and other major stock exchanges around the world. By listing China's Big Four state-owned commercial banks, phone carriers, oil and gas producers, plus mining, steel, and construction companies, the government hopes to enlist public investors and tighter regulatory regimes to compel these powerful giants to adopt market practices, something that it has trouble doing at home.

However, making SOEs adopt market discipline is like parents sending a child to school to get educated. School and family represent two different authorities. However, there is no question which one is more important. During the day, the child attends school to get his formal education. When he comes home from school in the afternoon, he gets a lesson on life from his parents. His parents are the real authority, and the child knows it. If he wants to go to the mall with his friends or get that new gadget, he must please his parents first. If he does poorly at school, he has to face the ire of his parents, not his teachers.

If the child has disciplinary problems, he may be suspended from school. His parents may give him a tongue-lashing, shame him with guilt or reduce his privileges. They may appeal to his teachers and principal for leniency, and pull all kinds of guanxi to keep him in school. If these don't work, they may send him to another school, if they have the means. However, if the child disobeys his parents or behaves badly towards them, he has a real problem. In a filial society, being disrespectful to one's parents is odious and repugnant. His relatives will shun him and his friends will be ordered by their parents not to associate with him. He has few allies and no real means of support, so he is in a seriously bad situation. Unless he wants to wander the streets, he has to go home and face the music.

By the same token, SOEs are like members of a big extended state family. The market is like the boarding school where management goes for its education. Periodically, the report card will show the company's sales and asset size, margins, price-earnings ratios, leverage ratio, return on assets, return on equity and all kinds of financial metrics that investors love to look at. However, as long as management remains in the SOE system, its fate will be determined by the state, not by the market.

If his company does well, the manager will humbly acknowledge it. If the results are poor, he will get a serious lecture from his superiors, even though they may not have the expertise to judge his performance. But regardless of how the manager performs, he is still treated as a member of the state family. If he does well, he will get respect from his peers, pay himself a big bonus or get promoted. If he does poorly, he will be relieved and reassigned somewhere else in the state system. The risks and rewards for SOE managers are asymmetric. The risks are underwritten by the state, while the management reaps the rewards.

The market that the state depends on to help supervise SOEs is seriously handicapped. Investors cannot force a change in management in the way that most publicly traded companies have to because the state maintains control by appointing friendly board members and loyal senior managers.

The only thing the frustrated investors can do is sell their shares and drive down the share price. But that doesn't bother the management or the state either because none of them are personally affected by it. As a result, errant SOE managers will never have to lose their jobs or suffer the kind of public indignity that their unfortunate Western counterparts have to face.

To further reform its economy, China must improve the performance of its giant SOEs by making them compete according to market rules. To do so, the state must allow the market to perform its supervisory functions, fully and unconditionally.

Bibliography

Fung Yu-lan, *A History of Chinese Philosophy, Vol.1, p. 2,* translated by Derk Bodde, Princeton University Press, 1953.
Deng Xiaoping quotes, www.brainyquote.com, reviewed Jan 2016.
Lucien W. Pye, *China: Erratic State, Frustrated Society,* Foreign Affairs, Sep 1, 1990.
Zhang Weiwei, *The China Wave, Rise of a Civilization State,* Ch. 1, 3.2, World Publishing Corporation, 2012.
Martin Jacques, *When China Rules the World,* P. 505–507, Penguin Books, 2012.
Francis Fukuyama, *The China Model: A Dialogue between Francis Fukuyama and Zhang Weiwei,* New Perspective Quarterly, Vol. 28, Number 4, Fall 2011.
J.E. Manning, *Membership of the 112th Congress: A Profile,* Congressional Research Service, November 26, 2012.
C. Rampell *First Thing We Do, Let's Elect All the Lawyers,* The New York Times, Feb. 23, 2012.
www.gov.cn
Jack Weatherford and Dulmaa Enkhchuluua, *Mongols; Children of the Golden Light,* P. 23, The Lonely Planet, 2008.

Bibliography

11

Moral Hazard or Moral Imperative?

Is a Chinese Minsky Moment Coming?

China's binge investments since 2008 have racked up a huge amount of debt in its financial system. Much of it went for fixed asset investments, especially property development. This raises the concern that if the Chinese property bubble was to burst, it could lead to a Minsky moment (see below), followed by a devastating Lehman moment and a financial collapse.

According to McKinsey, China's total debt to GDP reached a staggering 282 percent in the middle of 2014, up from 158 percent in 2007, if financial sector obligations are included (the comparable US figure is 269 percent.) Such a rapid increase in system leverage is indeed alarming, especially when much of it comes from property development, shadow banking and local government borrowing. The last two financing venues were practically non-existent a few years back.

The late economist Hyman Minsky described three stages of debt financing and their impact on financial system stability. Let's see whether it can be applied to China.

From best to worst, the three stages are: hedge, speculative, and Ponzi financing. In hedge financing, a borrower is financially strong enough to meet interest and principal repayments with internally generated cash flows. In speculative financing, the borrower can only afford interest payments and is no longer able to make any principal repayments. In Ponzi financing the borrower cannot satisfy either interest or principal repayments. He has to keep borrowing to refinance his debt and stay in business. The result is a continuous buildup of debt without any viable means of reducing it.

During a period of prosperity, investors grow complacent about the investment environment. They chase after deals and flood the market with plenty of risk capital. Credit standards are lowered and investors shift from hedge financing into more speculative financing. They reason that even if the borrowers' credit metrics have declined, their cash flows should at least allow them to cover their interest payments. Plus, over time, growth should allow these issuers to build up cash to make the principal repayments.

However, when growth stalls, the financial circumstances of these speculative borrowers can deteriorate faster than the financiers can react. Now the issuers can no longer pay interest on the mountains of debt that they have incurred, not to mention make any principal repayments. In fact, they have to keep borrowing new money just to stay afloat. In credit rating terms, this type of credit is firmly in the highly-likely-to-default category.

While investors may have started out doing hedge financing, they become reluctant Ponzi financiers because of the rapidly deteriorating financial circumstances of the borrowers. When they realize this, they cut their credit lines or call their loans back. This puts further upward pressure on the pricing of credit and may even shut off the borrowers' access to funding. This scenario is referred to as a Minsky moment.

Minsky further stipulated that if more investors practice Ponzi financing, the entire financial system could be destabilized. When that happens, the government has no choice but to step in and launch a rescue. This is a potential scenario for China. However, the Minsky moment is less likely to happen there because of the culture.

Sunset for Suntech

Suntech is a typical indebted Chinese company that went through debt restructuring and reorganization.

Debt-fueled boom-and-bust cycles have decimated many industries in China. After the government had anointed certain industries, such as solar power, coal and steel, investors and lenders loosened their purse strings without considering the inevitable. The Minsky moment can arrive in one of these hot industries when it is least expected. Solar power is one such example.

Suntech Power was once the largest solar panel manufacturer in the world and a poster child of China's emerging predominance in solar manufacturing. The company had a successful initial public offering (IPO) on NASDAQ in 2005. With an ambitious CEO and an abundance of investor funding, the company grew its production capacity to a massive 2 GW annually in 2008. However, its downfall began shortly afterwards when demand for solar panels plummeted as a result of the global recession.

Like many other industries also heavily dependent on fixed asset investments, solar has a typical cyclical dependence. With low barriers to entry, supply can overwhelm demand very quickly. Prices will drop, operating cash flows will turn negative, and borrowers will find it difficult to meet both interest and principal payments. Companies in such dire straits must borrow more just to stay afloat. The music stops when creditors realize the severity of the problem and pull the plug. This typically occurs when the industry outlook is at its bleakest. This is the Ponzi financing scenario described by Minsky.

Sure enough, the Chinese solar industry became massively overbuilt relative to actual demand. Exports fell when European governments rolled back panel subsidies and the US put anti-dumping duties on imports. With USD 2.3 billion of debt, owed mostly to Chinese banks, including USD 541 million of senior notes and USD 50 million of convertible debt owed to foreign investors, Suntech's debt was too great for the new business reality. Cash flow was tight and the company missed scheduled debt payments.

In March 2013, Suntech filed for bankruptcy protection in China. In April 2014, Shunfeng Photovoltaic International Limited acquired Suntech's major subsidiary, Wuxi Suntech, for RMB 3 billion (approximately USD 492 million), or roughly one-third of the company's outstanding domestic debt. In early 2014, the company filed a petition for Chapter 15 bankruptcy in the US to stave off an involuntary bankruptcy petition sought by foreign investors.

Suntech's journey towards bankruptcy took some twists and turns. When its financial travails first emerged, there were rumors of an old-fashioned bailout by the local government, but the higher authorities likely discouraged it in favor of a market solution. There are a number of reasons why Suntech's bankruptcy was handled this way. First, it was an extremely high-profile case with lots of media attention. Plus, there were many different stakeholders involved, including domestic lenders, foreign bondholders, shareholders, local government and, last but not least, the employees.

Not only did these stakeholders not share the same interest, but their priorities were different from a US-style bankruptcy process, where employees stand in line to receive some of the back pay they are owed. However, they are not a central party in the bankruptcy discussion—the capital providers are.

In Suntech's bankruptcy reorganization, stakeholders were affected to different extents. Domestic banks fared best since they had access to pledged collateral of plant and equipment. Domestic creditors were also more amenable to a restructuring proposal because they wanted to maintain banking relationships and appear supportive in the eyes of the local government so as to participate in its future businesses.

Foreign investors with unsecured senior and convertible notes were effectively subordinated to local creditors. They had little recourse to Suntech's assets on the Mainland, so they couldn't pose much of a challenge. Suntech's NASDAQ-listed shareholders were mainly foreign investors, including hedge funds, and they were helpless at the bottom of the priority totem pole.

Looking back, the most important consideration in this bankruptcy exercise had to be social stability. Suntech's employees would be most affected if it ceased to operate so, in the end, a deal was struck to allow the company to keep its factories humming and get 10,000 employees back to work, thus concluding a chapter in debt resolution with Chinese characteristics.

Market Reform with Chinese Characteristics

In China, investors, creditors and regulators often work together to help troubled borrowers get over their financial difficulties. In principle, these stakeholders have very adversarial mandates, as in the case of Britain or the US, both established markets with well-developed modern corporate capital structures and regulatory regimes. In China, however, these different stakeholders are more or less in it together, with the paternal government playing the important role of mediating behind the scenes.

In the US, creditors are normally behind the winding up of failed borrowers. In the bankruptcy recovery process, secured creditors rank highest in terms of payment priority, right behind the government and the employees. However, in China, no one seems to be that much more powerful than any other. There, borrowers often skillfully play the others in a game where they have supposedly few legal rights. The main reason is that all stakeholders must adhere to an important but unspoken rule—social stability.

Social harmony is an unwritten rule in Chinese decision-making. It is usually manifested in some version of the strong supporting the weak. Because this tradition has been further reinforced by socialism, the Chinese believe that those who are better off have a duty to assist those who are less fortunate.

For example, it is considered essential for a wealthy relative to take care of their kin in times of need. It is also reasonable for workers to accept across-the-board pay cuts to avoid layoffs when times are bad (Nucor, the largest and most profitable US steel company, also had a no-layoff rule during the recession); for a well-capitalized company to extend support to a related company in distress, or to hire workers who have been laid off from failed businesses; for a supplier to work around payment terms for a weakened buyer; for a bank to modify the terms for a troubled borrower; or for a regulator to practice forbearance.

This practice has both its pros and cons. In 2000 I caught the technology bug and left Lehman to become the CFO of iSwitch, a private tech company headquartered in Shenzhen. After raising a private venture round, we prepared the new business plan for this mobile interconnect player in earnest, including a potential IPO. However, shortly afterwards, the hot technology market stalled and the NASDAQ began dropping like a rock. This market reality forced us to re-evaluate our strategy.

We decided to adjust to the new reality. First, we would actively seek potential joint venture partners, such as some of China's giant telecom firms with deep pockets, to help defray the costs of development and marketing for our most promising products. Second, we would develop a contingency plan to downsize our ambitious targets, including potential layoffs.

In the 1980s, US companies regularly laid off their employees in large numbers to adjust to the Japanese manufacturing supremacy in auto, steel, televisions and even computers. Even blue-chip companies such as IBM had to restructure and implement large layoffs. In fact, being laid off was almost considered to be a rite of passage for many workers. As I had worked in the US, I proposed a US-style restructuring plan that refocused our businesses onto those that had the near-term visibility of cash generation, because cash is king in a recession. It called for us to reassign high performers to these more promising areas and to let go the poorer performers, albeit with generous severance packages. This plan was expected to allow us to ride out the tough financing environment for another two years.

The CEO and other senior managers had different ideas. Instead of announcing the plan on a Friday afternoon as they normally do in the US, they wanted to have a consensus on the problem. So for two long weekends, twenty of the senior managers holed up in the conference room and discussed what to do. As with most meetings that have too many participants with different ideas, it was unproductive and we were unable to reach agreement.

At the end of yet another day-long session, all of a sudden someone raised his hand and suggested that we should all cut our salaries to help the company ride out the storm. Surprisingly, everyone agreed, so that was settled. However, that solution also saw the strong performers leaving the company when they could while the dead wood remained in house.

This approach, where staff willingly work reduced hours or take a salary cut, is quite common in Chinese companies. However, while this practice may be socially acceptable, it prevents the management from making the necessary tough decisions. Therefore it doesn't make the company a stronger competitor in the long run.

The Chinese tradition of sharing the pains and gains coupled with an unwillingness to cause hardship to partners represents a significant departure from conventional business practices.

In the old days, a young man would begin his career in a Chinese family business as an apprentice. He would work in the shop during the day to learn his craft, and sleep on the floor at night. His pay would go up when business was good, and decrease when it was bad. He was treated as a family member and he acted like one. Over time, he also learned to think and behave like the owners. When workers and management share the same goals, they learn how to compromise and work out their problems together.

This runs counter to the adversarial labor and management relationship often seen in the West. This Chinese all-in-the-family approach may be irrational to Westerners but it is humane to the Chinese. It may be a moral hazard in the Western sense but is a moral imperative to Chinese people. These hidden cultural factors are also why it is so hard for Westerners to correctly forecast China's economy.

However, this also makes enforcing creditor rights, a basic tenet of the market economy, a challenging proposition in China.

In China, people are also very concerned about their own self-interests and will fight hard to protect them. However, few would want to be seen as that egregious person who would openly benefit from the miseries of others because doing so would destroy social harmony, invite public scorn and be against Ren.

Because of this matrix, the inevitable collapse of the Chinese banking system, a well-founded opinion drawn from the experience of developed countries, remains a speculation. This is not to say that some forms of financial system distress will not occur in China, but it will unlikely be as severe as a Western-style financial crisis.

The standard argument goes as follows. Massive numbers of Chinese loans have gone sour in financing ghost towns and redundant manufacturing facilities. Since the seriously indebted borrowers cannot afford to repay, banks will have to charge off their loans, which will deplete their precious capital. If banks don't meet capital standards, the regulators won't allow them to lend. This will cause the banks' balance sheet problems to develop into a liquidity crisis, and precipitate a downward economic spiral, much like what had happened in the West in late 2008. However, this dire scenario has yet to occur in China, despite the naysayers' impeccable logic.

Compared with the developed economies, China's financial system is still a work in progress. As such, it should be even more susceptible to the imbalances that can spin out of control and cause havoc to the broader economy. However, this scenario didn't materialize in the late 1990s, when Chinese banks were loaded with much higher levels of non-performing loans (NPLs) than they are today. (In the late 1990s, Standard & Poor's estimated that the Chinese banking system had upwards of 40 percent NPLs.) At that time the Chinese government had only a fraction of the resources that it has today. (According to the State Administration of Foreign Exchange, China's total foreign currency reserve was only USD 150 billion in December 1999 compared with USD 3.33 trillion in December 2015).

There are many reasons why a severe financial crisis has not yet happened in China and, even if it does happen, it is unlikely that it will follow the scenario that Western observers have laid out.

First, the Chinese traditions of tolerance and shared sacrifice have done much to ameliorate the self-interest forces that would drive large-scale financial collapse as a result of market panic. When most investors get nervous about the economy and sell, the market can crash overnight. When creditors all pull their lines at the same time, companies can collapse en masse. This kind of herd-driven volatility happens quite often in the Shanghai Stock Exchange (SSE), where the mostly individual investors gamble, sometimes with borrowed money. However, it hasn't yet happened in the corporate space, where large banks and institutions dominate and the government's strong arm is always in the background.

By definition, a missed payment or the restructuring of a loan agreement would constitute a credit default by a borrower. When that happens, it sets into motion an involuntary bankruptcy petition by the creditors. However, in China, creditor-driven insolvencies are not that common.

11 Moral Hazard or Moral Imperative?

When workers are willing to accept pay cuts, creditors are willing to restructure their loans and regulators are reluctant to enforce rules, instead opting for the parties to negotiate among themselves, financial disasters can't occur that easily. When players don't act rationally in the Western sense and the government is always there to act as a buffer, the outcomes are not that predictable. Also, China still has a restrictive capital account, where large currency outflows are limited. Therefore the Chinese financial system has yet to collapse. Instead it has morphed into a slow grinding workout process in the finest Chinese tradition.

China's high property prices and empty buildings have also frightened many foreign investors. However, the dynamics there are also different.

In the late 1990s, when the Chinese government practically gave away state-owned housing units to SOE employees, it instantly expanded the Chinese middle class, whose fortunes have since been closely aligned with the property market. With the stock market behaving like a casino and bank savings yielding meager returns, property continues to be a preferred way to save and invest for the long-term-minded Chinese.

Now, the Chinese homeownership level has reached a national urban average of over 90 percent (compared with 65 percent in the US). Such a high level suggests that property now represents a significant component of Chinese household net worth.

If a financial crisis occurs in China, and property crashes, it will decimate the largest single asset that most ordinary people have, or share with their families and relatives, and it will traumatize millions who labor hard to buy into the homeownership dream.

However, it is not just wealth that is of concern. Such a scenario, if it were to materialize, would affect ordinary people's confidence in their government's ability to provide financial stability, which indirectly undermines its legitimacy.

And if Japan and the US can serve as precedents, a significant loss of wealth from property can traumatize consumer confidence so much that it would take years or, as in Japan's case, even decades to recover.

A reasonable path to resolving the property overhang is for the government to control new supplies while allowing the market to slowly digest existing inventory through steady growth. If the government has any say, a Chinese real-estate crash will not happen with the same level of ferocity as in the global financial crisis, if it happens at all.

Industry over-capacity is another major concern, as China now has far too much hardware for an economy that aims to be consumer-driven. Massive layoffs can cause social instability, so that's not the preferred way to go. However, without the death and renewal process from a wretched recession, over-capacity will remain, asset prices will stay stubbornly high, bank asset quality will weaken, weak players will meander along and management skills will remain stagnant. It will also take much longer for the economy to work out its excesses.

There are two traditional ways of dealing with this type of problem. The first requires making painful adjustments to market forces. This means shutting down plants and laying off workers en masse to adjust to the slowing demand. The second way continues to rely on growth. This means churning out products to keep workers employed, and depressing prices and margins further.

The Chinese government is taking the Middle Way. It is pushing through market reforms and, at the same time, allowing excess capacity to be slowly digested through mergers and closures, some directly brokered by local governments. The government is also providing job training, early retirement and other assistance to laid-off workers to help them transition into the new consumer economy. These programs are not any different than what the US has done in its past recessions, except that they appear to be more gradual and deliberate.

Additionally, the opening up of new markets, such as through the One Belt One Road Initiative, can help create new markets for Chinese-manufactured products. In other words, the government's strong arms are being used in conjunction with the market's invisible hands in an attempt to bring about the desired economic transformation. However, just how fast and how well this scheme will work remains to be seen.

Sustainable growth is the only sensible path going forward. In order for growth to be sustainable, it should exhibit two quality characteristics: quality of earnings and quality of life. These two are closely related. The minimum requirement for a company to achieve financial sustainability is for its earnings to cover at least its cost of capital. If not, the more a company sells, the more losses it will make, and the more it must borrow to fund losses. The end result is a piling up of debt without any viable means of reduction. Over time, this Ponzi scenario will lead to financial instability.

To achieve sustainable growth, China should accelerate its financial reforms to promote a more efficient market that aims to reward strong performers and weed out the weak ones.

The quality of life requirement is just as important. As China is becoming a middle-income society, subsistence of its 1.36 billion people is no longer a major concern. Instead, quality of life has moved more front and center in people's minds. If growth at all costs ends up badly contaminating the air, the water and the food chain, it will be difficult for people to live healthy lives and raise their families in the traditional sustainable manner.

China's World Trade Organization (WTO) admission in 2001 helped to increase the competitiveness of domestic players to the point that foreign firms are no longer considered to be a serious challenge. In this environment, a new driver is needed to reinvigorate the economy. Private enterprises, especially those serving consumers, can be this new driver. With the private sector now accounting for over half of China's GDP and much of its growth, its future is bright. However, limited financing channels and government red tape continue to plague China's private companies. In order for them to drive the new economy, they should be provided with better access to credit by state banks and alternative financing channels.

In China the state's strong arms and the market's invisible hands have worked side by side before to transition to a market economy with Chinese characteristics, while avoiding the destructive boom-and-bust cycles often seen in Western markets.

Between 1998 and 2004, when China was carrying out its major SOE reforms, its economic conditions were a lot more fragile than they are today. Yet when more than 30 million state workers were laid off and had to fend for themselves, it unleashed their entrepreneurial spirit that helped to usher in today's market economy. Today, with an estimate of 5 million workers to be made redundant over a period of five years from heavy industry, such as steel and coal, but with a much larger economy and a stronger safety net, the situation is arguably a lot more manageable than back then.

While the Chinese government should not pick winners and losers in the marketplace, it can use its authority to enact forward-looking changes that are difficult to achieve in a Western system. In this respect, the government should further its reforms by tearing down bureaucratic barriers, strengthening the rule of law and eradicating official corruption. Over time, these changes should bring about an improvement in business efficiency that will help to drive sustainable growth in the Chinese economy.

Local Government Debt, Shadow Banking, Stock Market and ...

With Chinese characteristics, China's journey towards a market economy can be a bit confusing to observers. Very often, investors and market observers zero in on the latest troubling signs of the Chinese economy and sound the alarm. Local government debt, shadow banking and the stock market crash have all been cited as potentially disruptive events, any one of which could trigger a painful collapse of the Chinese economy. Although these are legitimate concerns, the Chinese situation is not necessarily as dire as some Western commentators have made it out to be.

China is fundamentally different from the West, where governments play mainly a passive supervisory role. In China the government is actively involved in many aspects of its markets, and almost all of the problems we see today have their genesis in some form of government involvement.

Local Government Financing Vehicles: Long-Term Good for Value

The rise of Chinese local government debt has raised the specter of a giant debt-fueled asset bubble that, if deflated, would have serious global ramifications. According to China's National Audit Office, at the end of June 2013, total local government debt and guarantees amounted to RMB 17.9 trillion (USD 3 trillion.) Much of it went into local government investments piggybacking on the central government's RMB 4 trillion (USD 586 billion) stimulus program set up in 2009 as a response to the global recession. This level seems staggering to Western hedge fund managers, who wager that the Chinese market will be undone as a result.

To get round the central government's iron grip on direct financing, China's local municipal governments created a funding scheme called the local government financing vehicles (LGFVs). It was estimated that by the end of 2015 almost half of the RMB 19 trillion (approximately USD 3 trillion) of outstanding local government debt and guarantees would be due and have to be refinanced. One may ask why the central authority has allowed LGFVs to grow so much so fast as to become a potential problem.

In China, local governments have always found ingenious ways to fulfill Beijing's directives for growth and self-financing. If land sales and tax receipts have slowed but growth and development targets are being held steady, local governments must borrow more to fund their programs. China's central government knew how this game was played, and it has turned a blind eye on the LGFV phenomenon for the sake of sustaining growth.

On October 14, 2014, China's State Council issued a stern decree stating emphatically that it would not bail out indebted local governments and that they were responsible for their own debt. This warning made it appear that the Chinese government really meant business this time round. However, in China the obvious is always deceptive and the non-obvious is what matters. What's more, the message is often mundane while the subtext can be the real message.

Without a comprehensive suite of laws and regulations to allow local governments to declare bankruptcy, and a liquid market for municipal bonds and distressed debt to trade, such a decree is impossible to enforce. As none of the prerequisites for a municipal debt-clearing process are currently in place, the central government is left with only political maneuvers and jawboning to keep the free-spending local governments in check. In the meantime, it must continue to reform the market and do whatever it takes to defuse the local debt bomb. As there are few viable options, the central government has no choice but to continue to be the reluctant but implicit guarantor of local government debt, at least for the foreseeable future.

In March 2015, Chinese central government indicated that it would allow indebted municipalities to issue up to RMB 10 trillion in bonds directly to refinance their maturing LGFV debts due in 2015. Under this program, each province will be given a quota for bond issuance. The total amount represents about a third of total local government debts outstanding, and it covers 53 percent of debts maturing in 2015.

Since LGFVs are quasi-local government entities established solely for the purpose of funding local government projects, local governments should be directly responsible for their obligations. The market should be allowed to determine which municipal credit to fund or not to fund, and on what terms.

In principle, better-run municipalities will enjoy lower funding costs. Bond terms will better match the underlying infrastructure project cash flows. Banks will also get precious capital and liquidity relief from stronger borrowers, even though they will have to settle for lower interest rates.

There is now yet another option: China's newly established local asset-management companies (AMCs). Provincial-level governments can now make use of the local AMCs to warehouse and slowly digest the NPLs that they had a hand in creating.

In late 2014, several direct municipalities and provinces obtained approval from regulators to set up their own local AMCs, in addition to some that were approved earlier in the year. Although the ultimate size, funding, valuation, loss-sharing mechanism and workout process of the various local AMCs are still a work in progress, they have the potential to catch on very quickly.

In China's current AMC reincarnation, municipal credit will substitute for local financing vehicle credit. The exercise will qualify as yet another form of government bailout. However, unlike the US Resolution Trust Corporation (RTC), whose mandate was to resolve the NPL from the savings and loans corporations, and return taxpayer funding on a timely basis, there is no time or taxpayer pressure on China's local AMCs to do the same. Therefore local governments have the luxury of warehousing distressed real-estate assets and waiting for the market to digest them over time. And if history is any guide, one day it will.

In 1999 I visited a number of bank-owned properties scattered over several cities in China, including some in Pudong, Shanghai, courtesy of Cinda AMC. These properties were in various stages of distress, and Lehman, being a big real-estate investor, was interested in acquiring them. Most of them were in prime locations near city centers. Some were half-finished commercial buildings; others were hotels or convention centers where the developers had run out of funds to continue. There were a couple of unfinished properties in Pudong that were literally only a stone's throw away from the landmark Oriental Pearl television tower.

As was usually the case, ownership of these buildings was not that clear and the banks that held them didn't have clean titles. In addition, their valuations seemed too high for the condition they were in. Thus the process of negotiation and converting ownership was going to be lengthy and messy. Also, Pudong was still being developed at that time, so there were plenty of empty lots and half-finished buildings around. This made it difficult for a US bank to develop a commitment to such a long-term investment. As a result, we passed on them and it was a huge missed opportunity for Lehman.

Today the areas where the distressed properties once were are now teeming with business activity, totally unrecognizable. Some appear to have been developed and redeveloped already. This lesson taught me that in China one must have a long-term view and look beyond the immediate hurdles. Patience is very important and one must accept that the Chinese have their own way of doing things.

The same lesson applies to the many empty building blocks and ghost towns dotted around the Chinese landscape today. In first-tier cities, such as Beijing, Shanghai, Guangzhou and Shenzhen, investors have already paid for most of the units from presales. In fact, house prices have already risen and inventories have dropped to single-digit months in these major cities. So with steadier prices, government subsidies or whatever creative schemes the developers, banks and authorities could come up with, the rest should be digested slowly over time. As long as there is stability, time will solve most problems in China.

Andy Rothman, now an equity strategist with Matthews Asia and a long-time China bull, once argued that because the same Chinese Communist Party runs both the central and the local governments, and banks, it will make sure that the various constituents work together to solve problems. Ultimately, they are all part of a big family where members stick together. This is only partially true. China's local governments don't always see eye to eye with the central government, and there is always a discrete tug-of-war going on between them.

Take golf courses, for example. Since 2004 the central government has banned the construction of any new golf courses in order to preserve the dwindling farmland and protect the environment. However, many beautiful world-class golf courses have continued to spring up all over China as parts of real-estate development projects that local governments wish to promote and the central government has turned a blind eye. When there is a decree from above there is also a response from below. The Chinese saying "The mountain is high and the emperor is far away" amply describes this mentality.

That's just how China is. The country is home to all kinds of contradictions. Different forces constantly jostle with each other, like yin and yang, but if any one side were to win big, it would upset the delicate balance and spell trouble for the rest. So there must be a conscious and balanced effort for creating change. At the end of the day, progress will be made the Chinese way.

Scared by the Shadows

Another popular concern is the Chinese shadow banking system, which is an alternative financing channel once encouraged by the government to take pressure off the banks after the onset of the global financial crisis. Most troubling is the Wealth Management Product (WMP) issued by loosely regulated trust or leasing companies for financially strapped issuers. Because of tightening lending criteria, companies in out-of-favor sectors are shut out of the conventional bank-loan market. WMP rose to offer an alternative. The typical WMP consists of a cocktail of stock and money market funds, corporate bonds and trust products, cobbled together and sold by banks to wealthy investors or companies hungry for yields. However, higher yields also come with higher risks.

In the West, only sophisticated investors such as hedge funds would dabble in such risks. However, in China these products are marketed to wealthy individuals and corporates, with banks functioning as arrangers and agents for their distribution. Many fixed-asset operators have

11 Moral Hazard or Moral Imperative?   211

found it difficult to borrow in China's new economic reality, and shadow banking rose to become a USD 3.2 trillion industry by the end of 2013. The potential collapse of this segment has created a lot of investor anxiety and weighed on global market sentiment.

In January 2014, all eyes were on China Credit Trust Co., the issuer of Credit Equals Gold No. 1, a RMB 3 billion WMP sold to investors. The product in question was to mature on January 31, 2014 when its principal was due. However, the underlying borrower, a coal miner, had already gone bankrupt and its owner was even arrested for conducting fraudulent activities, so no repayment was forthcoming.

In the West, if the issuer of a debt security has gone bankrupt and its owner is put in jail, then the best that investors can expect is to line up and wait for the bankruptcy process to run its course. With luck they will get some of their money back after the process is completed. However, given that this is China, things don't always work the way people expect them to.

On January 28, 2014, China Credit Trust announced that it was to be bailed out by a group of unnamed but most likely government-backed entities. The catch was that investors could only get back their principal investment, and they had to accept a haircut to the last interest payment if they decided to take the deal. Given that investors didn't really have too many good options, most acquiesced and a major financial default was averted.

In March 2014, Chaori Green Energy, a Shanghai-based solar energy supplier, announced that it could only afford to pay a fraction of the full coupon payment due to its bond investors. The market, however, reacted nonchalantly to the first ever onshore bond default by a Chinese issuer.

Even though investors were hoping that the government would again extend its helping hand, they were not exactly holding their breath. The Chinese government has repeatedly reaffirmed its position on risky lending in overheated sectors of the economy. Investors should be astute enough to understand that what they hold are risky investments with the potential for loss.

Another close encounter with default was the Huatong Road & Bridge Group Co., a construction company based in Shanxi province. At the last possible minute the issuer was able to scrape together enough funds to pay interest on its RMB 400 million bond so a much-anticipated default was averted. Again, the local government was rumored to have been involved in the rescue.

At this point it is not clear whether other major troubled Chinese trust companies will be resolved in this way. The most likely scenario is that the government will continue to let smaller issuers default so as to send a message that it is serious about reform.

According to *The Wall Street Journal*, by the end of 2014 the boom in shadow banking was effectively over. Tighter regulations and more investment options have reduced its attractiveness to investors. However, some of the risks have been effectively transferred to the stock market so officials now have a new headache to deal with.

The Shanghai Roller Coaster

While the government has managed for the time being to defuse the shadow banking and local government debt time bombs, the stock market pain is more acute. This time the securities regulator, the China Securities Regulatory Commission (CSRC), did not go slow in carrying out market reforms. Instead it opted for a big bang moment and ended up with a mess on its hands.

Against the backdrop of a slowing Chinese economy, the Shanghai Composite Index (SCI) went up an astonishing 150 percent between June 2014 and June 2015 before it crashed down to earth. By July 9, 2015, it had fallen over 35 percent from its peak and wiped out much of the gain from the previous year. Images of glum investors rushing to meet margin calls further supports the notion that the underlying Chinese economy was about to go into a tailspin and drag the world down with it. As if in sympathy, global markets also sold off. This is reasonable because in most advanced economies the stock market is a barometer of the real economy, and China is the second largest economy in the world. However, in China the SCI has not been a very good economic indicator, especially when it comes to the new economy.

First established in 1990, the original intention of the SSE was to provide large SOEs with an alternative funding channel, away from the state banks. As a result, the SCI, a market capitalization index tracking the equity performance of the more than 1,000 listed companies, remains heavily dominated by stodgy large-cap SOEs. Since it is skewed towards asset-intensive industries that are destined for a secular decline in China's new economic realignment, the index's dramatic rise can only be attributed to massive speculation.

The fastest-growing part of the economy is represented by the more than 40 million private enterprises, many of them catering to the growth sectors of consumers and consumption. However, they are hardly represented by the index. Economic data supports this thesis. China's December 2015 manufacturing Purchasing Managers' Index (PMI) stood at 49.7 percent, reflecting continued weaknesses in traditional manufacturing, especially in the state-owned sector. However, the tertiary sector, comprising consumption and services, has been expanding steadily. The December non-manufacturing PMI was a respectable 54.4 percent, a number that has been slowly trending up since the beginning of the year. In fact, the tertiary sector has been consistently growing faster than the secondary sector over the past decade, with the exception of the two years immediately after the onset of the global financial crisis of 2008, when consumers were jittery and the government had to introduce massive spending programs to take up the slack.

In 2015 the tertiary sector contributed 66.4 percent of GDP growth, 50.5 percent of GDP, which is 10 percent more than the secondary sector. The dreaded consumer slowdown from stock market crashes did not materialize because the wealth effect only affected about 5 percent of the population who dabble in stocks. As Chinese consumers become more affluent over time, the growth of this sector should continue.

China's two-speed economy has puzzled many of those who have known it primarily as a manufacturing and export powerhouse. This has prompted Rothman to ask, "Which China are you looking at?" If we look at the performance of the service sector and take into consideration sustainability, the answer should be obvious. However, for investors hoping for China to continue to drive international trade growth, the slowdown in the growth of imports remains a concern.

To stem further losses at the SSE, the government made SOEs purchase shares in the market. It also banned big shareholders from selling shares for six months and instituted a host of trading restrictions.

The market was whipsawed again in August 2015 when China's central bank, the People's Bank of China, announced a surprise devaluation of the RMB, just a month after the stock market carnage. These nasty surprises have become major publicity mishaps for the government and, at the same time, heightened regulatory risks for investors.

Instead of crossing the river by feeling the stones underneath, this time the regulators decided to jump in with both feet and were quickly in over their heads. Instead of liberalizing gradually in the proven manner and communicating their intentions to the public on a timely basis, they made abrupt decisions.

To manage volatility, the CSRC instituted a circuit breaker rule that halts trading for 15 minutes if the index has fallen by 5 percent, and stops trading for the day if it has fallen by 7 percent. On January 8, 2016, barely four days after this rule was put into effect, the index dropped by more than 7 percent and the authority had to abandon it for fear of triggering more losses. The reason is simple. While the market may behave irrationally, the regulators are not supposed to follow suit. Their major policy flip-flops have caused confusion and increased regulatory risk. As a result, jittery investors have to constantly speculate what it will do next. Since Chinese regulatory actions are often shrouded in political secrecy, investors will just hold on to their safest asset—that is, cash—whenever they can, and the SCI has continued to falter.

Moral Hazard or Moral Imperative?

As expected, the international chorus loudly denounces China for interfering with the market by not allowing poor performers to fail. But was what happened in China any different from what happened to the larger US financial institutions, such as Bear Sterns, AIG, Washington Mutual or even GM, where the US government either brokered or was directly involved in their rescues?

Market discipline stipulates that players should be responsible for their own actions, and be rewarded or punished based on their merits. If a company fails, shareholders should lose their investments, debt investors should accept haircuts and managers should lose their jobs for making the wrong decisions. Serious offenders should be punished according to the letter of the law.

But ordinary folk who are just trying to survive the daily grind and have nothing to do with any of the financial mishaps would be seriously affected if a systemic crisis erupts. Not only could they lose their investments but they could lose their jobs and homes. In this situation the silent majority, who cannot afford to play the financial game of chance, are made to pay for mistakes made by those who can afford to lose.

For any game to be played fairly, the rules must be clear and the referees must have the proper authority to enforce them. In a soccer match, when fights break out among the players, the referees should immediately stop the match and eject those involved. If they choose not to interfere and the fight spill onto the stands, it will be too late. A localized incident, if left uncontrolled, can trigger a violent stampede. Spectators can get trampled and injured for just being there. Market discipline is a great concept but is applicable only if all players behave rationally and abide by the same set of rules. Plus regulators must have unmitigated authority and the willingness to enforce them.

Any initiative with a global impact must be studied carefully before it is put into global practice. Consultation is more appropriate than dictating one's own rules onto others or, worse, unleashing one's own disruptive market forces on the rest of the world and then calling it market discipline at work.

Most Westerners would consider the bailing out of banks a moral hazard. No one would argue that the perpetrators of financial crimes should not be punished, but at what cost, and who should be responsible for the collateral damage?

Moral imperative is another frame of reference for this. The Chinese deem it morally imperative for the government to provide a stable environment in which people can live, work and raise their families peacefully. This traditionally Chinese mindset was derived thousands of years ago from their view of the natural order. Because of this, China has not been hesitant in bailing out its troubled institutions.

In the late 1990s I had the opportunity to work with my Lehman colleagues in advising the Chinese government on establishing their AMC. Our proposal was to set up one national AMC to resolve the huge number of bad loans accumulated in China's four large state-owned commercial banks. It called for these insolvent banks to funnel their NPL into the debt clearing house, which would hold public auctions to recover their value. After the NPLs were carved up the government would recapitalize the banks with fresh capital.

This was the model of the RTC set up in 1989 by the US Congress to resolve problem loans from thousands of failed savings and loan corporations taken over by the government. In fact the former Chairman of the RTC, Bill Seidman, was assisting us on this assignment. Besides being an affable gentleman from the US Midwest, he had a wealth of knowledge in finance, economics and politics. What was significant was that he was also the world's foremost expert on how to rescue financial institutions, based on his previous experience of running the US Federal Deposit Insurance Corporation (FDIC) and RTC. Because of that he was extremely well regarded by the officials we met.

Our team was recommending the US RTC model to Chinese officials. The rationale was that with such a large amount of bad debt residing in China's banking system, it would drag down economic growth for years to come. A rapid resolution was the best way to jump start growth, propel China into a market-based economy and recover the investments for the government. This was a Western practice and also the model that Lehman had successfully helped establish in Thailand and Indonesia shortly after the Asian financial crisis.

However, the Chinese had a different idea. They ended up setting up four separate AMCs, each tasked with resolving the NPL from a single state-owned commercial bank. So Cinda AMC was set up to resolve bad loans from the China Construction Bank, Huarong AMC was to resolve the bad loans from the Industrial and Commercial Bank, Great Wall AMC was for the Bank of China, and Orient AMC was for the Agricultural Bank of China. There were many reasons why the Chinese government had wanted to set up separate AMCs but none was obvious.

First, the government wanted to retain control of the debt-resolution process. It did not want foreigners managing sensitive auctions involving poorly documented legacy bad debt that didn't quite have the same purpose and definition as conventional bank loans in the West. The government specifically didn't want foreign hedge funds, which they viewed as vultures, to get involved and to sue them in foreign courts for recovery.

11 Moral Hazard or Moral Imperative?

It would be unseemly for a country as huge as China to be dragged into foreign courts and humiliated by some tiny but vicious vulture funds.

Second, the government believed that there was substantial value trapped in the legacy NPL, and they preferred domestic investors to acquire them. In the late 1990s, this meant only the mostly state-owned and local government entities were able to bid on NPL auctions.

Third, each one of the big banks wanted to have its own say in the AMC process. This was Chinese politics at play. Last and most important, the government didn't want the huge bankruptcies and job losses that come with a drastic debt-clearing process. It considered these to be culturally unacceptable.

So, in a sense, it was government funds going from one pocket to another. More importantly, it was obvious to us that the Chinese government was not interested in speeding up the NPL clearing process. This was a long-term internal affair involving the ongoing restructuring of SOEs, as far as the government was concerned. It wanted to clean up the banks at its own pace while stimulating the economy at the same time.

The Chinese government also believed strongly, as a result of its ongoing economic restructuring, including making the banks behave more commercially, that long-term Chinese economic growth would eventually raise the value of the NPL assets, either through monetization of equity from debt-to-equity swaps, or through the realization of the underlying collateral assets, most notably real estate.

As expected this all-in-the-family approach was called the mother of all moral hazards by Western observers. However, judging by the red-hot Chinese economy since the AMC exercise, the government's initial assessment turned out to be absolutely prescient, even though its solution was a bit unconventional.

China's homegrown approach worked quite well. While foreign observers may have misgivings about the moral hazard inherent in the exercise, the end result is that the economy kept growing and the Big Four banks are now much stronger and better-run commercial entities than before.

Just as in a family, when parents pull their children with love and support and, at the same time, push them with hard work and discipline, it can help them to develop into responsible adults, in a developing economy, the state and the market can work side by side without risking major market dislocations that can harm ordinary folk. China's AMC exercise is a fine example of this kind of thinking.

In 1998, a year after the onset of the Asian financial crisis, the Hong Kong government spent the equivalent of USD 16 billion buying up shares to shore up its stock market. Prior to the intervention, the stock market had been dropping like a stone and had lost over half of its market value from the high reached in 1997. Property values plummeted and many homeowners were deeply under water with their mortgages.

As a result of the government's intervention, Hong Kong's property and stock markets were stabilized and investor confidence was restored. However, market pundits argued that the intervention had tainted Hong Kong's image as one of the freest markets in the world. They also argued that it would make foreign investors hesitant about re-entering the Hong Kong market. The first assertion is subject to debate while the second one has turned out to be incorrect.

In 2008 the US government, under the authority of the Troubled Asset Relief Program, purchased equities in several major banks (including JP Morgan Chase and Bank of America), AIG, General Motors and Chrysler.

The US intervention was an about-face to the free-market system that it has always preached. The reasons were systemic stability and job preservation.

If General Motors was to go under, an estimated 2.5 million more US jobs could be lost, which would be a terrible shock to an already hemorrhaging economy. With government backing the rescued auto makers were able to breathe a sigh of relief. They consolidated their operations, restructured their significant legacy pension and healthcare liabilities, and lowered their costs significantly. With leaner operations and healthier balance sheets, they were able to make a fresh start.

The Hong Kong and US rescues had a similar motive. They put people first, and moral imperatives ahead of market principles. Market principles are fine as long as all players abide by the same rules and are well supervised. If not, self-interest can wreak havoc in the economy and hurt innocent folks. But regardless of whether the market is rational or not, the need to provide social stability is a moral imperative that falls squarely on the shoulders of every government. Perpetuating the human race is a universal mandate and the primary responsibility of our leaders.

11 Moral Hazard or Moral Imperative? 219

Bibliography

McKinsey Global Institute, *Debt and (Not Much) Deleveraging*, P. 75, Feb 2015.
Hyman Minsky, *The Financial Instability Hypothesis*, Working Paper #74, P. 7, Levy Economic Institute of Bard College, May 1992.
Hyman P. Minsky, Distinguished Scholar, Levy Economics Institute of Bard College, www.levyinstitute.org, reviewed Jun 2015.
Wayne Ma and Emily Glaser, *Suntech Is Pushed Into Chinese Bankruptcy Court*, The Wall Street Journal, Mar 20, 2013.
Katy Stech, *China's Suntech Power Plans U.S. Bankruptcy Filing*, The Wall Street Journal, Jan 31, 2014.
David E. Rovella, *Bankrupt Solar-Panel Maker Suntech Seeks Court Protection*, Bloomberg News, Feb 22, 2014.
Suntech Company Reports, reviewed Feb 2015.
Rick Barrett, *No Layoffs at Nucor Despite Bad Economy*, Milwaukee Wisconsin Journal Sentinel, www.jsonline.com, May 22, 2010.
Official Reserve Assets, Foreign Currency Reserves, safe.gov.vn, reviewed Jan 2106.
List of countries by home ownership rate, Wikipedia, reviewed December 2015.
Xing Yun, *Zero* Bailout Policy for Local Gov't Debt Leaves Doubts, CaixinOnline, Oct 9, 2014.
Don Weinland, *China Approves Second Batch of Asset Management Companies*, South China Morning Post, Nov 25, 2014.
Li Xiang, *More Local Govts Allowed to Establish AMCs*, China Daily, updated Nov 26, 2014.
Central Intelligence Agency, *The World Factbook, Country Comparison: Public Debt*, Jan 2.
Jack Perkowski, *China's Debt: How Serious Is It?* Forbes, Jan. 21, 2014.
The Economist, *Local-Government Debt, Counting Ghosts, China Opens the Books of Its Big-Spending Local Governments*, Jan 4, 2014.
Chen Weihua, *China's Local Government Debt in Spotlight*, China Daily, Nov 29, 2014.
Lu Jianxin and Gabriel Wildau, Reuters, *China Issues Rules to Limit Bond Investment by Shadow Bank Products*, Feb 13, 2014.
Bloomberg News, *First China Onshore Default Looms as Chaori to Miss Payment*, March 5, 2014.
Grace Zhu, Lingling Wei and Wynne Wang, *China's Huatong Road & Bridge Avoids Bond Default*, The Wall Street Journal, Jul 23, 2014.

Local government debt in spotlight, China Daily, Nov 29, 2014.
The Wall Street Journal, *Shadow Lender Strives to Avert Loss*, Lingling Wei, Jan 27, 2014.
Bloomberg News, *China Credit Repays Principal to Bailed-Out Trust Holders*, Jan 30, 2014.
Kate Mackenzie, *Moral Hazard, the Chinese Way*, FT Alphaville, Aug 19 2013.
Jack Perkowski, *China's Debt: How Serious Is It?* Jan 21, 2014.
Grace Zhu, Lingling Wei and Wynne Wang, *China's Huatong Road & Bridge Avoids Bond Default*, The Wall Street Journal, Jul 23, 2014.
Bloomberg News, *China Credit Repays Principal to Bailed-Out Trust Holders*, Jan 30, 2014.
Shen Hong, *China's Shadow-Banking Boom Is Over*, The Wall Street Journal, Dec 23, 2014.
Kate Mackenzie, *Moral Hazard, the Chinese Way*, FT Alphaville, Aug 19 2013.
Reform of State-owned Enterprise in China, China Labor Bulletin, last updated Dec14, 2007.
Prudence Ho, *Investors Pile into Cinda IPO*, The Wall Street Journal, Nov 24, 2013.
General Motors Chapter 11 reorganization, Wikipedia, reviewed June 2015.
Wikipedia, *List of Countries by Home Ownership Rate*, reviewed December 2015.
Shanghai Stock Exchange website, reviewed January 2016.
National Bureau of Statistics of China website, reviewed January 2016.

12

Exporting China Inc

As the Chinese economy slows down from its rapid pace, its businesses face intensifying domestic competition, rising costs and tightening environmental regulations. As a result, many Chinese companies, flushed with cash and confidence from years of phenomenal growth at home, are actively seeking opportunities overseas with the tacit encouragement of the central government.

China's so-called Going Out strategy was first announced by President Jiang Zemin in 2000. Its original intentions were to develop new overseas markets and prepare domestic companies for the expected onslaught of foreign firms after China's WTO entry. On December 11, 2001, after China had successfully become a full member of the WTO, the preparation of Going Out by Chinese companies began in earnest.

In 2005 the NDRC mentioned Going Out in its 11th five-year plan as a strategy to enhance international cooperation, which in Chinese speak is a synonym for overseas development. In March 2011 the theme was again repeated in China's 12th five-year plan.

Since the pronouncement of the initial Going Out strategy, many Chinese companies have made overseas acquisitions. Some have succeeded but a large number have failed. The incompatibility of the Chinese management style with foreign practices was to blame for a large number of these.

The kinds of Chinese company going out also mirrors China's ongoing development strategy. One of the persistent Chinese growth themes has been urbanization and the associated demand for commodities. According to the World Bank, China's urbanization rate reached 52 percent in 2012, a hefty increase from 48 percent in 2009, but still far below that of the US (83 percent), Britain (80 percent) and Germany (74 percent). During this three-year period, China urbanized 63 million of its rural inhabitants, the equivalent of the entire population of Britain. Even with this rate of urbanization there is still a long way to go before China can catch up with the developed nations.

As China builds new towns and roads to accommodate its newly urbanized citizens, it needs to import more iron ore, copper and other building materials. It also needs imported oil to feed its growing fleets of autos, and chemicals to keep its factories humming. These commodities are strategic to China's growth and they have been an area of intense interest overseas.

While China's quest for commodities will continue for some time, the domestic focus has now shifted from fixed-asset investments towards consumer, industrial-upgrade and quality-of-life sectors. China needs advanced technologies to upgrade its manufacturing capabilities, and new markets for its manufactured products. Many of the industries and markets that China covets are located in countries where such industrial transformation has already taken place, such as in Europe and North America.

Going Out requires Chinese companies to upgrade their management skills to a level closer to international standards. There is also the unspoken desire of Chinese managers to compete with international rivals on their own turf, and to reciprocate what foreign firms have done to them during the past three decades. Since Chinese companies have honed their skills at home, it is now time to let them go out and play with the big boys, the government also reasons.

What's more, China's massive USD 3.33 trillion foreign currency reserve (December 2015) can provide support to qualified companies going overseas. It is also an effective means of reducing the country's huge foreign currency stockpile accumulated from years of trade surpluses and foreign direct investment (FDI).

According to China's Ministry of Commerce, Chinese overseas direct investments totaled USD 90.17 billion in 2013, up by 16.8 percent from 2012. Of this, USD 72.77 billion was made in equity and other forms of investments. From January to July in 2015, Chinese overseas investments rose to USD 63.5 billion, representing a 20.8 percent increase from the same period a year ago.

While the number is big and expected to get even bigger, the total stock of Chinese overseas direct investments is dwarfed by that of the other developed nations. In 2012, total overseas Chinese investment was only USD 509 billion, ranking it 15th in the world, behind the US (USD 4.4 trillion, #1), Britain (USD 1.8 billion, #2), Spain (USD 710 billion, #12) and Italy (USD 528 billion, #13).

As a comparison, China has received much more in FDI into the country than what has gone out. In 2012 it had USD 1.34 trillion of total FDI, making it the number-three investment destination in the world on a stock basis, behind only the US (#1) and Hong Kong (#2). The number for China could be even higher if some of Hong Kong's direct investment destined for the Mainland is included. Even with its current economic slowdown, China still received FDI inflows of USD 289 billion in 2014 and USD290.9 billion in 2013, according to the World Bank.

Europe and North America have become favorite destinations for Chinese companies going overseas. In 2013, Chinese investments in these geographical areas rose by 218 percent and 135 percent compared with 2012, respectively.

Also, the makeup of the investor base has shifted away from SOEs towards local and private enterprises. These accounted for 35 percent of the total overseas investments during the first ten months of 2013, a 23.4 percent increase over the same period a year ago and 3.9 percent higher than the overall growth rate. This should not come as a surprise because China's private sector economy has been growing much faster than the overall economy and it is now responsible for more than 60 percent of its GDP growth.

To sustain their growth, private companies want new markets, technology upgrades and global brands. They are much nimbler than the lumbering SOEs, which continue to be saddled with their aging mandates, labyrinthine organizational structures and outdated approval processes. In addition, private companies are better suited to dealing with the consumer and quality-of-life sectors that the government is now promoting.

According to Forbes, of the 13 major Chinese companies that went global in 2013, ten were private. This diversified group of leading names included Lenovo, Huawei and ZTE in technologies; Tencent and Alibaba in e-commerce; Dalian Wanda in property and entertainment; Sany in industrial machinery; Li Ning in athletic apparel; Geeley in automotive; and Haier in white goods. Only CNOOC, Shangdong Heavy and Bright Foods were SOEs. In 2014, ten Chinese companies made overseas acquisitions. They are Lenovo, Huawei, Dalian Wanda, Fosun, Alibaba, Tencent, Bright Food plus newcomers Wanxiang (automotive and new energy), Xiaomi (smartphone) and Baidu. With the exception of Bright Food, the rest are private companies.

It will be interesting to see how these Chinese investments are faring a few years from now. It will be even more interesting to see how the Chinese acquirers overcome cross-cultural management issues.

When Going Out, Do What the Foreigners Do

The success of Chinese companies in their domestic market is undisputed. Familiarity with local conditions and culture has contributed much to their success. However, these success factors are absent overseas.

Operating environments in developed markets are more established and sophisticated as a result of decades of market development and validation. A Chinese company going overseas has to sink or swim on its own. It has to play by the local rules and can't rely on guanxi for much support, nor can it rely on politicking skills to get things done. Competition is stiff and local players are entrenched, sometimes favored. Rules and regulations are more stringent, and regulators are more vigilant. Labor unions can be powerful and difficult to deal with, especially in Europe and Australia.

Chinese companies accustomed to freewheeling through a fuzzy domestic environment will find it difficult to operate in the same manner overseas.

The long distance from the home office further adds to the challenge. Chinese expatriate managers who are used to deferring decisions to their superiors at home now find they must make them on their own. As a result, some become timid and unable to act quickly enough, while others feel so liberated that they become reckless.

Because they have a limited relationship with foreign domestic banks, most overseas Chinese companies have to continue to rely on Mainland China's banks for funding. If they approach local banks they must demonstrate strong standalone credit fundamentals because parental support is not always accepted as a given. The huge Chinese foreign currency reserve is always tantalizing, but getting a piece of it is never easy.

Foreign labor laws and safety standards are strictly enforced. Relationships with local government are at arms length only. Mindful of conflicts of interest, officials often shy away from assisting Chinese companies in the manner that officials often do in China.

While the host government may welcome Chinese direct investment for jobs and taxes, it has little influence over the regulators. What's more, the media is always watching Chinese companies like a hawk for potential shenanigans.

Vendors and suppliers in developed markets often stick to the letter of any agreement and expect payments on time. Some may even take advantage of Chinese companies that are unfamiliar with local practices to drive up bids. Labor laws can also be overly protective of domestic workers, thus neutralizing any low-cost Chinese labor advantage.

Foreign business practices are different as well. The guanxi that Chinese businesses rely so much on in their home country does not work the same way in developed markets. Lavish gifts are rare and reciprocity is not a given. Rights and responsibilities of all parties are clearly documented, and laws and regulations are strictly enforced rather than renegotiated on the fly.

To Chinese expatriate managers assigned overseas, language and cultural barriers are significant. Some have to rely on translators to communicate with locals. As a result, nuances in communications are often missed. This creates problems later on as the parties may have a different understanding of what has been discussed, or the context in which an agreement was made.

Work cultures are also quite different. Employees in developed countries adhere to strict working hours. Chinese managers, who are accustomed to working 24/7 to boost output, must prioritize and organize their time efficiently. They also have to be nice to their workers and not be too bossy in the manner that they are used to.

For the above cultural reasons, few Chinese companies have been able to replicate their domestic successes in overseas ventures.

For Chinese companies going out to developed countries, they must adjust to a different management style—one that places professionalism over hierarchy, rules over guanxi, and process over practicality. Chinese managers should also be more open-minded and strive to understand the host country's culture, instead of repeating what they have done at home. In addition, they should familiarize themselves with the local language and business etiquette.

Journey to the West

Below is a description of two Chinese companies with overseas ventures. They are Haier, the appliance giant, and China Aviation Oil, the jet fuel trader. They were chosen because they had majority Chinese control, and management culture played a big part in their success or failure. Plus there exists a fair amount of public information about them.

Haier: The Lower Sea

In 2012, Haier, China's best-known consumer brand, also became the world's largest appliance-maker by unit sales. Its success is a testament to the skillful application of traditional Chinese cultural values layered on top of modern management practices in a foreign context.

Like many Chinese companies, Haier can trace its origin to a collective enterprise. Its predecessor, Qingdao General Refrigerator Factory, was one of the many Chinese makers of poor-quality refrigerators in the early 1980s. However, its fate changed forever after it managed to acquire a joint venture partner, the German manufacturer Liebherr. In 1991 the company changed its name to Haier and its business began to take off.

Haier had total revenue of more than USD 23 billion in 2011. If it had been a US company it would have ranked in the upper tier of the Fortune 500. Its success as a foreign entrant in the highly competitive US consumer market mirrors the experience of Japanese automakers in the 1960s and 1970s. At the beginning, Nissan, Toyota and Honda were all selling entry-level compact cars in the US. After familiarizing themselves with the US market and gaining initial acceptance, they localized production and successfully broadened into mid-size sedans, trucks and luxury cars.

In the 1990s, with success at home, Haier ventured overseas. It started small, and it successfully built and operated manufacturing facilities in Indonesia, the Philippines and Malaysia. Its humility allows it to learn the best of foreign cultures and incorporate that knowledge into a local development strategy. Sticking to what it knows best before attempting new ventures is a prudent business strategy, especially for a Chinese manufacturer new to the foreign environment. Its ability to go with the flow and make incremental changes also follows the Tao Chinese management style.

In 1999, Haier entered the US market, and it built a manufacturing facility in South Carolina the following year, supplying small refrigerators to Wal-Mart and other big-box retailers. Although the US was the most sophisticated and competitive appliance market in the world, the compact refrigerator market for dormitories and offices was fragmented and ignored by established manufacturers. The likes of Whirlpool, Frigidaire, Maytag and GE were more interested in the full-size segment where the margins were much higher. This left Haier with a market niche that it could penetrate and expand.

After initial success in the compact refrigerator segment, Haier moved into the full-size market, and began to challenge the established market leaders. It managed to do well in the US, the Mecca of consumerism, by starting small, and attempted only what it knew well.

Much has been written about Haier's success in books and case studies. However, few have related its achievements to the cultural traditions of its founders. My view is that a large part of its success is due to the founders' skillful application of modern management techniques layered on top of a set of traditional Chinese values.

Haier's success was attributed to its visionary founder, Zhang Ruimin, and his right-hand woman, Yang Mianmian. In 1984, when Yang first came to the Qingdao factory, she could not even find a single soul on the shop floor. Despite an official roster of 600 employees, no one was making refrigerators. All the windows in the factory were broken, and the offices were so cold that they felt like the inside of the refrigerators that they were tasked to build. Needless to say, morale was also poor.

In fact, the Qingdao factory was typical of many collective enterprises at the time. It was unproductive, seriously in debt and on the verge of going bankrupt. To survive, it needed a foreign joint venture partner to help it modernize. It found Liebherr, the German manufacturer best known for its heavy machinery such as cranes, mining equipment and refrigerators.

When Yang was attending her training in Germany, her handler remarked that she was different than the other Chinese people who came before her on similar training missions. He said that she had both passion and ideals, while the others were more interested in sightseeing and collecting travel subsidies. Yang was indeed different. Instead of feeling disillusioned about the disastrous Cultural Revolution that ended in the mid-1970s, she buckled down and went to work.

Later, as she ran the factory, she instituted a code of conduct and enforced it diligently. This was also quite unusual. Traditional Chinese behavioral guidelines leave plenty of room for interpretation, not to mention the fact that most workers were still mildly rebellious and looked upon management directives as tricks of the exploitative class.

To be fair, most Chinese companies do have rules, but they often have too many conflicting rules, and too many exceptions to them. As a result, few people follow them. When disputes arise, rules are pushed aside and workers look for senior management to adjudicate. It then becomes a game of who has the best guanxi with the boss, not who is right or wrong according to the rules.

Without effective enforcement, rules are only worth the paper they are written on. A well-crafted set of rules that is diligently enforced makes for successful companies. However, enforcement is also what most Chinese organizations lack most. Sun Tzu said that it is the responsibility of the commander to be impartial and strict in enforcing military discipline.

Similarly, in business it is senior management's responsibility to follow the rules and set an example for its team to follow. If senior managers don't comply with the rules that they ask others to adopt then they have no credibility.

Haier's Chairman and CEO, Zhang Ruimin, is not only a successful Chinese businessman but also a global thought leader. In *The Haier Way* by Jennie Yi and Shawn Ye, Zhang attributed part of his success to his traditional Chinese cultural values. This is indeed true if we examine his management philosophy closely.

Zhang's motivation for constantly reinventing Haier's corporate culture mirrors the tireless motion of celestial bodies, as described in *I Ching*. To win, Zhang strives to understand his competitor's strengths and his own weaknesses. This comes from *The Art of War*. Zhang's depiction of Haier as a corporate family where employees feel supported follows Confucian family values. His penchant for self-improvement comes from *The Book of Great Learning*. Haier's employee code of conduct mirrors Confucian Li virtues. So instead of vague concepts, traditional Chinese cultural values have found practical expressions at the company.

But practicing the Chinese style of management on foreign soil requires some management flexibility. On Haier shop floors there are footprints painted in red, green and yellow. Each color denotes a different status, from red for outstanding performance to yellow for underperformance. Employees belonging to these performance categories have to stand on the appropriate footprints and then tell their colleagues why they are there in front of them.

The system that combines reward and punishment for employees is practiced in China and much of Asia. Workers often get extra bonuses if they do well but have their salaries docked if they perform poorly. However, this system did not sit well with American workers, who considered the punishment part to be insulting. So Haier devised a more culturally amenable approach.

Instead of having employees describe what they have done wrong (a negative push), they have to stand on the red footprints and tell others what they did right (a positive pull). Hopefully over time, Haier managers can help to revitalize management culture back home.

An incident cited by Yi and Ye involved a worker in Haier's South Carolina plant. It speaks volumes about Haier's management flexibility.

The gentleman in question loved listening to rap music while he worked, even though it was against shop rules. But, instead of confronting the employee directly, which might make him feel resentful, Haier management applied the Chinese management practice of peer pressure and subtle influence. It promoted a fellow employee for good conduct and put him next to the employee who played the loud music. The rap-loving employee quickly got the hint and stopped playing music all together. With a simple maneuver, management turned around a problem employee.

Managing by example, going with the flow, eschewing open confrontation and using group pressure to achieve management objectives are all parts of the traditional Chinese culture, as exemplified by the wisdom of Lao Tzu and Sun Tzu.

Zhang's belief that his employees are like rivers whose ideas flow into the Haier Sea is consistent with the Taoist belief that the highest value is like water, which supports all things but does not compete with any. And because the Haier Sea sits below all employee streams, it is in a great position to capture their bubbling energy and innovative ideas. That the executives view themselves as below their employees is a major reason why Haier is so successful at innovating.

In March 2012, Haier spent USD 132 million to buy out its Asian joint venture marketing partner, Sanyo Electric. The deal, which included Sanyo's washing machine and refrigerator units in Japan and six Southeast Asian subsidiaries, at that time represented the largest overseas acquisition Haier had ever made, but it is not stopping.

In January 2016, Qingdao Haier, a Shanghai Stock Exchange-listed company 41 percent owned by Haier, announced the biggest coup of all by outbidding others at an auction to acquire GE's appliance unit for USD 5.4 billion. This purchase will catapult Haier into becoming one of the largest appliance makers in the US market, and put it in a position to challenge Whirlpool, the number-one player.

It will be interesting to see how Haier, which has been running its businesses with a unique management culture, fares with the acquisition of the GE unit, which has a long history and arguably one of the strongest corporate cultures in the US.

CAO: China after Oil

In November 2003, China Aviation Oil (CAO), a listed oil trader in Singapore, shocked the market by announcing that it had incurred USD 550 million in losses from errant derivative trades. As a result, the company had to file for bankruptcy protection from creditors.

Up until then, CAO was a darling of the Singapore Stock Exchange. It was 75 percent owned by its SOE parent, China Aviation Oil Holding Company (CAOHC), and it held a monopoly to import aviation fuel into China. The announcement made major financial headlines and sent a shockwave through the investment community.

The company's once high-flying CEO, a Chinese national named Chen Jiulin, was considered to be a rising star in the Singapore business community. A SOE manager with an entrepreneurial bent, he built CAO from a modest beginning into one of the largest oil traders in Singapore in just a few years.

Shortly after the announcement, Chen left for China. Everyone was on edge, and for good reason. It was barely eight years ago that Nick Leeson, a rogue trader in Singapore, brought down his employer, the venerable Barings Bank. Leeson's unauthorized derivative trading lost USD 1.4 billion for Barings, and in so doing bankrupted the UK's oldest investment bank. In the end, Barings was acquired by the Dutch ING Group for the nominal sum of £1.

In 1997, when Chen took over as CEO of CAO, it had no office and only one other employee, a secretary, according to Hamilton and Zhang. By 2001, through a series of skillful but aggressive maneuvers, CAO had become the sole supplier of jet fuel to CAOHC and an integral part of China's national energy strategy.

In December 2001, CAO was listed on the Singapore Stock Exchange. In 2003 it had total assets of SGD 378 million, SGD 2.4 billion of revenue, and net profit of SGD 54 million. However, in the following year it reported a loss of SGD 885 million, and its net worth plunged to a negative SGD 663 million. Speculative trading had wiped out all the profits the company had ever made.

As the subsidiary of a major SOE, CAO's mandate was to secure jet fuel for China's growing fleets of thirsty airplanes, and to fulfill a vital role in the country's economic development. As a listed company it had to reward investors by growing revenue and profits alongside the red-hot Chinese economy. Herein lies the dilemma.

Both investors and the Chinese government wanted CAO to grow, and grow fast. By acting as a principal instead of an agent, the company wanted to take advantage of market opportunities to make bigger profits. Public investors would benefit from rising stock prices, managers would get larger bonuses and everyone would be happy, or so it seemed. However, amid the enthusiasm for growth and more growth, CAO's management failed to adequately address traders' Achilles' heel: market risk and operational risk.

At the beginning, Chen's derivative trading produced modest profits. This initial success gave him confidence about his ability to call the market. But when oil prices continued to rise instead of fall as Chen had speculated, losses mounted.

After Chen's supervisors at CAOHC heard about the derivatives blow-up, they attempted a Chinese fix. Instead of disclosing the losses to investors immediately as responsible corporate executives would, they worked feverishly behind the scenes to mount a rescue. Their eagerness to support a SOE family member together with their ignorance of corporate governance made for a fatal error.

In order to raise cash to inject into the company, CAOHC sold 15 percent of its shares in CAO to investors without disclosing to them the derivative losses. This blatant act of insider trading would later land Chen and the CFO in a Singapore jail. The Singaporean court also fined three of Chen's superiors in China for insider trading and failure to disclose losses.

Most importantly, the court struck down a motion by the defendants to dismiss the case based on the argument that CAO was acting on behalf of the Chinese government and therefore should be granted sovereign immunity. This legal precedent made it absolutely clear that SOE managers can no longer hide behind the state for protection; they are responsible for their own actions, wherever they are.

The staff's deference to Chen was also a major contributory factor in his downfall. As he was the big boss reporting directly to Beijing, no one dared to challenge him. When an idea came from the boss, everyone would only look at its bright side and heap on praise. No one wanted to offend him by bringing up the risks.

At CAO the only people who could challenge Chen were his superiors in China, but they had no idea about business practices overseas, not to mention the finer points of the accounting treatment of derivatives and modern corporate governance.

It was also quite difficult to manage Chen from almost 3,000 miles away. To many Chinese managers, going overseas is freedom at last. The Chinese saying that a field marshal can even disobey orders from the emperor aptly describes the situation. Managers posted overseas feel that they can finally relax and do their own thing without having to constantly brief their many bosses, or get their approval for every little decision they have to make.

What was unusual, according to Hamilton and Zhang, was that a risk manager first came up with the idea to restructure the first errant derivative trade into a new one of larger size and longer tenure. In this situation a risk manager oddly crossed the line to become a deal maker, and then doubled down on a bad hand.

This type of management culture, where professionalism is subordinated to group unity, is typical of many Chinese companies.

When risks are collectivized and shared, everyone is supposed to be responsible for everything, but in reality no one feels particularly responsible for anything. This can lead to recklessness. In hindsight, CAO should have provided the company gatekeepers (i.e. its risk managers) with enhanced stature and authority to carry out their professional duties. When employees act professionally, the company always benefits.

From the very beginning, Chen enthusiastically endorsed the trade-restructuring idea, believing that oil prices would soon be moving lower to his benefit. To cover the losses, CAO used premiums received from selling options to close the loss-making contracts. If oil prices had dropped, his losses would have been covered by gains from the new contracts and his problems would have been over. But because oil prices kept rising, so CAO had to sell larger and larger contracts to cover the increasing losses.

The risks in these new contracts were poorly understood. They blew up when CAO ran out of cash and banking facilities to cover the margin calls.

What Chen did was akin to what a gambler who has been losing all night long at the blackjack table does. To recoup his losses, he borrows to place larger and larger bets, hoping that the next set of cards will give him the winning hand. He reasons that what goes up must come down, so eventually he should break even. But that's just wishful thinking, as cyclicality in businesses is never very regular or predictable. And even if a gambler has unlimited funds, he will eventually hit against the house limit and have to abandon this strategy.

In CAO's case, it ran out of money while waiting for the oil market to turn around. John Maynard Keynes once said that the market can stay irrational longer than one can stay solvent. But few managers heavily invested in their own ideas are willing to abandon them just to cut losses. The ego that drives them to succeed in the first place also prevents them from dwelling on the negatives.

This is where an important partner, such as a strategic chief financial officer, can bring a sense of objectivity. In a business run by a strong manager without a senior partner to provide the offsetting balance, he will always get his way. If he gambles he may be lucky a few times, but in the long run the odds are against him.

In the *Tao Te Ching*, Lao Tzu says that opposites are what drive the movement of the Tao. So if someone wants to take on an important task, he should not only have a good rationale for doing so but also understand and come to terms with the contrarian opinions before he acts.

Diversity and inclusion enhance the management decision process. The resultant decision will be more powerful because it comes from experts; and more resilient because more people have ownership of it.

A lax risk-management culture was also at fault at CAO. For risk management to work properly, every employee must be vigilant at all times. However, because most managers prefer positive and reinforcing messages, they often view risk management as an exercise for cowards. As a result, risks can grow unnoticed.

Chen was also overly confident about his outlook on the oil market. According to his Caijing interview before he returned to Singapore, he was convinced that oil prices would soon go back down. He had analyzed oil prices over a period of 21 years and found that even during times of war, prices had never exceeded USD 34 a barrel.

Having too strong a conviction can narrow your vision, which prevents you from seeing the big picture. It is also the kiss of death for traders.

What Chen did not realize, and what is now abundantly clear, is the effect that China has on the world of commodities. Its modernization drive ushered in a commodities supercycle that drove prices up for oil, iron ore and just about anything consumable. However, like a double-edged sword, China's current economic slowdown has also caused this sector to hemorrhage badly. Ironically, CAO's jet fuel business was also a part of the newfound demand that drove prices up far longer than it would have historically. Chen's inability to see the whole picture unfortunately also contributed to his demise. In the end, CAO negotiated with creditors to restructure its liabilities and stayed out of bankruptcy.

Chinese companies venturing overseas are often challenged by problems that they have don't have at home. Knowing the strengths and weaknesses of their own management culture and having an open mind can help to smooth the going-out process and increase its chances of success.

Bibliography

British Chamber of Commerce in China, *China's Twelfth Five Year Plan (2011–2015), The Full English Version*, Ch. 52, 2011.

National Development and Reform Commission (NDRC), *The Outline of the Eleventh Five-year Plan for National Economic and Social Development of the People's Republic of China*, 2006.

China Daily, *Reserves to Support Overseas Expansion, Jan 16, 2013.*

Urban Population (%), The World Bank, June 2015.

Central Intelligence Agency, *Stock of Direct Foreign Investments—At Home and Abroad*, The World Fact Book 2014.

The World Bank, *Foreign Direct Investment, Net Inflows (BoP, Current US$)*, January 2016.

english.people.cn, *Going Overseas Holds the Key to Development*, September 2, 2013.

MOFCOM, *Business Review 2013 (II): Sound and Rapid Development in Overseas Investment & Cooperation*, December 2013.

MOFCOM, Brief Statistics on China's Non-Financial Direct Investments Overseas in January–July 2015.

Joel Backaler, *13 Chinese Companies Going Global inn 2013*, Forbes December 21, 2012.

Joel Backaler, *14 Chinese Companies Going Global in 2014*, Forbes Jan 10, 2014.
Joel Backaler, *10 Chinese Companies Going Global in 2015*, Forbes Jan 14, 2015.
Firms Heading Overseas Should Play by Market Rules, english.caixin.com/2014-11-26.
The Tao of Power, Lao Tzu's Classic Guide to Leadership, Influence and Excellence, Ch. 66, R.L. Wing, Doubleday & Company, Inc. 1986.
Haier.com May 2013.
Sun Tzu, *The Art of War*, translated by Lin Wusun, Long River Press, Ch. 11, P. 120, 2003.
Confucius, *The Analects*, Book 15, P. 228, translated by D.C. Lau, Penguin Books, 1979.
The Tao of Power, Lao Tzu's Classic Guide to Leadership, Influence and Excellence, Ch. 66, R.L. Wing, Doubleday & Company, Inc. 1986.
Cheng Shubo, Qiao Yuling, Hao Gengchao, Gao Tianxia, *Chief Executive, The Management Methods of Yang Mianmian*, P. 14, 20, 64, China Industrial and Commerce Press, 2006.
Jeannie J. Yi & Shawn X. Ye, *The Haier Way, The Making of a Chinese Business Leader and a Global Brand*, P. 171–181, Homa and Sekey Books, 2003.
Bill Fischer, Umberto Lago and Fang Liu, *Reinventing Giants, How Chinese Global Competitor Haier Has Changed the Way Big Companies Transform*, P. 53, Jossey-Bass, 2013.
R.L. Wing, *The Tao of Power, Lao Tzu's Classic Guide to Leadership, Influence and Excellence*, Ch. 8, Doubleday & Company, Inc. 1986.
Vladimir Pucik, Katherine Xin, Donna Everatt, *Managing Performance at Haier (A)*, Harvard Business Review, Jul 30, 2003.
Thomas W. Lin, CMA, *Effective OEC Management Control at China Haier Group*, Strategic Finance, May 2005.
Beyond China: Can a New Acquisition Help Haier Crack Japan? Knowledge@Wharton, 9 Nov 2011.
Carlos Sanchez-Runde, Yih-teen Lee and Sebastian Reiche, *How Haier handled Foreign Traditions*, Financial Times CASE STUDIES, April 1, 2013.
Sandra Bell, *International Brand Management of Chinese Companies, Case Studies on the Chinese Household Appliances and Consumer Electronics Industry Entering US and Western European Markets*, Physica-Verlag Heidelberg, P. 193–196, 2008.
Laurie Burkitt, Joann S. Lublin and Dana Mattioli, *China's Haier to Buy GE Appliance Business for $5.4 Billion*, The Wall Street Journal, 15 January 2016.

Stewart Hamilton & Jinxuan (Ann) Zhang, *Doing Business with China, Avoiding the Pitfalls*, Ch. 7, Palgrave Macmillan, 2012.
Wayne Arnold, *After Crash, China Aviation Oil Offers Creditors Sweeter Repayment Deal*, New York Times, 13 May 2005.
China Aviation Oil (Singapore) Corporation Ltd., Statement of Phase 1 Findings, PricewaterhouseCoopers, 29 March 2005.
The Tao of Power, Lao Tzu's Classic Guide to Leadership, Influence and Excellence, Ch. 40, Doubleday & Company, Inc. 1986.
Douglas R. Conant, *How to Make Diversity and Inclusion Real*, Harvard Business Review, 28 July 2011.
Ignorance, Violations, Hesitation Sink CAO Singapore, english.caijing.com.cn, 10 Dec.
China Becomes World's Top Oil Importer, Financial Times, 4 March 2013.
CAO Annual report, 2003.
CAO Company reports.
Stewart Hamilton & Jinxuan (Ann) Zhang, *Doing Business with China, Avoiding the Pitfalls*, Ch. 7, p. 70, Palgrave Macmillan, 2012.
Singapore Levies Fines after Firm Hides Loss, New York Times, 2 March 2006.
Ignorance, Violations, Hesitations Sink CAO Singapore, 10 Dec 2004, english.caijing.com.cn
Diversity and Inclusion at Google, Google.com
Oil Executive Sentenced, New York Times, 22 March 2006.
CAO company website.

13

Cross-Cultural Lessons

Revisiting Traditional Values

Although we live in the twenty-first century, traditional values are still important to us. Chinese traditions of benevolence, moderation, self-discipline, scholarship, respect for order and family values are universal and timeless. The Greek traditions of logic, science and ethics have expanded human frontiers and raised our standards of living, and their sports tradition has established competition as a way of life. Taken together, they can help us better deal with the future.

In the Internet age, we are constantly bombarded by new information every second of every day. With the tap of a finger we can get the latest news and expert advice about anything, at any time, from almost anywhere and on any device. This surfeit of information empowers us and makes us feel sophisticated. However, that's not always a good thing. Today, we have way too much information about everything. We have far too many easy answers and no real solutions. What's more, what we see and hear don't always make us wiser or more content.

In fact, the opposite may be true. When we watch terrorist acts on television, we feel susceptible. When we look at the stock market, we feel worried. When we read news about global warming, we feel vulnerable. When we hear about other people's successes, we feel jealous. When we see how others suffer, we feel ashamed. When we see thin people, we feel fat. When we see strangers, we feel threatened. When we have too many choices, we feel overwhelmed. The avalanche of information does not make us feel better. Instead it stresses us out.

The issues that affect us most today, such as economic survival, personal growth, the welfare of loved ones, our health and wellbeing, how to get along with others and the quest for meaning in our lives are all manifestations of the same human nature that has been around ever since humans knew how to think and reason. And as long as our DNA remains unchanged, we will have to deal with the same eternal issues in our lives.

Life is like an opera. The performers on stage may be wearing costumes that are no longer in fashion and singing arias in Italian or Chinese that were written a long time ago, but the emotions they seek to portray, whether it is the desire for love and affection, despair from loss and betrayal, or a struggle for survival and justice, are what make us unique as human beings. And we can be sure that our children and their children will have to deal with the same challenges in their lives. The fact is that advances do not change how we feel and behave as human beings. What's more, technology doesn't always offer us better solutions.

A long time ago, wise men from the East and West found ways to deal with these eternal problems. Let's examine a few of them.

Family Values

The family should be the foundation of all our relationships. A strong family provides stability for all members and allows children to grow up as well-adjusted young adults. A long time ago, Confucians assigned a set of corresponding rights and responsibilities to parents, children and siblings. The ancient Greeks and Jews had similar roles for family members and placed a strong emphasis on their relationships.

Traditional Chinese parents care for their children with kindness and affection. In return, children should be respectful to their parents and find ways to honor them. Being filial is a way for children to repay their parents' love and sacrifices in bringing them up. This relationship is a bilateral exchange that has stood the test of time.

The Chinese parent–child relationship is materially different from the Western concept of parenting with unconditional love, where parents give their children a lot and ask for little in return. In some families the parent's authority is supplanted by a religious figure, which provides the necessary anchor. But when an authority figure is absent, children can grow up feeling entitled. They don't necessarily listen to their parents much, nor do they feel particularly indebted to anybody. As a result, they are more likely to misbehave.

In today's China, where parents and grandparents compete to spoil their only child with material comforts that they never had, the traditional bilateral relationship has effectively become one-way. Parents enroll their only child in all kinds of afterschool classes and give him the latest electronic gadgets and clothes because they think their precious little one needs all the advantages he can get to compete with other privileged kids. As a result, the child is accustomed to receiving everything but not having to give anything back. Without strict parents or religion as the authority, this style of parenting spoils the child rotten and makes him ill-prepared to take on responsibility in the real world.

A strong relationship between parents and children is important in any family—anywhere. In today's information-rich world, family values are disintegrating faster than the bandwidth is increasing. The speed at which this is happening is quite alarming. The poor parents, who already have to adjust to the new openness now find themselves increasingly ceding the education of their precious ones to the airwave authorities, whose values they don't necessarily concur with.

No wonder children are getting more disoriented and parents exasperated. Now more than ever, young people need to have something solid to hold onto in their formative years so that they don't get pulled all over the place by the vicious social currents. With fewer distractions they can focus on making themselves more productive and valuable to others.

Family can provide just such an anchor, and traditional China was very good at that.

The story of Hua Mulan is a good example of filial piety. Legend has it that the Chinese heroine learned martial arts from her father. When government officials came to her village to draft a man from each household to serve in the army, Mulan put on a disguise and volunteered. She did it so that her aging father could be exempted from the hazardous military duty.

Chinese people adore Mulan for her filial piety—she sacrificed herself to fulfill her solemn duty as a daughter. Disney made her story into a successful Hollywood animated film, replete with martial arts and budding romance. Americans loved Mulan's heroism and femininity but found little resonance with her sense of duty. Being filial to one's parents is not quite befitting to individualistic Americans. It is just the opposite for the Chinese, who believe that Mulan exemplified this very important virtue.

Perseverance

Perseverance is a characteristic common in many cultures. Today, even with the abundance of technology, we still need to work hard if we want to accomplish something significant. Nothing can replace hard work and perseverance.

Thomas Edison, perhaps the greatest inventor of all time, failed hundreds of times before he finally invented the light bulb. Because of his perseverance, mankind was able to leave gas lamps behind.

It is a commonly accepted notion that in order to be really good at any endeavor, you have to invest at least 10,000 hours of hard work into it. Without perseverance you won't succeed. Athletes and entrepreneurs all know this rule well.

There is a Chinese story about a foolish old man who believed that he and his offspring could move a mountain—one shovel at a time. They did it because they didn't want future travelers to struggle with the difficult mountain passage. Like many Chinese tales, the foolish old man exalted a grand virtue, which is to sacrifice short-term comfort for long-term gain, and the self for greater good. However, the lesson of this tale really applies to everything that we do, which is to set long-term goals and chip away at them a little bit at a time. If we are foolish enough and don't take no for an answer, eventually we will succeed.

Tolerance and the Middle Way

The Middle Way favors moderation and eschews extreme behavior. It has both Greek and Chinese origins.

Relatively speaking, Asians prefer moderation while Westerners enjoy extremes. Most extreme sports, such as downhill racing, marathon running, base jumping, skydiving, cage fighting and even competitive eating, come from the West.

We are reminded by our competitive society everyday to push our limits and do our personal best. However, too much of a good thing can be bad.

Overeating can lead to obesity and a host of other medical conditions, such as high blood pressure and diabetes. The remedies are not pleasant at all. After we have become fat from feasting, we go on a crash diet and seriously deprive ourselves so as to get rid of the extra baggage. This feast-or-famine routine severely disrupts the body's natural balance and puts it through undue stress. Did we have to have that extra piece of cheesecake in the first place?

Here the Middle Way guideline suggests that we should eat appropriately for what we do, and not too much or too little. If we labor outdoors, which all of us should do once in a while, we should eat more than we would normally do for our age and physique. If we sit in front of a computer all day long, we should reduce our intake. The old Chinese saying that one should eat only up to 70 percent of capacity is a good Middle Way guideline. And if we do deviate from our mean sometimes, because of holidays or whatever, it's fine, as long as we revert to it over time.

Spending more than we can afford can lead to personal bankruptcy, followed by painful rehabilitation of our finances. Chasing higher highs can lead to substance abuse and addiction, followed by lengthy drug rehabilitation at great expense and stress to our bodies. Why can't we just have a glass of wine or two with family and friends, and achieve a smooth mental high instead? Over-exerting ourselves in sport can lead to serious injuries, followed by costly surgery and physical therapy. Would a moderate but persistent level of exercise not be good enough maintain our health?

While some of the consequences are reversible, others are more permanent. In our competitive society, balance is often overlooked and moderation is usually an afterthought. The Middle Way guides us to a more balanced way of living. Tolerance is another way for us to get there. These two virtues go hand in hand. Therefore we should be tolerant of others with different opinions. We should avoid taking an extreme position just because we are different and we have to show that we are. We should try to persuade those whose ideas we don't necessarily agree with, and not judge them with our own biases. If we are intolerant of others we will stray from the Middle Way and become extremists

The Chinese have a saying, "To seek similarities and tolerate differences." The way Asians like to deal with different people is to first identify their common ground, which is where most people would feel comfortable standing. From there they look at where most people would prefer to go, which is the Middle Way. Our common interests lie in the intercept of our desires. If we focus on the common ground and take the Middle Way, we should be able to comfortably split our differences and arrive at win–win solutions.

In Books there Are Houses Made of Gold

There are many Chinese stories about the virtue of studying hard. There is an old saying that goes, "In books there are houses made of gold; in books there are true beauties." The implication is that everything would be fine if we just study hard and do well in school. This will lead to a good job, a wife and family, and success. Education allows a person to become successful, regardless of his background. Young men can get everything they want by studying hard.

In one such story, a young boy's family was so poor that they could not afford to buy oil for the lamp. So in the evenings he would go outside of the house to catch fireflies, then put them inside a pouch so that he could study under their flickering luminescence. He later did well in the government exams and was appointed as an official. Another boy tied his hair to the ceiling beam so that his head wouldn't drop from dozing off. As an added insurance, he held a knife above his thigh so that he would stab himself if he ever fell asleep. The sharp pain would wake him up so he could study some more.

The message, which is constantly reinforced by Chinese parents and teachers, is that excellence in academia can lead to success in life. Chinese students generally follow this age-old advice and apply themselves diligently in school. If not, their "tiger moms" make sure they do.

In traditional China, virtues were revered over wealth. The proper conduct of a gentleman could only be acquired by studying the classics and practicing the virtues diligently. Today the marketplace is gradually replacing the schools in dictating values.

Back then, success meant doing well in the government exams and receiving an appointment as an official. Your family would be very proud of you for this important accomplishment. Future generations of your clan would remember that one of their ancestors had achieved high honors in a government exam and that they should all try to emulate him. Your achievements would be proudly recorded in the clan registry in the village temple where such records are kept. Your success meant that your village was no longer just any village in China. It had produced someone prominent, and you were the one who put it on the map. Compared with this, going into business was considered a less noble pursuit and not an activity befitting a Confucian gentleman.

Today, more options are available to ambitious young Chinese people. Being an entrepreneur is quite acceptable, and getting rich is no longer frowned upon. Instead it is envied. However, wealth without conscience is fragile. It is also against traditional Chinese values.

Out-of-the-Box Thinkers

The US is the land of entrepreneurs. Many people have good ideas and work on them diligently to create innovative products and services. Those who are successful share a common trait—the ability to think outside of the box.

As a result, we have Apple Computers, Microsoft and Facebook—hugely successful companies all founded by brilliant young men who all happened to be college dropouts. They were able to create entirely new industries, even without a formal education.

Chinese people also love out-of-the-box thinkers. They admire those who can conjure up clever schemes to solve difficult problems, seemingly with ease. These individuals can strategize like a grand chess master, see several steps ahead of their opponents, and they have a perfect countermove for every move. They can take incredible shortcuts that somehow always work out flawlessly.

In the classic Chinese novel *The Romance of Three Kingdoms*, a military strategist by the name of Zhuge Liang was considered the genius of geniuses. One day he was asked by his commander to procure a 100,000 arrows for battle and was given less than a week to accomplish the task. It was a test.

Instead of getting flustered, Zhuge Liang came up with a clever plan. He put uniforms on straw soldiers and stood them on boats. On a foggy day, he sent the boats sailing into enemy territory. To make sure that they were noticed, his soldiers beat drums and made loud noises along the way. The enemies saw the boats cutting through the fog and sailing towards them, and thought it must be a ruse, so they didn't dare engage the invaders directly. Instead they shot arrow after arrow at the straw soldiers. When the fog broke, Zhuge Liang pulled his troops back. The straw soldiers now looked like agitated porcupines covered from head to toe with enemy arrows.

With a stroke of genius and a keen understanding of human nature, Zhuge Liang had turned his weakness into a strength. Not only did he exceed his quota of arrows, he also won the confidence of his commander. Stories like this abound in Chinese history. The moral is that clever ideas can trump routine work.

Today Chinese society supports innovators, and there are many success stories. Entrepreneurs who didn't have much social status before have managed to ride China's high-speed economic train to phenomenal success.

Below I highlight the story of Jack Ma, the founder of Alibaba, as a successful entrepreneur from a humble background. He is also a traditional

Chinese thinker and a cross-cultural manager who takes advantage of China's growing consumer class. In the process he has become a billionaire.

Alibaba: A Crocodile in the Yangtze

Jack Ma, the founder of e-commerce giant Alibaba, failed his college entrance exams several times before graduating with an English degree from a local college. Before Alibaba, Ma was an English teacher, a translator and sometime tour guide. At the time when China was opening up to the world, being an English teacher was considered to be a reasonable profession for a young man like him. But times they are a-changin.

Ma had bigger ambitions. After visiting the US in 1995 and seeing what the Internet could do for commerce, he founded Alibaba. The company started out as a business-to-business e-commerce trading platform connecting overseas buyers with Chinese manufacturers. After a few years it evolved to take advantage of China's growing entrepreneur class and increasingly affluent Internet-friendly consumers, expanding rapidly. Its Internet platforms handily flattened the traditional distribution model and allowed businesses and consumers to trade with each other directly. In many ways, Alibaba is like a crowded and noisy Chinese bazaar where spirited buyers and sellers come to make deals.

Alibaba now runs the world's largest e-commerce marketplace with Taobao (consumer to consumer), TMall (business to consumer) and a host of other related Internet companies. Its platforms account for over 80 percent of e-commerce activity in China. But Alibaba is not stopping; it is moving into financial services by providing innovative solutions to its millions of business owners and customers.

On November 11, 2013, China's Singles Day, the Alibaba websites took in US$ 5.75 billion of online payments, surpassing by two-and-a-half times the total receipts for all US retailers on Cyber Monday in 2013, traditionally the biggest e-shopping day in the country that invented the Internet. The 2014 Singles Day saw Alibaba take in US$ 9.3 billion in sales, surpassing its 2013 record by a whopping 57 percent. The 2015 Singles Day extravaganza was even more incredible. At US$ 14.3 billion of gross merchandise sales, it easily obliterated the previous record.

What was remarkable was that Alibaba was able to deliver this sizzling growth against the backdrop of a slowing Chinese economy.

While many people may consider the Singles Day phenomenon to be just an adaptation of the online shopping model for China, and benefitting from the country's large population, there is more to it. The original Singles Day concept was created by a group of lonely college students celebrating singlehood by shopping for themselves because they didn't have girlfriends to shop for. This concept, while originated in China, is universally applicable. The Singles Day online shopping festival has the potential of becoming a new global cultural phenomenon, where people can shop online for everything and anything round the clock, take in the carnival-like atmosphere and enjoy the camaraderie developed with fellow shoppers for good deals.

The 2015 event was also global in design. It was kicked off with a three-hour extravaganza in the former Olympic swimming venue in Beijing called the Water Cube, replete with famous actors such as Kevin Spacey and Daniel Craig making sales pitches for Alibaba. The scale and breadth of this marketing innovation and, more importantly, the speed of its adaptation is truly breathtaking.

Alibaba is unquestionably a phenomenal success in China. Ma's massive ambitions and belief in the Chinese people is characteristic of many Chinese leaders. With persistence and a heavy dose of Hollywood hype, he succeeded in building Alibaba into the giant that it is today.

When the company went public on September 19, 2014 in New York, it raised almost US$ 25 billion and had an initial market capitalization of over US$ 225 billion.

Alibaba's successful IPO highlights two emerging trends: the shift in commercial gravity from the US, the richest country in the world, to Asia and particularly China, the most populous nation and fastest-growing major economy; and the emergence of a new breed of cross-cultural executives.

When Ma was asked on the morning of his company's IPO where he got his inspiration, he said *Forrest Gump*. Indeed, the Chinese executive chairman of the world's largest e-commerce marketplace loves a stoic American movie character, presumably for his humility and steadfastness, which are also traditional Chinese traits. The ability to integrate Western knowhow with Chinese sensibilities can be the making of a new breed of global executives.

Alibaba's motto is to put customers first, employees second and shareholders last. This simple slogan has a tinge of socialism as well as traditional Chinese values of fairness and paternalism. In fact, the company's broad employee share ownership scheme has allowed many of its employees to also become wealthy from the IPO.

While many Western companies espouse a similar motto, when push comes to shove it is always the owners (i.e. shareholders) who come first. When times are tough, layoffs are implemented and employees become disillusioned. Product and service quality decline, and customers defect to competitors. Putting the customers and employees ahead of the owners may affect a company's profitability in the short run but in the long term it's the right thing to do.

Jack Ma is sometimes compared to Steve Jobs, the former CEO of Apple. Indeed, these two disruptive visionaries shared some similar qualities. Both CEOs headed technology companies even though neither was technically trained. (Ma is now Alibaba's Executive Chairman having relinquished his CEO role in 2013.) Ma studied English while Jobs dropped out of college after one semester. Both had outsized egos and both were able to marshal their troops to achieve the nearly impossible.

Jobs wanted to build insanely great products that could change the world, while Ma wants to build the best platforms for consumers and businesses to trade on. Even though Ma did not create an entirely new industry like Jobs did, he was able to combine Western knowhow with Chinese characteristics to strike it big in China. It will be interesting to see whether Alibaba, which Ma once described as a crocodile in the Yangtze River, will be able to expand his innovative Chinese bazaar model successfully into the international marketplace.

Sports and Business

Sport as a tradition dates back to the ancient Greeks, who founded the Olympic Games.

In ancient Greek murals, one can see many different athletic contests, including foot races, equestrian events, wrestling, long jump, discus, javelin, boxing and pankration. The last one is a particularly gruesome event combining boxing and wrestling. All kinds of moves, with the exception of biting and eye gouging, were allowed, so not too different from today's mixed martial arts.

In ancient China, archery and horsemanship were two of the six subjects young noblemen studied. Soccer, basketball and other team sports are more modern imports. In historical paintings, the Chinese were seen playing their versions of polo, golf and soccer. These were more pastimes for the upper class that never became as popular as their Western counterparts.

Sport in China is traditionally viewed as a means to get fit and as a pastime. In schools the focus is on the mind rather than the body, and sport is considered secondary to academic subjects.

In the West, sport is as much a way of life as a means of achieving physical fitness. In sport a person can develop an important life skill, which is to set goals and go after them assiduously. You learn to train hard, savor the joy of winning and accept the agony of defeat. To win you must do your best, play by the rules and have respect for the competition. You must win a point at a time and not take shortcuts. Winning is a reward for a job well done but not necessarily a given.

Like sport, nothing beats the adrenaline rush from dealing with business challenges. Also like sport, a good businessman should be able to see the entire field and be keenly aware of his opponent's every move. Plus he should be able to think on the run, choose his best option and execute it with authority. No wonder many senior executives of major US corporations are former athletes from either college or professional teams. Their sporting experience provides them with the necessary confidence and discipline to compete in the cut-throat world of business.

Westerners are taught to defend their ideas and not shy away from confronting those who have different ones. Sport gives them the training to stand their ground while being challenged. In business meetings, Westerners often openly and aggressively challenge other participants' points of view, but it's about business and nothing personal.

Being direct and focused on issues removes emotion from the equation. It is good for business. After work, colleagues who fought earlier happily go out and have drinks together, just as they would after a friendly softball match. Any enmity in the office is forgotten after a few rounds of beers and snacks, self-deprecating humor and slaps on the back. To fight hard defending one's position and be able to shake hands afterwards follows the sporting tradition.

Sport helps to build character. Sportsmanship is developed from competing under fair rules. Confidence comes from overcoming failure—over and over again. Leadership is fostered from teamwork and self-sacrifice.

American football is a good analogy for business. Americans love their football. According to a 2014 Harris Poll, professional football is by far the most popular sport for adults over 18, with 35 percent of the votes, and 46 percent if college football is included in the count. American football is a full-contact sport best described as territorial conquest by strong men. Unlike the popular football game that is loved everywhere in the world but known as soccer in the US, American football is mostly played with the hands rather than the feet. Only kickers use their feet on the ball, and in special plays.

The football field is 120 yards long and divided into two halves of 50 yards each, with each half capped by a 10-yard end zone. The objective is for one team to carry the oblong football into the opponent's end zone to score a touchdown, which yields six points. Extra points are either kicked (for one point) or advanced over a goal line (for two points). The ball can be kicked through the goalposts after being held on the ground (a field goal for three points.) At the end of regulation play, the team with the most points wins.

In a football match, two opposing teams of eleven players spread out in formations. The offense rush or pass the football to gain yardage from the opponent's turf. Of course, the opponent's defense wants none of that and they will do their best to frustrate the offense, forcing a fumble if possible.

The speed and power of football means that winning or losing can literally happen in a split second, so there is rarely a dull moment. Sometimes it seems as if both teams expend a lot of effort contesting over a few yards in the mid-field. At other times a quarterback can unleash one of those magnificent long "bombs" to score a touchdown that instantly changes the dynamics of the game.

To the uninitiated, football looks more like a brutal conquest than a game of skill and strategy. In fact, the football game is as American as capitalism, the main difference being that it occurs on an athletics field rather than in the world of business. But the strategizing, running, passing, blocking and tackling are every bit as intense as real business activities.

In football, each team attempts to create an opening in the opponent's formation to run through. Running plays are less risky than forward passes, similar to a company's product extensions, which are capable of generating incremental revenue but nothing too dramatic. Long passes are spectacular but also riskier. As the football must stay in the air longer, it is susceptible to being deflected or intercepted. These passes are like a company's innovative but risky new products that can either become spectacularly successful or fail miserably. To win, management must carefully weigh its best options and execute the game plan diligently, and be flexile enough to react to the dynamics of a business.

The job of the National Football League, professional football's governing body, is like that of regulators in business. Its has to make sure that football is professionally run, with rules that are fair and getting fairer over time. Referees are there to enforce the rules but not to influence the outcome of a game. Under their watchful eyes, the play advances. The tenet is that in a level playing field, the strong and agile will have a better chance of winning, just as in business. If athletes compete vigorously and fairly, both fans and owners will be happy, and everyone will come out a "winner," even for the losers.

Bibliography

J.V. Luce, An Introduction to Greek Philosophy, P. 114, Thames and Hudson, 1992.

Victor Luckerson, *Meet the Visionary Behind the World's Largest IPO*, TIME, May 8, 2014a.

Telis Demos and Matt Jarzemsky, *Alibaba's IPO Priced at $68 a Share, The $21.8 Billion Offering by the Chinese E-Commerce Giant Is Among Biggest Ever,* The Wall Street Journal, Sep. 18, 2014.

Victor Luckerson, *China's Alibaba Finds Riches on Wall Street*, Time, Sep 19, 2014b.
What is Alibaba? Project.wsj.com
Crocodile in the Yangtze: A Westerner inside China's Alibaba.com, Directed by Porter Erisman, 2012.
Shanshan Wang and Eric Pfanner, *China's One-Day Shopping Spree Sets Record in Online Sales*, The New York Times Nov 11 2013.
Jenifer Booton, *Alibaba's 'Singles Day' Sales Top $9 Billion, Bigger than Black Friday*, MarketWatch Nov 111, 2014.
Paul Carsten, *Alibaba's Singles' Day Sales Surge 60 Percent to $14.3 Billion*, Reuters, Nov 11, 2015.
Helen H. Wang, *The Chinese Dream: The Rise of the World's Largest Middle Class and What It Means to You*, P. 162, Best Seller Press, 2010.
Greek Athletic Contests, The Getty Villa, Malibu, California.
Darren Rovell, *NFL Most Popular for 30th Year in Row*, ESPN.com

14

Two Systems: One World

*Oh, Till Earth and Sky stand presently at God's great Judgment Seat;
East is East, and West is West, and never the twain shall meet,
But there is neither East or West, Border, nor Breed, nor Birth,
When two strong men stand face to face, tho' they come from the ends
of the Earth.*

Rudyard Kipling

Culture affects how we live and make decisions. Because Chinese and Western cultures developed independently thousands of years ago, they remain separate and distinct despite periodic efforts to assimilate them. Suffice to say, their leadership and management styles are also quite different. If we compare these two styles from a cross-cultural perspective, we should be able to identify their relative strengths and weaknesses, and take the best from both worlds.

The powerful Western analytical approach is successfully applied to science, medicine, business and law. It works particularly well in situations where the problems are well defined, their facts undisputed and the outcomes measurable. However, the approach is less effective in areas that require substantial qualitative reasoning, or in matters that are heavily influenced by culture. In those cases the Western approach can be too narrow if it is pushed too far, or too polarizing when there are too many divergent opinions and no one is willing to compromise. Because it emphasizes detail in favor of the big picture, it has a tendency to underestimate global constraints, until it is too late. Also, since the approach is scientific, it assumes universality and downplays cultural factors.

Competition makes the economy productive by separating out the winners and losers. However, not everything important to us has to have a clear winner and loser, or benefits from competition. Unfettered competition can bring about unintended consequences that can harm innocent bystanders and, as a result, make losers of all of us.

In a family, if the parents fight non-stop, the children will become disoriented. It will cause them to look outside their homes for guidance and stability. In a business, if senior managers fight vicious turf battles, it will harm employee morale and productivity. If politicians fight only for their own agenda and lose sight of the common good, the conflict can paralyze the nation. In these situations, everybody is a loser regardless of who wins.

If we get involved in other people's business without understanding their culture, we may achieve initial victories but rarely any lasting peace. When these unfortunate events happen, the latent damage often overwhelms the initial justification. What's more, it is always the innocent people who suffer most. History is full of such examples.

At the other end of the management spectrum is the wholistic management style practiced by the Chinese and other Asians. This style is comprehensive and covers all bases. However, it can gloss over the detail and misdiagnose problems. Also, if there are too many issues to consider and too many constituents to please, it is difficult for management to prioritize and focus. This can lead to weak decisions and an execution nightmare.

The Chinese and many Asians like the Middle Way, an artful approach to life that leaves plenty of room for interpretation and creativity. The Chinese style also relies too much on people and guanxi for success. It over-emphasizes order and deference to authority, and it downplays the individual spirit, to the detriment of innovation. What's more, the

Chinese style has a tendency to comingle issues with personalities, and focus on practicality over process. This makes it difficult to gauge management performance and pursue accountability.

In business, where individual effort matters most, such as in the technology industry, the Western management style works best.

If a manager asks questions repeatedly in a Socratic manner and doesn't take no for an answer, he will eventually ferret out the problems and come up with improvements. If a manager empowers his employees to contribute freely towards the corporate good, he can tap into their boundless creative potential and follow the Tao to success.

The Chinese style works best in systems with constraints, where optimum solutions come from all members sharing the same goals and pitching in together to reach them.

Advances in communications have effectively made our world smaller. As such, actions from one part of the world can impact the rest of the world in ways that are difficult to fathom. In our constrained world, one's assets can become someone else's liability, and actions from one member of the community can one day subject all of us to the same fate. Lone rangers can upset the delicate balance and cause unintended consequences. Being less critical and more considerate can make life easier for everybody.

In this respect, the traditional Chinese management style of eschewing confrontation while conducting endless rounds of dialogue to reach consensus is both gentler and less disruptive. The promotion of mutual interests, while respecting our differences, can point to a path towards peaceful development.

Table 14.1 summarizes the different emphases of the Chinese and Western management styles.

When we compare the two different management styles we see dramatic differences.

The Western manager believes in individual accomplishment and accountability. This is fine as long as people are held accountable for what they do and the reward or punishment is appropriate. Often, liabilities are not obvious at the onset, while benefits are more easily justified. Most of the time, responsibilities and blame can only be assigned after considerable damage has already been done. By that time it may be too late.

Table 14.1 Differences in management emphasis

Western	Chinese
Manages resources to achieve corporate objectives	Leads the troops to fight in the trenches
Causality—understands why and seeks to visualize cause and effect	Heuristic—looks for how and practical ideas that work
Bottom-up problem-solving seeking context-independent solutions	Top-down approach favors strategy and diplomacy
Focus on detail—strives for clarity	Focuses on big picture—accepts ambiguity
Favors substance—ideas and track record Encourages diversity of opinion	Relies on formality—status, relationship and reputation Strives for consensus

Climate change is a case in point. In the past, when people drove their big gas-guzzling cars, they had no idea that the car exhaust would one day trap the heat of the sun and cause global warming. Another example is the trading of securities based on US home mortgages, where supposedly well-structured financial products failed and eventually brought the world down with them.

Having said that, the wholistic belief that our interests and liabilities are closely inter-linked is insightful. We should address our common concerns carefully and proceed deliberately to solve them. As global citizens, we must work hard to identify our mutual interests and work even harder to resolve our differences.

Table 14.2 compares and contrasts different aspects of the two distinct management styles.

This table is by no means exhaustive. The listed attributes are for comparison only. They would have little value if they were taken out of the context. In addition, these style differences are not binary because each person already has a mixture of both.

For example, an American businessman may find his German counterpart much less flexible than he is, but his Chinese colleagues may view him as a very rigid person. A French manager may find his English counterpart too subtle, but the English manager may say the same thing about his Chinese colleague. Or a Japanese manager may find his Chinese counterpart undisciplined, but the Chinese manager may say the same thing about some of his other Asian colleagues.

14 Two Systems: One World

Table 14.2 Cross-cultural comparison of management styles

Western	Chinese
Analytical—looks for why	Wholistic—looks for how
Adversarial—looks for differences	Consensual—seeks common ground
Individualistic—driven by personal responsibility	Group—led by a group mandate
Fairness to individuals	Responsibility to group
Protects the minority	Promotes the majority
Low-context	High-context
Invisible hand	Strong arm
Men's law	Heaven's way
Short-term focus	Long-term horizon
Linear	Comprehensive
Logical	Reasonable
Bound by legal contracts	Relies on mutual understanding
Depends on statistics	Driven by will power
Process-driven—do the right thing	Results oriented—do things right
Research to find the best solution	Feeling stones to cross river
Personal best	Best person
Strength from diversity	Unity is power
Disdain for authority	Reverence for status
Direct and critical	Warm and fuzzy
Open and vocal	Quiet and reserved

Westerners may find the comparisons helpful if they wish to communicate better with their Asian counterparts. This table offers them a different perspective to help them to refine their approach. Chinese or Asian managers may also use the table to understand how Westerners look at information and why they always seem so critical. Understanding the Westerner's cultural mindset can help them to respond appropriately.

Regardless of where we are from, Asia or the West, we have much in common but much more to learn from each other. Taking the best from both cultures allows us to be more effective across a range of personal and managerial endeavors.

The essence of Chinese and Western philosophical traditions has sustained us for more than 2,000 years. They have not faded away, even in the face of advancing technologies, changing governments and political systems.

In the future, these two cultures will increasingly engage with each other. Whether it is in head-to-head contest or cooperation will depend on the skill of our leaders. And, regardless of what space exploration has in store for us in the future, humans will still inhabit the same Earth our ancestors lived on. We should all therefore try to get along better.

Also, as human beings, we will continue to have the same aspirations and fears as our forefathers. Like them, we will continue to search for ways to make ourselves safe and fulfilled, and to provide for our love ones. These challenges will continue to occupy thinkers for years to come, as they did in ancient Greece and China.

If we know each other's culture better, we may be able to limit our misunderstandings or, even better, reduce unnecessary conflict. At the minimum, we should be able to reduce our stress levels as a result of not knowing what the other side is doing, or why it is doing it. This, I hope, is what this book can, in a very small way, help to accomplish for us.

Bibliography

Rudyard Kipling, *The Ballad of East and West*, 1889.
The Tao of Power, Lao Tzu's Classic Guide to Leadership, Influence and Excellence, Ch. 16, R.L. Wing, Doubleday & Company, Inc. 1986.
Josh Kerbel, *The Clash of Cognitions, The United States, China, and Strategic Thinking*, American Diplomacy, Feb. 2009.

Index

A
academics. *See* education
active learning, process of, 157
acupuncture, 19–20, 27, 180
Affordable Care Act, 32
Agricultural Bank of China, 216
agricultural communities, 121
AIG, 214, 218
Alan Goa, 187
alcoholic beverages, etiquette for, 166–168
Alibaba, 11, 224, 246–249
AMCs (asset management companies), 208–209, 215–218
American culture. *See* culture and traditions, Western; United States
American *vs.* Chinese Dream, 17, 66–67
Analects (Confucius), 2, 75, 155, 158

analytical thinking
 absolute *vs.* relative perspectives, 47
 benefits and limits of, 106–107, 255–260
 Chinese pragmatism *vs.*, 179–182
 critical thinking skills, 45, 157–159, 161–162
 decision-making processes, 10–11, 44–46, 64–66
 democratic *vs.* meritocratic approaches, 182–186
 logic and precision, emphasis on, 19, 72–73, 106
 management modes based on, 105–106
 market panic and freezes, effect of, 107–110, 202
 wholistic thinking *vs.*, 255–260
ancestor worship, 149, 179

Apple Computers, 86, 161–162, 246, 249
apples, giving, 12
Aristotle, 139
Art of War, The (Sun Tzu), 28, 34, 37–38, 229
Asian culture. *See* culture and traditions, Asian; culture and traditions, Chinese
Asian financial crisis of 1997, 4, 99–101, 210, 216, 218
asset management companies (AMCs), 208–209, 215–218
astrology, Chinese, 62
authority and power, Chinese
    Chinese government and state power, 186, 197, 205–206
    Chinese *vs.* Western approaches to, 18, 185
    in Confucian management style, 90–91
    in education, 191
    guanxi and managing upwards, 150–153
    labels and formalism, 74–76
    supernatural *vs.* ordinary power, 17–18
automotive industry, American, 214, 218
automotive industry, Japanese, 227

B
Bad Emperor Syndrome, 186
Baidu, 224
Baiju, 166, 168
balance. *See* harmony and balance

Bangladesh, rising sea levels in, 154
banking
    financial engineering, 97–99
    government bailouts, Chinese, 211–212, 215–218
    interest rates, profits from, 111, 116
    lending processes, Chinese, 141–142
    shadow banking in China, 210–212
Bank of America, 218
Bank of China, 216
bankruptcy processes, 109, 141–142, 198–199, 202–203, 207, 211, 217
banquets, Chinese, 122, 166–168, 178
Barings Bank, 231
Bear Sterns, 110, 214
benevolence, value of, 16, 134, 140–144, 148, 188, 239
big picture thinking, 31–34, 44, 79, 80, 86–87, 92
Black Swan, The (Taleb), 113
black swan events, 99, 107, 113
Book of Changes (I Ching), 26, 46, 229
Book of Great Learning, The (Zhu), 136, 229
boxing, 24, 27, 250
brands as soft power, 15
Brazil
    Asian financial crisis, effect on, 100
    as high-context culture, 73
Bright Foods, 224
Britain
    overseas direct investments, 223
    urbanization in, 222

Brown Center Report on American Education, 156
Buddhism, 128
Buffett, Warren, 55, 85, 110
business models
    American tech company business models, 50–51
    Chinese government model, 182–183
    Chinese vs. Western, pros and cons of, 13–14
    family model, 89–91, 187–192
    US government model, 184–186 (*see also* state-owned enterprises (SOEs))
business plans, 87–88
business project launches, 129–130, 176–177, 248
business rules, differing views on, 56, 228
business self-help books, 85
business success factors, differences in, 56–60, 224–226, 255–260

C
(CAO) China Aviation Oil, 226, 231–235
capitalism
    American culture and, 252
    Asian financial crisis and, 100
    business benefits of, 14
    Chinese perceptions of, 12–13
    concerns about, 86–87, 97, 99
    social stability *vs.*, 101
cartoon characters, 16–18

CDOs (collateralized debt obligations), 97–99, 111
center of gravity, concept of, 38–39
center of mass, concept of, 39
Chaori Green Energy, 211
Chengdu, 130
Chen Jiulin, 231–235
chess, 34–36
Chiang Kai-shek, 39–40
China Aviation Oil (CAO), 226, 231–235
China Credit Trust Co., 211
China Securities Regulatory Commission (CSRC), 212
Chinese Characteristics (Smith), 11
Chinese civilization, origins of, 121
Chinese copper coins, 172
Chinese Cultural Renaissance Movement, 120
Chinese culture. *See* Confucianism; culture and traditions, Chinese; management styles, Chinese; wholistic thinking
Chinese language
    high-context nature of, 74
    study of, 2, 15–16
    Western culture, influence on, 8–9
Chinese New Year festivals, 143–144
Chinese Republic, founding and unification of, 119, 129
Chinese sayings. *See* proverbs and sayings, Chinese
Chinese *vs.* American Dream, 17, 66–67
Christianity, 94, 128

Christmas, 12
Chrysler, 218
Civil Rights Movement, US, 185
Clausewitz, Carl von, 37–39, 41
climate change, 153–155, 258
CNBC, 168
CNOOC, 224
Coates, John, 116
Coca-Cola, 15, 55
co-existing opposites, concept of, 26, 46–47, 101–102, 234
cognitive styles, 45. *See also* analytical thinking; wholistic thinking
cognitive styles, differences in, 44
collateralized debt obligations (CDOs), 97–99, 111
comfort zones, Chinese, 19
common good, value of, 71–73, 90, 151–152, 256
common sense, 112, 138–139
communication and expression
  Chinese language, study of, 2, 8–9, 15–16, 74
  Confucian views on, 113, 115
  decision-making, importance to, 10
  high-*vs.* low-context cultures, confusion in, 78–80
  math as language, 114
  reserved manners *vs.* speaking out, 2, 3, 28, 35, 90–91, 157, 169–174, 250
  Taoist thinking and subtleties, 113–115
communism, 12, 15, 39–40, 65–66, 69, 120, 177
compensation structures, differences in, 83–84, 182–186

competition
  benefits and limitations of, 101–102, 144–145, 256
  business success factors, differences in, 56–60, 224–226
  Chinese moderation *vs.* Western extremes, 243–244
  military strategies on, Chinese *vs.* Western, 37–40
  sports and business, 250–252
  winning, Western emphasis on, 24–27, 32, 34, 250–252
conflict management
  avoiding confrontation Chinese strategy of, 23–27, 30, 32, 34–37, 105–106, 257
  dialog *vs.* combat, 36–40
  military strategies on, Chinese *vs.* Western, 37–40
  Weiqi *vs.* chess, 34–36
conformity, Chinese emphasis on, 3, 45, 137
Confucian humanism, 120
Confucianism
  ban on, 119–120, 129
  common good, value of, 71–73, 90, 151–152, 256
  conformaty in, 137
  education, virtue of, 53–54, 128–129, 244–245
  family, value of, 119, 190, 240–242
  foundations of, 128–130, 133–134
  gentleman, concept of, 68, 75–76, 115, 136–138, 245

global populations influenced by, 43–44
Inner Sage and Outer King, 135–136
on labels and formalities, 75–76
on language and expression, 113, 115
Mencius, 2, 119, 126, 134, 141, 145
Middle Way, 5, 10–11, 35, 106, 134, 138–139, 204, 223, 243–244, 256
new Confucianism and modernity, 120–121
reciprocal relationships, 89, 151–152, 190
relevance and resilience of, 120, 259
self-education, 128
shendu, concept of, 136–138
teaching of, 119–120
virtues of, 133–135
Confucian management style, 89–91, 122, 151–152, 187
Confucian virtues
foundations of, 133–135
Li, 134, 140, 148–150, 152, 229
Ren, 134, 139–143, 147, 186, 201
Yi, 134, 145–148
Zhi, 134, 155
Confucius, 64, 127–129, 149
Analects of, 2, 75, 155, 158
Confucius Institute, 15–16
congestion in China, 19, 71
context
big picture thinking, 31–34, 44, 79, 80, 86–87, 92
concept of, 72–78
culture, effect on, 73–74
decision-making processes, 72–74
high-*vs.* low-context communication, 78–80
high-*vs.* low-context cultures, 73
labels and formalities, 72–78
relationships, high-context concept of, 60–61
in wholistic management style, 44–45
contracts
Chinese *vs.* Western concepts of, 58–59
relationships, quantitative aspects of, 60
control engineering, 69
corporate families, 89–91, 187–192
corruption
in China, 30, 137, 142–143, 186
US insider trading, 137
Craig, Daniel, 248
creativity. *See* innovation and creativity
credit and liquidity, 97–98
credit derivatives, 109
creditor rights, enforcement of, 199, 201
creditors, concept of, 141–142
credit ratings, 32, 111
critical thinking skills, 45, 157–159, 161–162
CSRC (China Securities Regulatory Commission), 212
Cultural Revolution, 15, 69, 119–120, 177, 228

culture
  context, effect on, 73–74
  differences in, co-existence of, 1, 3–4, 50–52, 255–260
  information overload, effect on, 239–240
  soft power and, 14
  work styles, influence on, 166
culture and traditions, Asian
  alcoholic beverages, etiquette for, 166–168
  education systems, 154–155
  face, concept of, 174–178
  family relationships in, 52–53, 190, 240–242
  as high-context culture, 73–74
  labels and formalities, 74–75
  no and negative answers, 78–79, 169–172
  reserved manners, 2, 3, 28, 35, 172–174, 250
  Western culture, influence on, 8–9
  wholistic thinking, 43–47
culture and traditions, Chinese
  ancestor worship, 149, 179
  benevolence, 16, 134, 140–144, 148, 188, 239
  business, perceptions of, 12–13
  characteristics of, 11–14
  Chinese language, study of, 2, 8–9, 15–16, 74
  Chinese vs. American Dream, 17, 66–67
  clothing and dress, 12
  comfort zones, 19
  common good, value of, 71–73, 90, 151–152, 256

  complexity and uniqueness of, 9–10, 18, 79
  conformity, Chinese emphasis on, 3, 45, 137
  efficiency, 70–72
  face, concept of, 174–178
  family, value of, 52–53, 119, 149, 179, 187, 190, 240–242
  food and eating, 12, 19–21, 166–169
  foreign confusion about, 15–16, 78–79, 143–144
  foreign cultures, influence on, 11–13
  frugality, value of, 53, 55, 134, 149
  global perceptions of, 14–16
  government jobs, focus on, 53–54, 159–160, 182–183, 245
  government promotion of, 15
  greetings, etiquette for, 61, 169–170
  history, cultural importance of, 9, 18–21, 55–56, 66, 121
  humility and modesty, 24, 92, 93, 113, 123, 134, 155, 171–178, 187, 227, 248
  labels and formalism, 74–76
  medicine, 19–20, 27, 51, 180
  Middle Way, 5, 10–11, 35, 106, 134, 138–139, 204, 223, 243–244, 256
  moderation, virtue of, 134, 138–139, 239, 244
  nature, value of, 46, 101–106, 119, 123–126, 133, 144, 186, 215, 259

no and negative answers, 78–79,
 169–172
perceptions about, 15–16
perseverance, 242–243
populations included, 5
pragmatism, 179–182
public vs. private morals, 88–89
relevance and resilience of,
 120, 259
religious diversity, 128, 179
reserved manners vs. speaking out,
 2, 3, 28, 35, 90–91, 157,
 169–174, 250
self-discipline, 134, 137–138,
 143, 239
self-improvement, 53–54,
 135–138
shared sacrifice, value of,
 167–168, 198–203,
 249, 259
socialism, 10, 12–13, 65–66, 69,
 121, 199, 249
sports and athletics, 23–24,
 37, 250
teaching of, 119–120
Warring States Period and, 37,
 121–123, 127–128
welcoming guests, 122–123
Western culture, influence on,
 8–9, 11–14, 165
Zhou Dynasty, 122–123 (*see also*
 Confucianism)
culture and traditions, Greek
 boxing, 27, 250
 education systems, 44–45
 family values, 240
 food and medicine, 20
 Hippocrates, 20

human virtues, 134
moderation, virtue of, 134, 139,
 243–244
Plato, 134, 161
social stability, 136
Socrates (Socratic method), 45,
 128, 135, 158–159, 161,
 162, 184, 257
sports and athletics, 156, 239,
 249–250
Western culture, influence on,
 43–45, 239
culture and traditions, Western
 American vs. Chinese Dream,
  17, 66–67
 confidence vs. humility,
  175–176
 details, Western narrow focus on,
  10, 31–34, 46, 56, 67–68,
  88, 167, 180–182
 extremes vs. moderation,
  243–244
 food and eating, 12, 19–21,
  167–168
 global dominance of, 8–9
 greetings, etiquette for, 61,
  169–170
 individualism, 3, 15, 19, 50,
  167–168, 178, 188–189,
  242, 257–259
 medicine, 19, 180
 names and titles, 62–64
 nature, exploitation of, 120,
  153–154
 no and negative answers, 170
 personal space, concept of, 19
 populations included, 5
 private vs. public morals, 88–89

culture and traditions, Western (*cont.*)
  speaking out and expressing opinions, 90–91, 157, 173–174, 250
  underdogs, success of, 18, 185, 248
  winning, emphasis on, 24–27, 32, 34, 250–252
  work ethic, 54–55, 89 (*see also* analytical thinking)

D
Dalian Wanda, 224
debt financing, 195–196, 202, 208, 215–218
decision-making processes, Chinese
  commonalities, Chinese focus on, 31–34, 67–68, 259
  context and, 72–74
  group consensus, focus on, 67–68, 71–72, 183, 200–201
  Middle Way, 5, 10–11, 35, 106, 134, 138–139, 204, 223, 243–244, 256
  responsibility and accountability for, 82–84
  social stability, emphasis on, 11, 101, 119, 142, 198–201, 218
  Western processes *vs.*, 10–11, 44–46, 64–66
decision-making processes, Western
  Chinese processes *vs.*, 10–11, 44–46, 64–66
  risks and opportunities, emphasis on, 10–11, 54–55

Dell, Michael, 185
democratic *vs.* meritocratic approaches, 182–186
Deng Xiaoping, 12–13, 180
derivatives, 109–110, 231–233
details, Western narrow focus on, 10, 31–34, 46, 56, 67–68, 88, 167, 180–182
Disney, 16, 242
diversity
  equal rights and diversity in US, 49–50, 185
  religious diversity in China, 128, 179
Dulles, John Foster, 175

E
economic development, Chinese
  Asian financial crisis, effect of, 4, 100–101, 218
  foreign direct investment (FDI), 223
  housing market, risks to, 101, 102, 202–203, 208–209
  lending processes and, 141–142
  overseas direct investments, 223–226
  positive actions supporting, 99–102
  slowdown and challenges to, 210–212, 221
  socialism and, 12–13, 65–66, 69
  societal consensus on, 71
  sustainable growth, achieving, 204–205
  Wealth Management Products (WMPs), 210–211

Index 269

economy, Chinese
 consumer markets, 8, 15
 financial crisis, potential for, 101
 forecasting on, difficulty in, 201
 foreign currency reserve, 202, 222–223, 225
 GDP, rates of, 7, 195, 213, 223
 global influence of, 7–8
 government bailouts, 211–212, 215–218
 growth of, 1, 7–10, 13, 15, 121, 213, 223
 homeownership, rates of, 203
 reforms and political movements, effects on, 69
 slowdown and challenges to, 210–212, 221
economy, US
 debt-ceiling debacle and, 31–34
 government bailouts, 214–215, 218
 Treasury obligations, credit risk of, 33
Edison, Thomas, 242
education, Chinese
 Confucian virtue of, 53–54, 128–129, 244–245
 math and science education, 156
 modern changes in, 54
 rote learning, 2, 159–160
 self-improvement, 53–54, 135–138
 social status and, 84
 Western systems vs., 1–2, 155–160
 Zhi (wisdom), virtue of, 134, 155
education, Western
 active learning, process of, 157
 in business, emphasis on, 54–55
 Chinese students in US, 158
 Chinese systems vs., 1–2, 155–160
 critical thinking skills, 45, 157–159, 161–162
 knowledge for knowledge sake, 135, 158
 math and science, 156–157
 Socratic method, 45, 128, 135, 158, 161, 162, 184, 257
 sports and athletics, emphasis on, 27, 54, 156, 249–252
efficiency, Chinese, 70–72
Einhorn, David, 109
elections and political campaigns, US, 31–34, 153, 184–186
England. See Britain
Enron, 141
entrepreneurship, 11, 85–86, 162, 245–249
environmental protection, need for, 71, 113, 153–155, 258
etiquette. See culture and traditions
Europe
 overseas direct investments, 222, 223
evasive tactics, Chinese, 39–41

F

face, concept of, 174–178
Facebook, 51, 86, 246
Fairbank, John, 123
fairness and justice
 Heaven's Way, 123–126, 133, 186, 259

fairness and justice (cont.)
  Middle Way, 5, 10–11, 35, 106, 134, 138–139, 204, 223, 243–244, 256
  Ren, virtue of, 134, 139–143, 147, 186, 201
  sportsmanship and, 251
  Yi, virtue of, 134, 145–148
fake products, Chinese, 30, 142
family business model, 89–91, 187–192
family relationships, Chinese
  ancestor worship, 149, 179
  hierarchal structures in, 74–76, 122–124, 126, 135–136, 240–242
  labels and formalism, 74–76
  mutual support in, 61, 187, 190–191, 199
  parent-child relationships, 81–82, 90, 160–162, 188–189, 240–242
  unity in, 187
  value of, emphasis on, 52–53, 119, 190, 240–242
family relationships, Western
  individualism vs. family, 149, 190
  parent-child relationships, 81–82, 160–161, 188–189, 242
farming communities, 121
Federal Reserve, 110, 116
feedback, importance of, 68–69
feng shui, 62, 63
financial bailouts, 211–212, 215–218
financial crisis and bubbles
  Asian financial crisis of 1997, 4, 99–101, 210, 216, 218
  Great Depression of 1930s, 100
  interest rates and risks causing, 116, 202–203
  market panic and freezes, 108–110, 202
  US tech bubble of 2000, 97
financial crisis of 2008, US
  global financial risks of, 97–99
  housing market, collapse of, 101, 102, 202–203, 208–209
  Lehman Brothers, collapse of, 32, 97–100, 110–111, 141, 195, 209
  long-term thinking, 86–87
  new financial products causing, 97–99
financial defaults, 110, 202–203, 210–212
financial derivatives, 109–110, 231–233
financial engineering, 97–99
financial trading
  derivatives, 109–110, 231–233
  interest rates and, 111, 116
  markets, irrationality of, 114–115
  risks in, 109–110 (see also investor behavior)
fish frying analogy, 60
Fitch Ratings, 111
flexibility, Chinese emphasis on, 39, 71–72, 91–93, 227
flow, Tao management of, 91–93
food and eating
  alcoholic beverages, etiquette for, 166–167
  Chinese banquets, 122, 166–168, 178
  Chinese vs. Western approaches to, 12, 19–21, 51–52, 166–169

food as medicine, 19–21
soup vs. salad analogy, 51–52
Tao management compared to, 92
football, American, 27, 251–252
Forbes, 224
foreign direct investment (FDI), 223. See also overseas development, Chinese
Forest Gump, 248
Fosun, 224
freedom, American value of, 15, 66
free market economics
  Asian financial crisis and, 100
  business benefits of, 14
  capitalism, 12–13, 100, 252
  concerns about, 86–87, 97, 99
  social stability vs., 101
Frigidaire, 227
frugality, value of, 53, 55, 134, 149
Fukuyama, Francis, 182, 186
Fung Yu-lan, 74, 84, 135, 179

G

Gang of Four, 119
Gaokao test, 157
Gates, Bill, 85
Geeley, 224
GE (General Electric), 227, 230
General Motors (GM), 214, 218
gentleman
  Confucian concept of, 68, 75–76, 115, 136–138, 245
  Western concept of, 75
Geography of Thought, The (Nisbett), 45
Germany
  urbanization in, 222
  us high-context culture, 73
  World War II, 30

gift giving, etiquette for, 12, 123, 137, 138, 152, 172
global financial system. *See* financial crisis and bubbles; financial trading
Global Trends 2030, 7
global warming, 153–155
GM (General Motors), 214, 218
Going Out strategy, 221–222
Golden Mean, 139
government bailouts, 211–212, 215–218
government interventions, Chinese
  authority and power of state, 186, 197, 205–206
  bailouts and market interventions, 211–212, 215–218
  social stability, emphasis on, 101, 203
government jobs, Chinese focus on, 53–54, 159–160, 182–183, 245
government management models
  Chinese model, 182–183
  US model, 184–186
Great Depression of 1930s, 100
Great Leap Forward, 65–66, 69
Great Wall, 129
greetings, etiquette for, 61, 169–170
gross domestic product (GDP), Chinese, 7, 195, 213, 223
guanxi
  in business, emphasis on, 56–60, 150–153
  Confucian management style, 90, 151–152
  environmental responsibility and, 153–155, 258
  managing upwards and, 150–153
  problem solving and, 44, 45, 54

272   Index

Guoxue (traditional Chinese culture)
(*see* culture and traditions,
Chinese)

H
Haier, 224, 226–230
Haier Way, The (Yi and Ye),
229, 230
Haight-Ashbury, San Francisco, 3
Hall, Edward T., 72–73
Hamilton, Stewart, 231, 233
Han Dynasty, 11, 129, 133,
144, 148
happiness, differences in, 52–53
harmony and balance
Chinese cognizant styles, 45–47
co-existing opposites, concept of,
26, 46–47, 101–102, 234
conflict, Chinese strategy of
avoiding, 23–27, 30, 32,
34–37, 105–106
food and eating, 19–21, 166–169
medicine and healing, 19–20
Middle Way, 5, 10–16, 35, 134,
138–139, 204, 223,
243–244, 256
in names, 63
natural order and value of nature,
46, 101–106, 119,
123–126, 133, 144, 186,
215, 259
qi, flow of, 20, 27, 51
social stability, emphasis on, 11,
101, 119, 142, 198–201,
218
in Tai Chi, 24–27
Harris Poll, 251

health
medicine, differences in, 19–20,
27, 51, 180
physical exercise, benefits of,
27, 156
wholistic thinking, benefits of,
27, 46–47
heaven, Chinese concept of, 125
Heaven's Way, 123–126, 133, 186,
259
hedge financing, 196
Heisenberg's Uncertainty
Principle, 92
herbal medicine, 19, 27, 51, 180
hierarchical structures, Chinese
in Chinese families, 74–76,
122–124, 126, 135–136,
240–242
in Confucian management style,
89–91, 122, 187
innovation, influence of, 75
labels and formalism, 74–76
self-family-society order,
135–136
workplace relationships, 61,
69–70, 74–81, 88–90, 126,
165, 178, 259
in Zhou Dynasty, 122–124
high-context cultures. *See* context;
culture and traditions,
Chinese
Hippocrates, 20
history, Chinese
Chinese civilization, origins of, 121
cultural importance of, 18–21,
55–56
as justification for plans, 66
length of, 9, 259

history, Western, 19. *See also* culture and traditions, Greek
Hitler, Adolf, 30
Hong Kong
  Asian financial crisis, effect on, 218
  Lehman mini-bonds, effects of, 98
  math and science education in, 156
  overseas direct investments, 223
  protest movements in, 2–3
  stock markets, government intervention in, 218
  traditional Chinese culture, teaching of, 120
hotpots, 12
House of Rothschild, 187
housing markets. *See* real estate development
Hua Mulan, 242
Huatong Road & Bridge Group Co., 211
Huawei, 224
humility and modesty
  Chinese emphasis on, 24, 92, 93, 113, 123, 134, 155, 171–178, 187, 227, 248
  face, concept of, 174–178
  gift giving and, 123
  no and negative answers, 78–79, 169, 171–172
  praising employees, 81–82, 90, 160, 171–172, 176–177
  reserved manners *vs.* speaking out, 2, 3, 28, 35, 90–91, 169–174, 250
  water analogies on, 93, 94
  Western confidence *vs.* humility, 175–176

IBM, 200
I Ching (Book of Changes), 26, 46, 229
India
  Buddhism from, 128
  as high-context culture, 73
  math and science education in, 156
individualism, Western emphasis on, 3, 15, 19, 50, 167–168, 178, 188–189, 242, 257–259
Indonesia
  Asian financial crisis, effect on, 99, 100, 216
  corporate families in, 188
  US RTC models in, 216
  Industrial and Commercial Bank, 216
information overload, 239–241
information warfare, 38
infrastructure projects, Chinese, 70–72
Inner Sage and Outer King, 135–138
innovation and creativity
  in Chinese management styles, 58, 91
  computer and Internet technology, 11, 85–86, 161–162, 224, 246–249
  entrepreneurship, 11, 85–86, 162, 245–249
  learning styles and education, 156–157, 161–162
  out-of-the box thinking, 245–247
  perseverance and, 242–243

innovation and creativity (*cont.*)
   personal passions and, 84–86
   speaking up and expressing ideas for, 90–91
   underdogs, success of, 18, 185, 248
   in Western management styles, 84–86, 90–91
insider trading, 137, 232
interest rates, 111, 116
International Monetary Fund, 100
Internet. *See* technology
intuitive thinking. *See* wholistic thinking
investor behavior
   debt financing and, 196
   market panic, 108–110, 202
   market panic and freezes, 107–110, 202
   markets, irrationality of, 114–115
   quantitative finance and irrationality, 109–113
   stress and trading, 115–116 (*see also* banking; financial trading; stock markets)
iPhones and iPads, 162
Islam, 128
iSwitch, 200
Italy, overseas direct investments, 223

J

Jacques, Martin, 7, 182
Japan
   automotive industry in, 200, 227
   corporate families in, 188
   culture, Confucian influence on, 43
   names and titles, 62
   no and negative answers, 169
   real estate property crashes, 203
   reserved manners, culture of, 173–174
Jesus, 94
Jiang Zemin, 221
Jobs, Steve, 85–86, 161–162, 249
Johnson, Lyndon, 29
JP Morgan Chase, 218
justice. *See* fairness and justice

K

Keynes, John Maynard, 234
King, Martin Luther, Jr., 185
Kipling, Rudyard, 255
Kissinger, Henry, 34, 86
Korean culture. *See* South Korea
Korean War, 65
Kung Fu movies, 23
Kuomintang regime, 65

L

labor laws and standards, 199, 224, 225
language. *See* communication and expression
Lao Tzu, 2, 23, 26, 60, 92, 93, 101–102, 113–115, 127–128, 230, 234
layoffs
   Chinese approaches to, 141, 199–201, 205
   Western approaches to, 11, 200, 249
Lee, Ang, 77
Lee, Bruce, 24, 93
Leeson, Nick, 231

left-brain thinking. *See* analytical thinking
legal frameworks
  contracts, Chinese *vs.* Western views on, 58–59
  lawsuits, Chinese *vs.* Western views on, 59
  weakness in Chinese systems, 137
  Western emphasis on, 14, 58–59, 153, 184, 224, 225
Lehman Brothers, 32, 97–100, 110–111, 141, 195, 209, 216
Lenovo, 224
Li, virtue of, 134, 140, 148–150, 152, 229
Liang Shuming, 88–89
Liebherr, 226, 228
Lincoln, Abraham, 31, 137
Li Ning, 224
local asset management companies (AMCs), 208–209, 215–218
local government financial vehicles (LGFVs), 206–210
logic and precision. *See* analytical thinking
Lombardi, Vince, 27
Long-Term Capital Management (LTCM), 110
long-term thinking, 44, 86–87, 102, 242–243, 259
Lou Jiwei, 102
low-context cultures. *See* context; culture and traditions, Western
LTCM (Long-Term Capital Management), 110
Lu, kingdom of, 128

luck and fortune
  co-existing opposites, concept of, 26, 46–47, 101–102, 234
  names and, 62–63

M

Ma, Jack, 11, 246–249
Malaysia, corporate families in, 188
management emphasis, differences in, 258
management styles, Chinese
  benefits and limitations of, 101–102, 144–145, 255–260
  big picture thinking, 31–34, 44, 79, 80, 86–87, 92
  business plans, 87–88
  business project launches, 129–130, 176–177, 248
  business success factors, 56–60, 224–226, 259
  commonalities over differences, focus on, 31–34, 67–68, 259
  Confucian management style, 89–91, 122, 151–152, 187
  decision-making processes, 10–11, 44–46, 64–66
  evasive tactics, 39–41
  face, concept of, 174–178
  family, value of, 52–53, 119, 190, 240–242
  flexibility, emphasis on, 39, 71–72, 91–93, 227
  group consensus, 67–68, 71–72, 183, 200–201

management styles, Chinese (cont.)
  guanxi, emphasis on, 44, 45, 54, 56–60, 90, 150–155
  leaders vs. managers, 81
  long-term thinking, 44, 86–87, 102, 242–243, 259
  motivations of managers, 52–56
  motives, importance of justifications for, 64–66
  natural order and value of nature, 46, 101–106, 119, 123–126, 133, 144, 186, 215, 259
  negotiation, 28–29, 31–34, 67–68, 184–185, 259
  politics, emphasis on, 31–34, 56–60
  reserved manners vs. speaking out, 2, 3, 28, 35, 90–91, 157, 169–174, 250
  responsibility and accountability, 82–84
  self-family-society order and, 135–136
  social stability, emphasis on, 11, 101, 119, 142, 198–201, 218
  Tai Chi compared to, 28
  Tao management style, 91–94
  three Ps of business, 28–31, 39, 93
  Western styles vs., cross-cultural comparison of, 255–260
  workplace relationships and roles, 61, 69–70, 74–81, 88–90, 126, 165, 178, 259 (see also wholistic thinking)
management styles, cross-cultural Chinese vs. Western styles, comparison of, 255–260

cross-cultural executives, emergence of, 248–249
cultural differences, co-existence of, 1, 3–4, 50–52
management styles, Western
  benefits and limitations of, 101–102, 144–145, 255–260
  business plans, 87–88
  business rules, respect for, 56
  business success factors, 56–60, 224–226, 259
  Chinese styles vs., cross-cultural comparison of, 255–260
  decision-making processes, 10–11, 44–46, 64–66
  details, narrow focus on, 10, 31–34, 46, 56, 67–68, 88, 167, 180–182
  differences over commonalities, focus on, 31–34, 67–68, 259
  education, emphasis on, 53–54
  history, cultural importance of, 55–56
  legal frameworks, emphasis on, 14, 58–59, 153, 184, 224, 225
  out-of-the box thinking, 245–247
  praising employees, 81–82, 90, 160, 171–172, 176–177
  responsibility and accountability, 82–84
  risks and opportunities, focus on, 10–11, 54–55
  servant leadership, 93–94
  Socratic method of learning, influence of, 45, 128, 135, 158, 161, 162, 184, 257

sports and athletics, emphasis on, 27, 54, 156, 249–252
statistics, emphasis on, 109–113, 259
winning, emphasis on, 24–27, 32, 34, 250–252
work experience, emphasis on, 54–55
workplace relationships and roles, 61, 69–70, 74–81, 88–90, 259 (*see also* analytical thinking)
Manchu culture, 11, 12
Mandate of Heaven, 123–126
manufacturing, Chinese
  economic development and growth, 204–205
  overseas direct investments *vs.*, 222
  weakness in, 213
Mao Zedong, 39–40, 65–66, 120, 177
mapo doufu, 21
market discipline, 214–215
market panic and freezes, 108–110, 202
market reforms, Chinese
  banking system collapse, potential risk of, 201–203
  government bailouts, 211–212, 215–218
  housing market, risks to, 202–203, 208–209
  industry over-capacity, 204
  local asset management companies (AMCs), 208–209, 215–218
  local government financial vehicles (LGFVs), 206–210

manufacturing and growth, 204–205, 213
moral imperative *vs.* market principles, 214–218
Ponzi financing, 196, 197, 204
recessions, recovery from, 204–205
regulations, need for, 212, 214–215
social stability, focus on, 198–201, 203
stock markets, 206, 212–214
markets, irrationality of, 114–115
martial arts, 23–24, 37. See also Tai Chi
math and science education, 156–157
math as language, 114
May Fourth Movement, 119
Maytag, 227
MBS (mortgage-backed securities), 98–99, 111–112
McKenzie, Scott, 3
McKinsey Global Institute, 195
medicine, differences in, 19–20, 27, 51, 180
melting pot analogy, 49
Mencius, 2, 119, 126, 134, 141, 145
Meno (Plato), 161
Mercedes, 15
meritocratic *vs.* democratic approaches, 182–186
Mickey Mouse, 16–18
Microsoft, 246
Middle Way, 5, 10–16, 35, 134, 138–139, 204, 223, 243–244, 256
Ministry of Commerce, China, 223
Minsky, Hyman (Minsky moment), 195–197

Minutemen, 185
mission statements, 64, 187
moderation, virtue of, 134,
   138–139, 239, 244
modernity
   Confucian approach to,
      120–121
   culture and traditions, effect on,
      77
   environmental harm and,
      153–155, 258
   Internet and information
      overload, 239–240
   new Confucianism and, 133–134
   urbanization and, 222
modesty. *See* humility and modesty
Mongolians, 11–12, 187
Monkey King, 16–18
Moody's, 111, 173–174
moral hazard *vs.* imperative,
   214–218
morality
   Heaven's Way, 123–126, 133,
      186, 259
   Inner Sage and Outer King,
      135–138
   market principles *vs.*, 214–218
   Middle Way, 5, 10–11, 35, 106,
      134, 138–139, 204, 223,
      243–244, 256
   public *vs.* private morals, 88–89
   Ren, virtue of, 134, 139–143,
      147, 186, 201 (*see also*
      fairness and justice)
mortgage-backed securities (MBS),
   98–99, 111–112
motion
   Newton's Laws on, 25, 44
   in Tai Chi, 24–27

motivation in Chinese management,
   52–56
Mulan, legend of, 242
mutual support, value of
   in business, 144–145, 175
   in families, 187, 190–191, 199

N

names and titles, 62–64
NASA, 153
National Development and Reform
   Commission (NDRC),
   87, 221
National Football League
   (NFL), 252
nature, value of
   animal kingdom and, 144
   Confucian emphasis on, 144
   Heaven's Way, 123–126, 133,
      186, 259
   natural order and harmony with,
      46, 101–106, 119,
      123–126, 133, 144, 186,
      215, 259 (*see also* Taoism)
NDRC (National Development and
   Reform Commission), 87,
   221
negotiation
   Chinese Middle Way, 5, 10–11,
      35, 106, 134,
      138–139, 204, 223,
      243–244, 256
   commonalities *vs.* differences, focus
      on, 31–34, 67–68, 259
   dialog *vs.* combat, 36
   group consensus, Chinese focus
      on, 67–68, 71–72, 183,
      200–201

legal frameworks, Western focus on, 184–185
management styles, Chinese vs. Western, 28–30, 184–185
winning, Western emphasis on, 24–27, 32, 34, 250–252
Newton, Sir Isaac (Newton's Laws), 25, 39, 44, 112
Nicomachean Ethics (Aristotle), 139
Nisbett, Richard E., 45
Nixon, Richard, 175
no and negative answers, 78–79, 169–172
Nobel laureates, 156–157
non-performing loans (NPLs), 202, 208, 215–218
Nucor, 199
Nye, Joseph S., 14

O

Obama, Barack
  budget battle, 2011, 32–33
  Xi Jinping, visits with, 40, 67–68
Olympic Games, 249–250
On China (Kissinger), 34, 86
One Belt One Road Initiative, 204
On War (von Clausewitz), 37–38
Open Door policy, 9
opposites, co-existing, 26, 46–47, 101–102, 234
Outer King and Inner Sage, 135–138
out-of-the box thinking, 245–247
overseas development, Chinese business success factors for, 224–226

China Aviation Oil, 226, 231–235
  cultural differences, challenges of, 223–226
  foreign regulations, challenge of, 224, 225
  Going Out strategy, 221–222
  government support of, 221–222
  Haier, 224, 226–230
  overseas direct investments, growth of, 223–226

P

pankration, 250
parent-child relationships, 81–82, 90, 160–161, 188–189, 240–242
Paris Climate Conference, 155
Park Geun-hye, 147
parrying (three Ps), 27–30, 39
People's Bank of China, 213–214
perseverance, value of, 242–243
personal integrity, 137–138
personal space, concept of, 19
Pew Research studies, 14
phase transitions, 107
Plato, 134, 161
Politburo, 184
political processes
  China's influence on, 8
  elections and campaigns, US, 31–34, 153, 184–186
  lobbyists, US, 153
  yin and yang in, 31–34
politics, Chinese emphasis on, 31–34, 56–60
pollution, 71, 113, 154

Ponzi financing, 196, 197, 204
pop culture
American pop culture,
perceptions of, 14, 16–18
Chinese martial arts, 23–24
Chinese pop culture, Western influence on, 8–9
power. *See* authority and power; social status
pragmatism, Chinese, 179–182
presidential campaigns, US, 31–34
privacy, concept of, 19, 33–34
Problem of China, The (Russell), 9
problem solving, Chinese
guanxi and, 44, 45, 54
incremental river crossing approach, 4, 48–49, 214, 259
intuitive *vs.* Western analytical approach, 10–14, 44–45, 80–81, 92, 180–182, 259
pragmatism and, 179–182
Tao management style, 92
problem solving, Western
analytical *vs.* Chinese intuitive approach, 10–14, 44–45, 80–81, 92, 180–182, 259
details, narrow focus on, 10, 31–34, 46, 56, 67–68, 88, 167, 180–182
Socratic method of learning, 45, 128, 135, 158–159, 161, 162, 184, 257
procrastination, 60, 94, 181–182
proverbs and sayings, Chinese
on context and experiences, 73
on cross-cultural management, 5
on cultural contradictions, 210
cultural importance of, 160
on education and learning, 160, 244
on long-term thinking, 102
on moderation and tolerance, 243, 244
on perseverance, 242–243
on problem solving, 181
on socialism, 10
on soup, 51
on tradition *vs.* individualism, 53, 54, 233
on wholistic thinking, 100
pulling (three Ps), 27–31, 93
pushing (three Ps), 27–31
Pye, Lucien, 182

Q

qi, flow of, 20, 27, 51
Qin Dynasty, 127, 129–130, 133
Qingdao General Refrigerator Factory, 226
Qingdao Haier, 230
Qing Dynasty, 119, 148
qipao traditional dresses, 12
quantitative finance, 109–113

R

Reagan, Ronald, 93–94
real estate development
American housing market, collapse of, 101, 102, 202–203, 208–209
Chinese housing market, risks to, 202–203, 208–209
Chinese property ownership, rates of, 203
reciprocity, 89, 93, 123, 126, 150–153, 190
Red Guards, 177
Reform and Opening Up, 69, 135

regulations, Chinese
 in banking, 142, 199
 enforcement of, difficulty in, 49, 191, 209, 214
 market reforms for, 212, 214–215
 overseas development, challenges of, 224, 225
regulations, Western
 for corporate capital structures, 199
 labor and safety standards, 224, 225
 Lehman Brothers collapse, effect on, 97–99
 in sports, 251
relationships, Chinese
 guanxi, 44, 45, 54, 56–60, 90, 150–155
 labels and formalism, 74–76
 mutual support in, 144–145, 175, 187, 190–191, 199
 quantitative vs. qualitative aspects of, 60–61
 reciprocity in, 89, 93, 123, 126, 150–153, 190
 Ren, virtue of, 134, 139–143, 147, 186, 201
 workplace relationships, 61, 69–70, 74–81, 88–90, 126, 165, 178, 259 (*see also* family relationships, Chinese)
relationships, Western
 business rules vs. guanxi, 151–153
 family relationships, 149, 160–161, 188–190
 workplace relationships, 61, 69–70, 88–90, 188, 259

relative vs. absolute perspectives, 47
religious diversity, Chinese, 128, 179
Ren, virtue of, 134, 139–143, 147, 186, 201
Resolution Trust Corporation (RTC), 209, 216
respect, Chinese
 face, concept of, 174–178
 Li, virtue of, 134, 140, 148–150, 152, 229
 in parent-child relationships, 188–189, 242
 social status and, 2, 84–85, 149, 174–178
 for teachers, 149
 traditions and culture, effect on, 2, 3, 18, 119, 174–178
right-brain thinking. *See* wholistic thinking
risks and opportunities
 Chinese emphasis on avoiding, 102, 105–106
 market failures and investor behavior, 108–109, 115–116
 Western acceptance of, 10–11, 54–55
river crossing analogy, 4, 48–49, 214, 259
Rockefeller, John D., 82
role models, differing views of, 18
Romance of Three Kingdoms, The, 246
Rothman, Andy, 209, 213
RTC (Resolution Trust Corporation), 209, 216
Russell, Bertrand, 9, 120, 155
Russia
 Asian financial crisis, effect on, 100

Russia (cont.)
  default of 1998 and market crashes, 110
  World War II, 30

S
safety and wellbeing, differing views on, 52–53
safety regulations and standards, 224, 225
salad vs. soup analogy, 49–50
Sandel, Michael, 146
San Francisco hippie movement, 3
Sany, 224
Sanyo, 230
Sanyo Electric, 230
scholarship. See education, Chinese; education, Western
SCI. See Shanghai Composite Index (SCI)
science and math education, 156–157
sea levels, rise of, 153
Seidman, Bill, 216
self-defense. See Tai Chi
self-discipline, value of, 134, 137–138, 143, 239
self-education, 128
self-improvement, 53–54, 135–138
self-interest, 146–148, 202–203
servant leadership, 93–94
Sewol (ship), 146
shadow banking, 210–212
shadow boxing. See Tai Chi
Shangdong Heavy, 224
Shanghai Composite Index (SCI), 212–214

Shanghai Stock Exchange (SSE), 202, 212, 213
shared sacrifice, value of, 167–168, 198–203, 249
shendu, concept of, 136–138
Shunfeng Photovoltaic International Limited, 198
Sima Qian, 129
Singapore
  China Aviation Oil (CAO), 226, 231–235
  math and science education in, 156
  traditional Chinese culture, teaching of, 120
Singles Day concept, 247–248
Smith, Arthur Henderson, 11
social hierarchies. See hierarchal structures, Chinese
socialism, 10, 12–13, 65–66, 69, 121, 199, 249
social stability
  Chinese emphasis on, 11, 101, 119, 142, 198–201, 218
  Li, virtue of, 134, 140, 148–150, 152, 229
social status, Chinese
  education and, 84
  face, concept of, 174–178
  names and titles, 62–64
  perceptions of others and, 84–85
  respect and, 2, 84–85, 149, 174–178
Socrates (Socratic method), 45, 128, 135, 158–159, 161, 162, 184, 257
SOEs. See state-owned enterprises (SOEs)

soft power
  American soft power, 16
  brute force vs., 24, 26–28
  Chinese soft power, 8, 14–16
  defined, 14
  Li, virtue of, 148
  pop culture icons analogy, 16
  Tai Chi as, 23–24
  in Tao management style, 93
solar power industry, 197–199
soup vs. salad analogy, 51–52
South Korea
  alcoholic beverages, etiquette for, 166–168
  Asian financial crisis, effect on, 99, 100
  Confucian influence on, 43, 74–75
  corporate families in, 188
  family and relationship roles in, 74–75, 190
  math and science education in, 156
  names and titles, 62
  self-interest, examples of, 146–148
Spacey, Kevin, 248
Spain, overseas direct investments, 223
speculative financing, 196
sports and athletics
  American football, 27, 251–252
  in ancient China, 250
  benefits to business of, 249–252
  boxing, 24, 27, 250
  martial arts, 23–24, 37
  physical exercise, benefits of, 156
  Tai Chi, 23–28
  Western emphasis on, 54, 251–252

Spring and Autumn Period, 121, 124, 128
SSE (Shanghai Stock Exchange), 202, 212, 213
Stalin, Joseph, 30
Standard and Poor's, 32, 111
standardized tests, American, 156, 158
Standard Oil, 82
state-owned enterprises (SOEs)
  business model and management of, 83, 90, 191–192, 203, 231–232
  prevalence of, 83, 188
  private sector companies vs., growth of, 223–224
  reforms of, 192, 205–206, 217
  stock markets and funding for, 192, 212–213
  statistics, Western emphasis on, 109–113, 259
stock markets
  Chinese government interventions, 206, 212–214
  Chinese stock market crashes, 107–108
  financial engineering, effect on, 97–99
  market panic and freezes, 107–110, 202
  Shanghai Stock Exchange (SSE), 202, 212, 213
  Wall Street crashes and failures, 97–100, 107–108, 110–111
stock options, 109
structured financial products, 97–99
Suntech Power, 197–199
Sun Tzu, 23, 28, 34, 37–40, 59, 93, 228–230
  Art of War, The, 28, 34, 37–38, 229

Sun Wukong (Monkey King), 16–18
Super Political Action Committees (PACs), 153
swearing-in ceremonies, 176

T
Tai Chi, 23–28
Taiwan
    Chinese Cultural Renaissance Movement, 120
    films from, 77
    math and science education in, 156
Taleb, Nassim, 113
Taobao, 247
Taoism
    actions and reactions in, 26
    co-existing opposites, concept of, 26, 46–47, 101–102, 234
    communication and expression, 113–115
    definition of Tao, 47, 113, 114, 128
    flow, Tao management of, 91–93
    Tai Chi, origins in, 24
Tao management style, 91–94
Tao Te Ching (Lao), 23, 26, 93, 101–102, 113, 234
Teacher's Day, China, 149
teaching methods, differences in, 158–159. *See also* education, Chinese; education, Western
tech bubble of 2000, 97
technology
    American tech company business models, 50–51
    information overload, 239–240
    information warfare, 38
    innovation and, 11, 85–86, 161–162, 224, 246–249
Tencent, 224
Thailand
    Asian financial crisis, effect on, 99–100, 216
    US RTC models in, 216
think tanks, 87–88
three Ps
    of Chinese business, 28–30
    of Tai Chi, 27–28
3 Ss in business, 181
titles and names, 62–64
TMAll, 247
tolerance, value of, 14, 16, 19, 68, 202, 243–244
    Middle Way, 5, 10–11, 35, 106, 134, 138–139, 204, 223, 243–244, 256
    self-interest *vs.*, 146–148, 202–203
trading. *See* financial trading
Troubled Asset Relief Program, US, 218
Tu Wei-Ming, 120

U
Uncertainty Principle, Heisenberg's, 92
underdogs, success of, 18, 185, 248
United States
    American football, 27, 251–252
    American *vs.* Chinese Dream, 17, 66–67
    cultural values, 66
    education systems, 157–158

elections and political campaigns, 31–34, 153, 184–186
equal rights and diversity in, 49–50, 185
food and eating, etiquette for, 19–21
global perceptions of, 14–16
homeownership, rates of, 203
housing market, collapse of, 101, 102, 202–203, 208–209
individualism, emphasis on, 3, 15, 19, 50, 167–168, 178, 188–189, 242, 257–259
math and science education in, 156–157
Nobel laureates, 156–157
overseas direct investments, 223
recessions, recovery from, 204
urbanization in, 222
Vietnam War, 2–3, 29–30, 40 (*see also* culture and traditions, Western)
unity, value of
family unity, 187
group consensus, 67–68, 71–72, 183, 200–201
sportsmanship and teamwork, 50, 251
urbanization, 222
US National Intelligence Council, 7

V
value at risk (VaR), 109
Vietnamese culture, Confucian influence on, 43
Vietnam War, 2–3, 29–30, 40

W
Wall Street
crashes, 97–100, 107–108
financial engineering, 97–99
quantitative finance and failures on, 110–111 (*see also* financial crisis and bubbles; financial trading)
Wall Street Journal, 212
Wanxiang, 224
war
in business, 36
military strategies, differences in, 37–40
modern definition of, 36
Sun Tzu on, 23, 28, 34, 37–40, 59, 93, 228–230
Warring States Period, 37, 121–123, 127–128
Washington Mutual, 214
Washington Post, 55
water analogies
crossing river feeling stones, 4, 48–49, 214, 259
evasive war strategies, 39–41
humility and flexibility, 93, 94
phase transition and market freezes, 107
wealth
education valued over, 53–54
ethics of emphasis on, balancing, 15, 135–138, 146–148, 245
frugality *vs.*, 53, 55, 134, 149
virtues valued over, 245
wealth gaps, 32, 47
Wealth Management Products (WMPs), 210–211
weather systems analogy, 47
Weiqi, 23, 34–36

When China Rules the World
(Jacques), 7
Whirlpool, 227, 230
Whitehead, Alfred North, 113, 114
wholistic management models,
  13–14
wholistic thinking
  absolute *vs.* relative perspectives,
    47
  analytical thinking *vs.*, 255–260
  benefits and limitations of,
    255–260
  big picture thinking, 31–34, 44,
    79, 80, 86–87, 92
  Chinese cognizant styles, 45–47
  co-existing opposites,
    concept of, 26, 46–47,
    101–102, 234
  democratic *vs.* meritocratic
    approaches, 182–186
  on food and medicine, 19–21
  Middle Way, 5, 10–11, 35, 106,
    134, 138–139, 204, 223,
    243–244, 256
  shared sacrifice, value of, 167–168,
    198–203, 249, 259
  winning, Western emphasis on,
    24–27, 32, 34, 250–252
wisdom (virtue of Zhi), 134, 155
work ethic, differences in, 54–55,
  89, 135
work experience, Western emphasis
  on, 54–55
workplace relationships
  Chinese *vs.* Western approaches
    to, 61, 69–70, 88–90,
    188, 259
  in Confucian management
    style, 90

hierarchical structures, Chinese,
  74–76, 126, 165, 178
labels and formalities, 74–78
meritocratic *vs.* democratic
  approaches, 182–186
names and titles, 62–64
praising employees, differences in,
  81–82, 90, 160, 171–172,
  176–177
World Bank, 7, 153, 222, 223
World Trade Organization (WTO),
  205, 221
World War II, 30
Wozniak, Steve, 85, 161
WTO (World Trade Organization),
  205, 221
Wuxi Suntech, 198

X

Xiaomi, 224
Xi Jinping
  on Chinese Dream, 66
  Obama, visits with, 40, 67–68

Y

Yang Mianmian, 228
Ye, Shawn, 229, 230
yes and positive answers, 79–80
Yi, Jennie, 229, 230
Yi, virtue of, 134, 145–148
yin and yang
  in Chinese medicine, 19
  co-existing opposites, concept of,
    26, 46–47, 101–102, 234
  motion in Tai Chi, 24–27
  in politics, 31–34 (*see also*
    harmony and balance)

Z

Zhang, Jinxuan (Ann), 231, 233
Zhang Ruimin, 228–230
Zhang Weiwei, 182
Zhengzhou, 41
Zhi, virtue of, 134, 155
Zhong Rong. *See* Middle Way
Zhou Dynasty, 46, 121–124, 140, 148, 172
Zhou Enlai, 175
Zhuangzi, 2, 92, 135
Zhuge Liang, 246
ZTE, 224
Zuckerberg, Mark, 86

The manufacturer's authorised representative in the EU is Springer Nature Customer Service Centre GmbH, Europaplatz 3, 69115 Heidelberg, Germany. If you have any concerns regarding our products, please contact ProductSafety@springernature.com

Printed and bound by CPI Group (UK) Ltd, Croydon, CR0 4YY
23/03/2026
02076674-0009